ASSEMBLY LANGUAGE PROGRAMMING FOR THE 68000 FAMILY

Related Titles of Interest from John Wiley & Sons

PROGRAMMING WITH MACINTOSH PASCAL, Swan
EXCEL: A POWER USER'S GUIDE, Hodgkins
JAZZ AT WORK, Venit & Burns
MACINTOSH LOGO, Haigh & Radford
DESKTOP PUBLISHING WITH PAGEMAKER FOR THE MACINTOSH, Bove & Rhodes
SCIENTIFIC PROGRAMMING WITH MAC PASCAL, Crandall

ASSEMBLY LANGUAGE PROGRAMMING FOR THE 68000 FAMILY

Thomas P. Skinner

John Wiley & Sons, Inc.
New York • Chichester • Brisbane • Toronto • Singapore

Publisher: Stephen Kippur
Editor: Therese A. Zak
Managing Editor: Ruth Greif
Editing, Design, and Production: Publishing Synthesis, Ltd.
Composition: McFarland Graphics

Library of Congress Cataloging-in-Publication Data

Skinner, Thomas P.
Assembly language programming for the 68000 family/Thomas P. Skinner.
p. cm.
ISBN 0-471-85357-7
1. Motorola 68000 series microprocessors—Programming.
2. Assembler language (Computer program language) I. Title:
QA76.8.M695S58 1988 87-20293
005.265—dc19 CIP

Printed in the United States of America

88 89 10 9 8 7 6 5 4 3 2 1

To my wife Linda

PREFACE

This book deals specifically with the Motorola 68000 family of microprocessors. It is primarily about assembly language programming. Chances are that a reader interested in assembly language programming is familiar with computers and their programming; In the unlikely event that you are not, and have picked up this book expecting to learn all about computers, I want to urge you to start elsewhere. In order to gain the maximum knowledge from this book, you should already be familiar with computers in general and have written some programs in a high-level language such as BASIC or Pascal. It is not necessary to know another assembly language or be an expert in computer programming. I start at a fairly low level but get up to speed pretty quickly. Those who already know another assembly language will be able to progress rapidly through the material. In the writing of this book I attempted to strike a balance between a beginner-level tutorial and the brief format of a reference manual. This level of presentation should appeal to the majority of readers.

There are 15 chapters plus a number of useful appendices. Chapter 1 covers number systems. This is mostly general information, but there is a little bit of 68000-specific information here. You should look through it even if you know number systems inside out. Chapter 2 describes microcomputer architectures in general, and the 68000 specifically.

Chapters 3 through 5 provide enough information to start writing complete programs. Chapters 6 through 8 cover more advanced topics such as addressing modes and subroutines. Once through chapter 8 you will have a substantial background in 68000 assembly language. At this point Chapter 9 presents a major program, a linked list manager. This helps to cement the techniques from Chapters 1 through 8.

Chapters 10 through 12 cover advanced topics such as exception handling, shift and rotate instructions, and advanced arithmetic. By the end of Chapter 12 you will know all the instructions of the 68000. Chapters 13, 14, and 15 cover the newest members of the 68000 family—the 68010, 68020, and 68030. Chapter 15 should be of special interest, since it provides an introduction to the latest and most powerful 68000 processor. You will be hearing more about the 68030 as it is introduced into systems. It is destined to have a major impact on the computer systems of the next decade.

Of special note is Appendix B, which provides program shells. These shells allow you to start programming with the Atari ST, the Apple Macintosh, or the Commadore Amiga. Without these program shells it would require a good deal of effort just to learn how to interface to your operating system.

A number of people provided assistance along the way. Among my students who helped out were Carol Cook and An-Ping Chi. Special thanks to Mike Mellone and John Saywell, who helped prepare the appendices. Finally, I would like to thank Motorola for their cooperation and permission to reprint information from their 68000 manuals.

Thomas P. Skinner

CONTENTS

INTRODUCTION

Why learn assembly language? Most people do so out of a need to perform programming tasks that are not easy, or not possible, with other languages. The popularity of the 68000 family of microprocessors, as exemplified by the sales figures of the Apple Macintosh, Commodore Amiga, Atari ST, and others, certainly makes it worthwhile to learn more about this line of micros. The particular microprocessor chip your computer uses will remain an abstraction unless you get down to the machine language level; but since no one really programs in machine language, assembly language is the way to gain the most complete knowledge of the 68000 family capabilities.

Programming in assembly language allows the control of every aspect of the computer hardware. Many applications require procedures that are either impossible or inefficient with computer languages such as BASIC. You may be a professional computer user who has a need for a laboratory control computer, such real time applications often require some assembly language programming. Regardless of your reason for learning assembly language, it is challenging and rewarding when your programs start to run. You will feel—and be—"in control."

This book is about programming the 68000 microprocessor, not a particular computer using this chip. For this reason there will be some specifics about your computer and operating system that are not covered. Since you are more than likely experienced in using your computer for other applications, it would be a waste of time to attempt to cover all the small details. Instead, I will present the material in a general manner such that it will be easy to locate the specifics for your particular machine in your manuals. As an aid to those individuals having one of the aforementioned computers, some specific input/output subroutines and a program shell are provided in the appendices.

Before we get started, let's pause to review the steps required to write a program and run it. Programming in assembly language, like programming in a high-level language, requires entering the "source code" into the computer. Unless all of your programming has been in BASIC, using its built-in editing features, you have probably used some form of text editor. It really doesn't matter which editor you use as long as you can create a source file for input to the assembler. An assembler is similar to a compiler in that it "translates" a source language into machine language.

The output from an assembler is called the *object code.* Normally this is machine language put into a special format that combines it with other object modules into an *executable image.* This file is essentially a picture of what goes into memory. When you finally run the program, this file is brought into memory so that the microprocessor may execute the instructions.

The operation of combining object modules is called *linking.* A special program called a *linker* is used to perform this function. Figure 1 shows the steps used to produce an executable program. The details will differ from computer to computer. Your system may have a program similar to a linker that converts the output of the assembler into an executable form, but does not allow combining object modules. You should have no trouble in learning the commands that perform these steps on a particular machine.

There are quite a few 68000 assemblers available for a range of computer systems. It is not possible to present all the variations in assemblers in this book. Motorola, as the designer of the 68000 microprocessor family, originated its assembly language. The most important task of the assembly language designer is to devise a set of symbolic names for each instruction the microprocessor can execute. These symbolic names are known as *mnemonics.* For example, an instruction to move data from one place to another has the mnemonic MOVE.

In order to allow the greatest flexibility, this book will use the standard Motorola assembler syntax and mnemonics. There will probably be some minor variations with the assembler you use. However, most of the pieces of an assembly language program will be identical regardless of the assembler used, and you should not find it difficult in relating the material to your particular assembler. If you don't presently have an assembler and linker for your computer system, check with the manufacturer, who probably sells a "developer's package" that contains an assembler, a linker, and the system documentation you will need. Many independent software houses also supply development packages. Go to your local computer store and compare these for compatability with the Motorola standard. If the syntax or mnemonics of the assembler are very far from the standard, you should probably consider another one. Other items that are sometimes provided are an editor (a must if you don't have one), an interactive debugger, and other utilities to assist in rapid program development. This book does not assume any specific development aids or utilities.

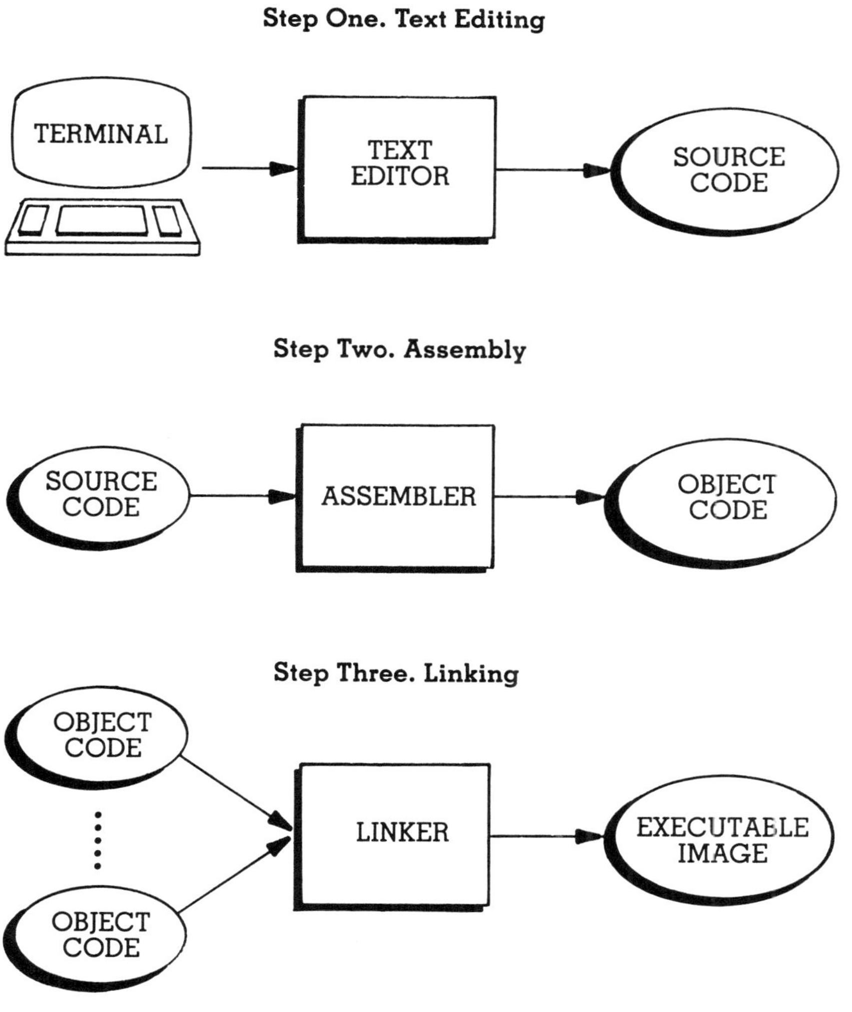

Figure 1 Assembler Operation.

In Chapter 1 I will review number systems. If you are an experienced assembly language programmer in another language you probably know most of this material. However, it is a good idea to review the chapter, especially as it presents some details specific to the 68000.

CHAPTER 1

NUMBER SYSTEMS

Throughout history mankind has used a variety of methods to represent numerical quantitites. Early man used piles of stones, each stone representing one unit of those items being counted. It soon became obvious that for large numbers, a large number of stones were required. One solution to this problem was to use stones of different sizes. A single large stone could be used to represent a pile of smaller stones. This is similar to the use of the denominations of paper currency. Schemes like this work well for physical entities like coins or stones. However, to represent quantities on paper we would be forced to draw pictures of our piles of stones.

Decimal

Our decimal number system is a product of all these schemes. Instead of piles of different numbers of stones or stones of different sizes, the Arabic numerals 0 to 9 and the relative position of these numerals are used to represent the number of stones in a pile and the relative size of the stones. The numerals 0 to 9 can represent quantities from zero to nine. Position can be used to represent any number of sizes. For example, the decimal number "23" can be thought of as representing three small stones and two larger stones. If each larger stone is equivalent to ten small stones, this number represents the equivalent of twenty-three small stones. This may seem obvious to most readers, but it is the basis of all the number systems we will study.

In the decimal number system, each digit's position represents a different power of 10. For example, the number 7458 is equivalent to:

$$7(10)^3+4(10)^2+5(10)^1+8(10)^0$$

The choice of 10 as the numerical base, or *radix*, as it is sometimes called, is arbitrary. We can create a number system using any base we desire.

Binary

Virtually all computers use 2 as the base for numerical quantities. The choice of 2 as a base for computers is not arbitrary. Internally, the electrical elements, or *gates*, that collectively construct the computer are much easier to build if they are required to represent only two values or states, they are thus called *binary* state devices. Each element can only represent the values zero or one. Each one or zero is called a *bit*, or binary digit. In order to represent larger numbers, bit positions must be used. Binary numbers are based on powers of two rather than on powers of ten. For example, the binary number "1011" is equivalent to:

$$1(2)^3+0(2)^2+1(2)^1+1(2)^0$$

This value is equivalent to:

```
8+0+2+1 = 11
```

in decimal representation. The positional values of the bits are thus:

$(2)^0 = 1$

$(2)^1 = 2$

$(2)^2 = 4$

$(2)^3 = 8$

$(2)^4 = 16$

.

.

$(2)^{16} = 65,536$

.

.

etc.

To convert a binary number to its decimal equivalent, merely add up the appropriate powers of two. If the binary position contains a 1, the decimal value of that bit position is added.

Conversions

Converting a decimal number to binary is not quite as simple as converting a binary number to decimal. One method is to work backwards.

We can look for the highest power of two that is not greater than the decimal number, place a 1 in the equivalent bit position, and then subtract this value from the decimal number. We repeat this operation until the number is zero. Bit positions not used in this subtractive process are set to 0. For example, we can convert 57_{10} (57 in base 10) to binary by the following steps:

$$57 - 2^5 = 25$$

$$25 - 2^4 = 9$$

$$9 - 2^3 = 1$$

$$1 - 2^0 = 0 \text{ (finished)}$$

This gives us the binary number

$$1(2)^5+1(2)^4+1(2)^3+0(2)^2+0(2)^1+1(2)^0 = 111001_2$$

Another method can also be used. We can divide the original decimal number by two and check the remainder. If the remainder is one, a binary one is generated. We repeat this division by two until we obtain a zero. This method gives us the bits in reverse. In other words, we get 2^0, 2^1, and so on. For example, using the same number as above:

```
57/2 = 28 R 1

28/2 = 14 R 0

14/2 = 7 R 0

7/2 = 3 R 1

3/2 = 1 R 1

1/2 = 0 R 1 (finished)
```

Reading the bits in reverse gives us 111001_2, which is the same number as we arrived at before. The method you use is up to you.

These methods can be used to convert from any number base to any other number base. However, the arithmetic must be done in the number base of the number being converted. As this becomes complicated when converting from a system other than decimal, you are better off to convert the number to decimal and then the decimal number to the new base. There are a few exceptions to this rule. One of these exceptions is the conversion of the hexadecimal (hex) base to or from binary. Since hex is used quite extensively with the 68000 family, it is the topic of our next discussion.

Hexadecimal

Hexadecimal, or base 16, uses positional values that are powers of 16. Each hex digit can take on 16 values. Since the decimal digits 0 through 9 only represent 10 values, 6 additional symbols are needed. The letters A through F are used to represent these additional values. Thus the hex digits are represented by 0, 1, 2, 3, 4, 5, 6, 7, 8, 9, A, B, C, D, E, and F, corresponding to the values from 0_{10} to 15_{10}. The positional values are:

$(16)^0 = 1$

$(16)^1 = 16$

$(16)^2 = 256$

$(16)^3 = 4096$

etc.

As you can see, these values increase rapidly. A hex number is usually larger than it looks. For example, $32BF_{16}$ is

$$3(16)^3+2(16)^2+11(16)^1+15(16)^0$$

$$= 12{,}288+512+176+15 = 12{,}991_{10}$$

We can convert from decimal to hexadecimal by either method discussed above. For example, to convert 387_{10} to hex, we perform the following:

```
387/16 = 24 R 3

24/16 = 1 R 8

1/16 = 0 R 1 (finished)
```

The result in hex is 183_{16}. Remember to list the hex digits in reverse order.

A nice property of hexadecimal numbers is that they can be converted to binary almost by inspection. Since $2^4=16$, there is a simple relationship present. Four binary digits grouped together can represent one hexadecimal digit. The binary values 0000 through 1111 represent the hexadecimal digits 0 through F.

HEX	BINARY	HEX	BINARY
0	0000	8	1000
1	0001	9	1001
2	0010	A	1010
3	0011	B	1011
4	0100	C	1100
5	0101	D	1101
6	0110	E	1110
7	0111	F	1111

To convert from hex to binary we merely write the equivalent of each hex digit in binary. To convert $6E3C_{16}$ to binary we would write:

```
   6    E    3    C

0110 1110 0011 1100
```

and our binary equivalent is 110111000111100_2. We can go from binary to hex in the same manner. 111100001010_2 is $F0A_{16}$.

Arithmetic in Binary and Hexadecimal

We can perform the normal arithmetic operations of addition, subtraction, multiplication, and division in any number base. Addition and subtraction are simple if we remember that a carry or borrow may be required. If the sum of two digits equals or exceeds the number base, a carry is generated. The value used as the carry or borrow is equal to the number base. For example, if we add two binary numbers together, we generate a carry if the sum of the bits in one binary position and a possible carry from the next lowest position is greater than or equal to two. Adding 1100101_2 to 0111101_2 gives us:

```
   1100101
 + 0111101
   -------
  10100010
```

Let's try adding $72A8_{16}$ to $1F08_{16}$.

```
   72A8
 + 1F08
   ----
   91B0
```

Subtraction is only slightly more difficult. If the individual digits cannot be subtracted from one another, we need to borrow from the next higher digit position. In other words, if the minuend (top digit) is less than the subtrahend (bottom digit) we need a borrow. In binary the value borrowed is always two. This borrow is added to the minuend, the subtraction is then performed on the two digits. To adjust for the borrow, just as we had to adjust for a carry, we must add one to the subtrahend in the next higher digit position. For example, in binary

```
   1111          1001
 - 0110        - 0110
   ----          ----
   1001          0011
```

or hexadecimal

```
  55F2
- 4A63
  ----
  0B8F
```

Hand calculations involving multiplication or division are rarely performed by programmers. However, conventional hand methods can be used. The basic principles we used for addition and subtraction are applied. Although I will not explain multiplication or division, those readers who desire can try some examples and verify their results by converting to decimal and repeating the multiplication or division in the decimal number base.

Bits, Bytes, Words and Longwords

So far in our discussion of numbers we have not indicated how large our numbers can be. If you want to write down a very large number on paper, the size of the number is only limited by the size of the paper. This is not the case for computers. Internally the computer must represent numbers by electrical signals. These signals represent the binary values 0 and 1. The maximum size of a number inside the computer is limited to the number of binary digits, or bits, used to represent the number. Theoretically we could use *all* the bits inside the computer to represent a *single* number. This, of course, is not practical. Internally it is convenient to limit the number of bits used for each number.

Many computers are organized around groups of eight bits, called *bytes*. The size of memory on many computers is measured in bytes. We might say a computer has 64 thousand bytes of memory. This is equivalent to 512 thousand bits. Modern computers often have memory sizes in the millions of bytes. A megabyte (MB) is equal to approximately one million bytes. As we will discuss shortly, a single byte is normally used to represent a single character of textual information. If we have a 2 MB memory, we can store 2 million characters of information. If we assume approximately 60 characters per line of printed material, and 50 lines per page, this is equivalent to over 650 pages.

Bytes can be grouped together. For most computers, including the 68000 family, two bytes grouped together form a *word*. A word is therefore equal to 16 bits. This is also equivalent to four hexadecimal digits. We can also have *longwords*, made up of four bytes or 32 bits. Larger groupings are possible but are not normally handled as a single value except by much larger computers. We will be dealing primarily with bytes, words, and longwords in 68000 assembly language programming.

Representing Negative Values

So far in our discussion of number representations, we have only been dealing with positive numbers. A method of representing negative numbers in the computer must be introduced. You have already learned that numbers are represented internally by binary digits. We must devise a way of including the conventional minus sign "—", used to indicate a negative number, with the number itself. But how does a minus sign translate into binary? Since numbers are either positive or negative, we can indicate this fact by using a single binary digit. A negative number can be indicated by using an "extra" bit rather than a minus sign. This may not work as well on paper, but it is essential for a computer's internal representations.

Numeric quantitites are normally restricted to fixed sizes—a single byte, a word, or some multiple number of words or bytes. It is not practical to append an extra "sign" bit to a fixed unit of storage such as a byte: the central processing unit (CPU) normally is restricted to manipulating integral numbers of bytes, and this extra bit would force the use of an extra complete byte. The solution is to sacrifice one of the bits of our number for use as the sign bit. The size of the largest number we can represent is reduced, but we can now represent the same number of positive numbers as negative numbers.

By convention, if a number is negative we indicate this fact by including a sign bit equal to one. The sign bit is normally the leftmost, or high-order, bit of the number. The simplest technique would be merely to indicate the magnitude of the number in the remaining bits, setting the sign bit to either one or zero to indicate a negative or positive number. This representation, called *sign magnitude,* has been used on older computers. It has a number of disadvantages, the most prominent to a programmer being the fact that both a positive and negative zero exist—both 10000000_2 and 00000000_2 are zero values for a single byte number. Without going into additional detail, suffice it to say that a better method is needed.

Virtually all modern computers, including microprocessors, use a representation called *two's complement.* The sign bit is still used to indicate whether a number is positive or negative, but the remaining bits do not directly indicate the magnitude of the number if it is a negative number. To represent a negative number in two's complement, we first form the *one's complement* of the number in its binary form. The one's complement is merely the number with all the one bits converted to zeros, and all the zero bits converted to ones. The one's complement of 01100011_2 is 10011100_2. So far this is quite simple. We are almost finished. To get the two's complement we add one to the one's complement. We perform this addition just as we have done in the previous examples. To complete the conversion of our example, we get:

```
   10011100
 + 00000001
   --------
   10011101
```

Let's convert 89_{10} to -89_{10} using two's complement. First we must convert 89_{10} to binary. $89_{10} = 01011001_2$. Now form the one's complement, 10100110_2; finally, to get the two's complement we add one. Our result is $-89_{10} = 10100111_2$.

The nice property of two's complement numbers is that we can add them together without concern for the sign. We do not have to perform any conversion. As a simple example, we should be able to add 89_{10} and -89_{10} and obtain a zero result.

```
   01011001     89₁₀
 + 10100111    -89₁₀
   --------
   00000000      0₁₀
```

We ignore any carry out from the sign bit position.

To subtract in two's complement, we merely negate the subtrahend and then add. This operation is performed regardless of whether the subtrahend is positive or negative.

ASCII Character Codes

In order to represent character information in the computer's memory, we must find a way to convert the such as CR (carriage return), LF (line feed) and HT (horizontal tab). There are other "control character" codes that are of general interest but are not necessarily available on all terminals. For example, a BEL (bell) might sound a beep on your terminal, or a VT (vertical tab) might be implemented. The other codes with values less than 32_{10} are used for a variety of purposes including the protocols used for data communications.

One special character should be mentioned. The DEL (delete) code, 127_{10}, which is sometimes called a *rubout,* is most commonly used by software to indicate the deletion of the last character typed. Some software uses the BS (backspace) character to perform this same operation. You should note that these are really two different character codes, 8_{10} and 127_{10}, and the interpretation as to what, if anything, these characters do is up to the software.

Some computers and terminals have incorporated additional characters as an extension to the standard ASCII character set. By allowing codes above 127_{10}, an additional 128_{10} characters can be specified. These might be from a foreign language, or for special graphics used by certain terminals. The IBM PC, which does not use the 68000, makes extensive use of such an extended character set. You should be aware that these special character sets are not part of the ASCII standard, when you use these codes, your programs will not necessarily be useful on *all* computers, even though they use the 68000 microprocessor.

Exercises

1. Binary numbers are based on powers of ________.
2. Give the decimal equivalent of the following binary numbers: a) 11100010 b) 111111 c) 10000000
3. Convert the following decimal numbers to binary: a) 126 b) 255 c) 100
4. Convert the following binary numbers to hexadecimal: a) 11111111 b) 10000 c) 11000101
5. Convert the following hexadecimal numbers to binary: a) 55 b) AB c) EE
6. Give the decimal equivalent of the following hexadecimal numbers: a) FF b) 55 c) DE
7. Perform the following binary additions:

```
a)   110000     b)   01111
   + 001111        + 11100
```

8. Perform the following hexadecimal additions:

```
a)   FFAA       b)   0123
   + A100          + A5EE
```

9. Perform the following binary subtractions:

```
a)   11111      b)   11001
   - 00101         - 10000
```

10. Perform the following hexadecimal subtractions:

```
a)   FFFF       b)   12AA
   - AAAA          - 02AB
```

11. How many bits are there in a byte?
12. How many bytes are contained in a 68000 word?
13. The 68000 uses what method to represent negative numbers?
14. Which bit is the sign bit?
15. If a number is negative, what is the binary value of the sign bit?
16. Convert the binary number 00111101 to an equivalent negative number.
17. What is the decimal equivalent of 11110000 in signed binary?
18. What is the equivalent of −100 decimal in a signed hexadecimal byte?
19. What number bases are convenient to use when programming the 68000?

20. Hexadecimal numbers use what number base?
21. What number base is used internally by the 68000?
22. Convert the following decimal numbers to binary and hexadecimal:
    a) 200 b) 5 c) 65000
23. Convert the following unsigned binary numbers to decimal:
    a) 11010101 b) 00001110 c) 11100000110
24. Convert the following unsigned hexadecimal numbers to decimal:
    a) ABCD b) 123 c) FF
25. Convert the following hexadecimal numbers to binary:
    a) FEAA b) 123A c) 0100
26. Convert the following binary numbers to hexadecimal:
    a) 1100110001 b) 00010000 c)11110111
27. Perform the following signed binary additions:
    a) 11111000 + 00111111
    b) 00010001 + 01000000
    c) 11111100 + 00000011
28. Perform the following signed binary subtractions:
    a) 11100000 − 00000001
    b) 00111000 − 11111111
    c) 10101010 − 00010101
29. What is the range of the ASCII codes that are printable?
30. Does the 68000 interpret the ASCII character codes?

Answers

1. two
2. a) 226 b) 63 c) 128
3. a) 1111110 b) 11111111 c) 1100100
4. a) FF b) 10 c) C5
5. a) 01010101 b) 10101011 c) 11101110
6. a) 225 b) 85 c) 222
7. a) 111111 b) 101011
8. a) 1A0AA b) A711
9. a) 11010 b) 01001
10. a) 55555 b) OFFF
11. 8
12. 2
13. two's complement
14. the high-order bit
15. one
16. 11000011
17. −16
18. 9C

19. decimal, binary and hexadecimal
20. 16
21. binary
22.
    a) 11001000_2; $C8_{16}$
    b) 101_2; 5_{16}
    c) 1111110111101000_2; $FDE8_{16}$
23. a) 213 b) 14 c) 1798
24. a) 43981 b) 288 c) 255
25.
    a) 1111111010101010
    b) 1001000111010
    c) 100000000
26.
    a) 331
    b) 10
    c) F7
27.
    a) 100110111
    b) 01010001
    c) 11111111
28.
    a) 11011111
    b) 00111001
    c) 10010101
29. 33_{10} through 126_{10}, assuming that space, 32_{10}, does not print.
30. No. Input/output devices and software interpret the ASCII codes.

CHAPTER 2

MICROCOMPUTER ARCHITECTURE

Before we begin to discuss assembly language, we should take time to explore the world of the microcomputer. Just what is a microcomputer? As the name implies, it is a small computer. This should not mislead you into thinking that a microcomputer cannot be a powerful computing tool. In fact, the microcomputers of today are as powerful as the minicomputers and mainframe computers of just a few years ago. The reduction in size has been a direct consequence of the development of integrated circuits (*chips*) that contain the functional equivalent of many thousands of transistors.

A microprocessor is an integrated circuit that is the basic functional building block of the microcomputer. Figure 2 shows the organization of a basic microcomputer system. The central processing unit (CPU) is the microprocessor chip itself. Electrically connected to the CPU chip is memory. Memory can be of various sizes—for example, over 16 million bytes for the 68000 microprocessor. Also connected to the CPU are input and output (I/O) devices that allow the CPU to communicate with the outside world through a terminal, as well as other information storage devices such as floppy disks and magnetic tapes.

The Motorola M68000 Family

The M68000 family of microprocessors is the current step in a continually evolving microprocessor technology. The M68000 family consists of a number of different CPU chips. Among these are the MC68000, MC68008, MC68010, and the MC68020, and the very new MC68030 (actual chips are designated with the prefix MC). Later on in this book I will refer to the M68000 family or the MC68000 CPU chip as just the 68000.

Motorola, like the other major microprocessor designers, didn't start with a chip as sophisticated as the MC68000. Prior to the introduction of the M68000 family, Motorola's bread-and-butter microprocessor line was

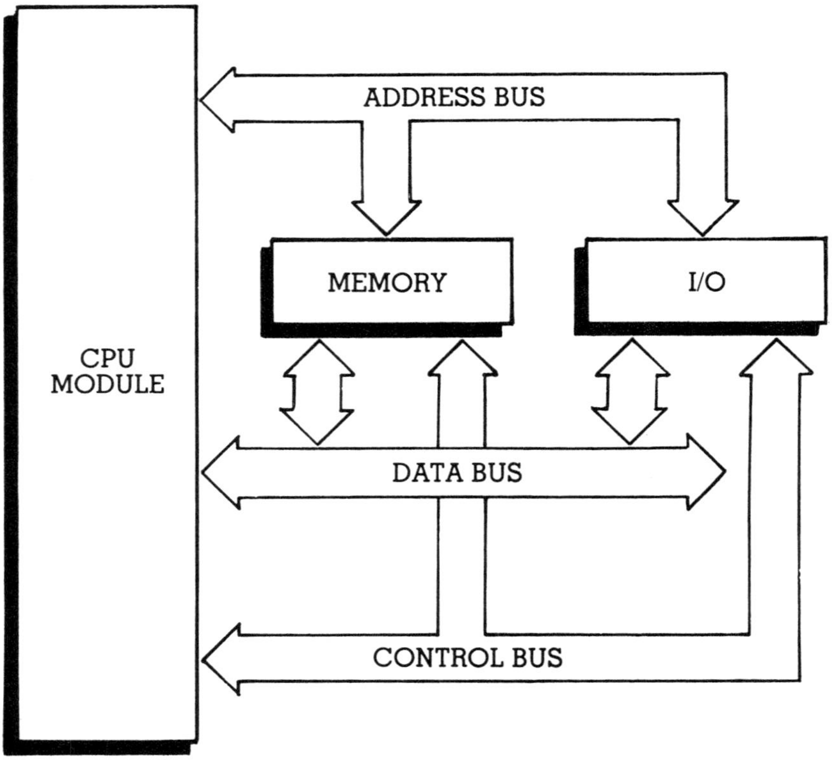

Figure 2 Organization of a simple microcomputer system.

the M6800 family. The MC6800 is strictly an 8-bit processor. Motorola attempted to bridge the gap with the MC6809, a pseudo-16-bit CPU. The 6809 never caught on like the Intel 8086 family. However, it did gain wide popularity in the Radio Shack Color computer.

A major issue that faces chip architects is how compatible to make their new chips with earlier chips. It is rarely possible to make a new chip completely compatible, at the machine code level, with prior designs. An alternative is to make the architectures *source code-compatible.* With this scheme, a programmer merely has to reassemble the program for the new chip. He or she is then free to use the features of the new chip in modifications to an already running program. This technique was adopted by Motorola when they jumped to the 6809.

The successor to the Intel 8080 family is the 8086 family. Intel chose to make the new chip family *somewhat* compatible at the source code level. This requirement may have bridled the new architecture to some extent. It is possible to convert an 8080 program to an 8086 program by a source code conversion program. The resulting program can then be modified by hand to allow for the differences in architectures. This scheme did have the advantage that it allowed software vendors to get their products to market quickly. However, the transposed code did not run as well as if it had been written for the target machine in the first place.

Motorola's MACSS (advanced computer system on silicon) project abandoned both object and source code compatibility with the older MC6800 line. While this decision forced a slower introduction of software for the M68000 system family, it allowed a completely unconstrained design. The only concession Motorola made was at the bus interface level: special pinouts are provided to accommodate the large number of 8-bit peripheral chips already in existence. It should be noted that this is a plus, and in no way affects the architecture or, for that matter, the M68000 bus interface.

The question always arises, is a chip 8, 16, 32, or some other number of bits? To properly answer this question requires setting a base of comparison; we must compare apples with apples and oranges with oranges. One basic metric that can be used is the *internal* register size. If 16-bit registers support 16-bit operations with the majority of arithmetic and logical instructions, the chip can be classed as internally a 16-bit architecture. If only a few of the registers and/or instructions are 16-bit, and the remainder are 8-bit, the chip should be classified as an 8-bit chip. The 8080 family is a good example of an 8-bit chip. Another perspective is the width of the data path to and from memory. Contrary to popular belief, the internal size does not have to be the same as the data path; the data path can be larger or smaller. The only restriction is that the data path always be a multiple of a byte (8 bits). The very popular 8088 is an 8-bit data bus version of the 16-bit data bus 8086. This is the chip found in the original IBM PC.

The M68000 family uses a 32-bit architecture internally. It fully supports its 32-bit registers with a rich instruction set performing 32-bit operations. The MC68000 and MC68010 have a 16-bit data bus. The MC68020 and MC68030 have full 32-bit buses. The MC68008 is an 8-bit bus version of the MC68000. Its position is similar to the Intel 8088 in that it allows interfacing to 8-bit buses and memory components.

The astute reader may be asking the question, what effect does the data bus width have on the microprocessor's speed? This is not a simple question to answer. A 16-bit bus does not necessarily allow a CPU to operate twice as fast as an 8-bit bus. It is true, however, that if the CPU desires to fetch a 16-bit value it will require two accesses to memory if an 8-bit bus is used. But even if the 16-bit bus *is* operating at twice the byte transfer rate of the 8-bit bus, there are many other factors that control the CPU speed.

A CPU requires a clock. The speed of this clock determines the internal rate at which operations are performed. The basic interval between clock pulses is the cycle time for the CPU. It takes a multiple number of cycles for the CPU to execute an instruction. Not all instructions require the same number of cycles, and not every cycle requires an access to memory. Furthermore, the M68000 family supports what is known as an *asynchronous bus:* the speed of the bus does not have to be directly related to the CPU clock. This is a major departure from the M6800 family design.

When you consider this information, together with some more exotic concepts such as instruction prefetch and pipelining, to be covered in later chapters, it is a complicated task to determine the exact relationship between the data bus width and the CPU speed. One thing is clear; the M68000 is a fast microprocessor. Microprocessor manufacturers are constantly designing benchmark tests to show the performance edge of their chips. It is always possible to design a program that shows up the good features of any chip in comparison with others. I will leave it up to you to decide for yourself how much faith you want to place in benchmark programs.

The CPU

Before starting on assembly language programming, it is essential that to take a look at the 68000 microprocessor architecture. We are not going to discuss all the details of the actual machine language used by the CPU, but we must know enough about the structure of memory and the internal CPU registers to use assembly language.

As you are probably aware from your experience with a high-level programming language such as BASIC or Pascal, all information in the computer's memory and acted on by the CPU must be represented as numbers. This includes textual information, which is represented by the numeric equivalents for each character as governed by an appropriate character set. You will learn more about character manipulation in later chapters.

The instructions of the 68000 microprocessor are designed to manipulate numeric information in a variety of ways. Data can be moved from one place to another in the computer's memory, or data can be moved from memory to registers contained in the microprocessor chip. Registers are special places to store and manipulate data. They are like memory locations except that they operate at much higher speeds and serve special purposes for the CPU. The most important use of the registers is in performing arithmetic operations. The 68000 is capable of performing the normal arithmetic operations on integer numbers, such as addition, subtraction, multiplication and division, as well as logical operations. Logical operations allow manipulation of the individual bits of the data. You will soon see how logical operations can be very useful.

Some instructions do not manipulate data but are instead used to control the flow of your program. Often you will desire to repeat an operation many times. Rather than repeat the instructions over and over when you write your program, you can use the control instructions to cause the microprocessor to automatically repeat a group of instructions that you have written only once.

Memory

The memory used with the 68000 consists of a number of locations or cells, each holding one 8-bit number or *byte*. Memory cells are numbered from zero up to the maximum allowable amount of memory. The 68000 allows a maximum of 16 megabytes of memory. A megabyte is equal to 2^{20} or $1{,}048{,}576_{10}$. Therefore, 16 megabytes is actually $16{,}777{,}216_{10}$ locations or addresses. Figure 3 shows the concept of memory cells and their corresponding addresses.

A program consists of instructions and data. Since everything in memory is a number, careful organization is required to prevent the computer from interpreting instructions as data, or data as instructions. This is normally the responsibility of the programmer.

One of the reasons for using assembly language is to free the program-

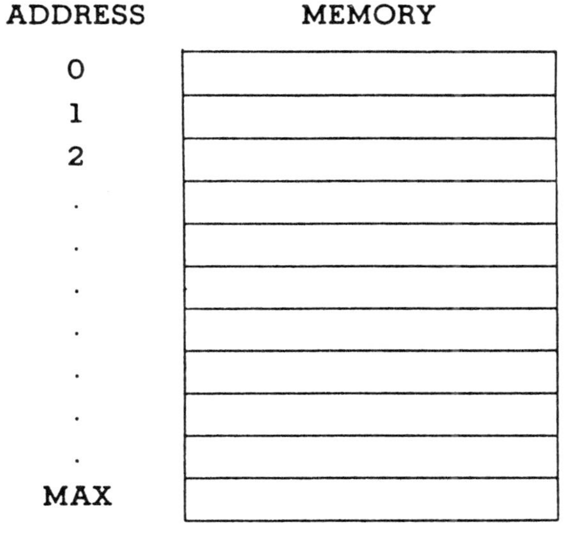

Figure 3 Memory Organization.

mer from having to worry about the exact representation of instructions and data in memory. However, a programmer usually finds the occasion when such knowledge is useful.

Recall that memory consists of an array of individually addressable bytes. If the data we wish to store in memory is only a single byte, there is no question as to *how* it is represented, only *where*. If, however, the data is a word or instruction consisting of more than one byte, it is not clear how this information is stored. Word data (16 bits) are always stored with the high-order byte stored in the lower memory address. This means that if we were reading a dump of memory, word data would be read directly. Many microprocessors have this order reversed, making it much harder to interpret the contents of memory. Figure 4 shows how byte, word and longword values are stored.

Instructions consist of one or more words. The first word always contains the operation code, or *opcode*. This specifies what the particular

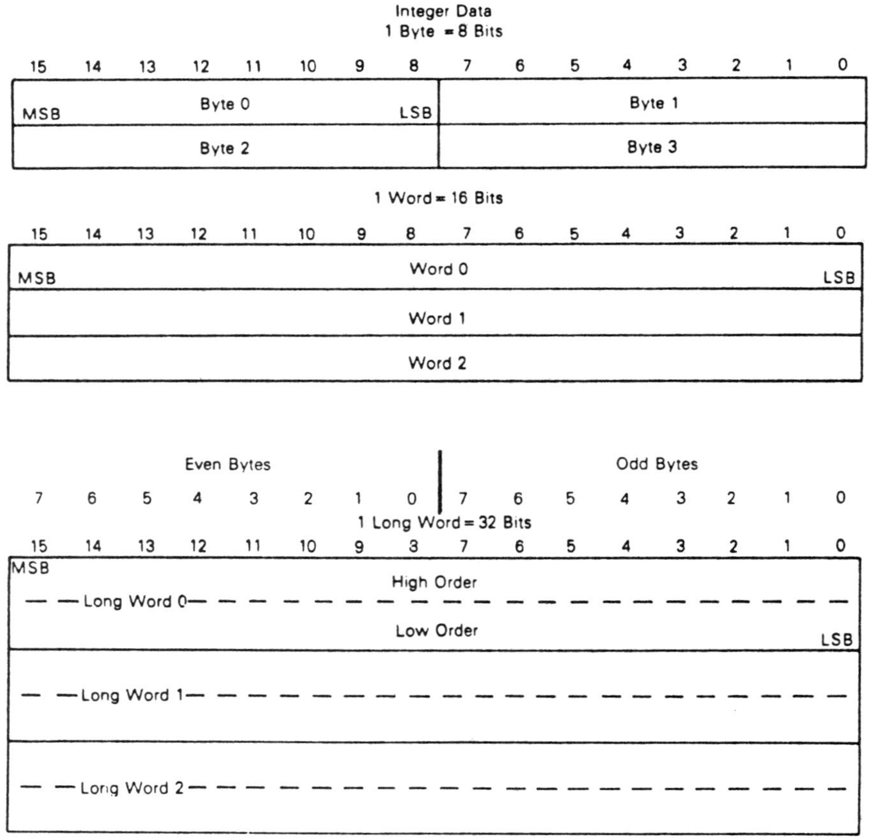

Figure 4 Bytes, words, and longwords memory. (Courtesy of Motorola, Inc.)

instruction is. Many instructions are actually represented by several different opcodes, each specifying a different version of the instruction.

Virtually all systems will have two kinds of memory: *read-only memory* (ROM) and *random-access memory* (RAM). Read-only memory, as its name implies, can be read but not written. How then is it possible to use it? Actually, ROM chips can be written, but not by a program. Certain types of ROM chips have data stored when the chips are manufactured. These ROM chips can never be changed; the data is part of the mask used to create the chips. Other types of ROM chips can be erased, either electrically or using ultraviolet light, and then "reprogrammed." There are special ROM programming devices to do this. ROM's can be used to store a program that will never change. A good example of this is an operating system. All or part of your operating system is more than likely in ROM.

RAM memory is something of a misnomer, since ROM is in fact also a random-access type of memory. By random access we mean that any location in the memory can be accessed in any order, without restriction to a sequential order. Read/write memory actually is what is normally meant by RAM. This is the memory that holds your program and data, as well as data that must be maintained by the operating system. The amount of RAM memory your system has will vary, but some amount of RAM is required with any system. The more RAM memory available, the larger your program and data can be if it is all to fit into memory at the same time.

User and Supervisor Modes

The 68000 executes programs in one of two modes, *user* or *supervisor*. If a program is running in the user mode, it is most likely a normal everyday program. You will more than likely be writing mostly user-mode programs. The supervisor mode is used by programs that require complete control over all aspects of the hardware. Your operating system is a prime example of a program that would run in supervisor mode.

If a program is running in the user mode, it is restricted in a number of ways. Some instructions are designated as privileged. One of these is the STOP instruction. A program in user mode cannot execute any of the privileged instructions. This helps to prevent a program with bugs from crashing the system it is running on. In a multiple user system it is important that one user not be able to do damage to another user. If a user crashes the system, or otherwise performs a privileged instruction, it could affect all users.

While not built into the 68000 CPU chip, many machines have implemented various forms of memory protection. The 68000 provides the user/supervisor mode information on every reference to memory. If the system is so designed, certain areas of memory can be restricted to references only when in the supervisor mode. If a user mode instruction were to try to access this "protected" area of memory, a special condition or "exception" would occur and the operating system could then take control before any damage is done.

The CPU Registers

In one sense, a register is a type of memory location. However, it is located right on the CPU chip itself. Registers differ from conventional memory locations in that they operate at a higher speed. In other words, if we use registers in a calculation, it will be faster to perform than if memory locations were used. Additionally, registers are specified by special names rather than just by numbers. The existence of a good register set is a major asset to the architecture of a particular microprocessor. The 68000 family is a good example of a microprocessor with a rich register set.

Depending on whether a program is running in user or supervisor mode, there is a slightly different view of the CPU registers. This view is known as the *programmer's model.* The following paragraphs discuss the programmer's model for the user mode.

The 68000 has sixteen 32-bit general-purpose registers. These are divided into two groups of eight. The eight data registers, D0 through D7, are the registers you would normally use to perform arithmetic operations. These can be used as bytes, words, or longwords. The second group of eight general-purpose registers are the address registers, A0 through A7. These registers can be used for arithmetic operations, but are primarily designed for use in the special *addressing modes* discussed in subsequent chapters. The address registers can be used as words or longwords, but not as bytes. In the next chapter you will learn more of the details concerning the use of the sixteen general-purpose registers.

Address register A7, also known as the *user stack pointer* (USP), has a special interpretation by the 68000. Some instructions affect this register without its being explicitly specified. You will learn all about stacks and the use of the USP in Chapter 7. For now, consider it as just one of the eight address registers.

Another very important register is the *program counter,* or PC. This 32-bit register is used to hold the memory address of the next instruction that the CPU will execute. The programmer never explicitly references this register; its contents are always updated by the CPU. Normally, the PC advances as the program executes sequential instructions that are in memory. If an instruction causes a branch to a part of the program other than the next sequential instruction, the PC will be updated automatically.

The final register in the user programmer's model is the *condition code register,* or CCR. This is an 8-bit register that contains individual bits that are set or reset as the result of arithmetic instructions. The CCR will be covered in detail in Chapter 5.

The supervisor programmer's model is identical to the user mode programmer's model with two exceptions. First, in the supervisor mode there is a different register A7, known as the *supervisor stack pointer,* or SSP. This register is totally distinct from the USP. Second, the condition code register is still present, but it is in a 16-bit form. Together with the new high-order 8 bits, it is known as the *status register,* or SR. Figure 5 shows the programmer's models for both the user and supervisor modes.

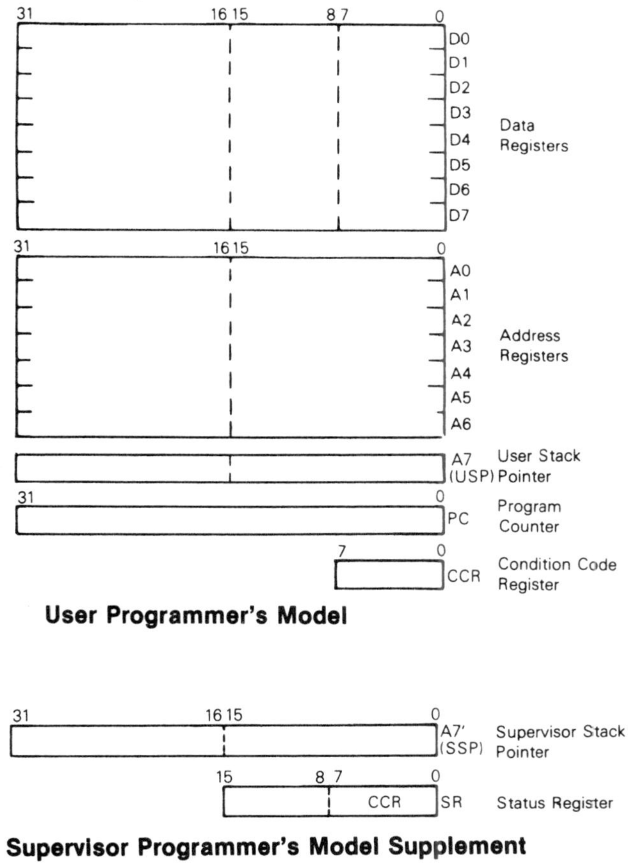

Figure 5 Programmer's models. (Courtesy of Motorola, Inc.)

Input/Output

It may come as a surprise to you that the 68000 does not have any input/output instructions. How then, is I/O performed? The 68000 family uses a technique known as *memory mapped I/O*. This means that input/output devices are connected to the system via interface chips that are connected to the CPU as if they were areas of memory. A small part of the huge amount of memory we are allowed must be sacrificed; it is now used for I/O and can't be used for main memory at the same time. The real advantage to the memory-mapped I/O technique is that rather than being restricted to a small number of special I/O instructions, we can use *all* of the 68000 memory reference instructions with I/O devices.

A large variety of I/O interface chips are available for the 68000 family. A number of these were formerly used with the M6800 family. The 68000 allows the use of these 8-bit chips as well as the newer 16-bit I/O devices specifically designed for the 68000. In Chapter 12 we will discuss the programming of a typical I/O chip. We will use an asynchronous serial I/O device or UART chip.

Exercises

1. What are the three main parts of a microcomputer?
2. What is the difference between the MC68000 and the MC68008?
3. What is the newest member of the M68000 family?
4. Is the M68000 family an extension of the M6800 architecture?
5. How many bits is the internal architecture of the 68000?
6. What are the data bus sizes for the M68000 family?
7. Is the M68000 data bus synchronous or asynchronous?
8. What is the difference between RAM and ROM?
9. What is the purpose of supervisor mode?
10. Are registers faster or slower than memory?
11. How much memory is allowed with the MC68000?
12. What are the 32-bit general-purpose registers?
13. Is multi-byte data stored with the high order byte in the lowest or highest address?
14. Are all instructions the same number of words?
15. What is the purpose of the program counter?
16. What register is used for the USP and SSP?
17. How many input/output instructions does the 68000 have?

Answers

1. CPU, memory, and I/O.
2. The MC68000 transfers two bytes of data to and from memory, while the MC68008 only transfers one byte.
3. The MC68030.
4. No.
5. 32 bits.
6. The MC68000 and the MC68010 are 16-bit buses, while the MC68020 and the MC68030 are 32-bit buses.
7. Asynchronous.
8. RAM can be read and written, while ROM can only be read.
9. Supervisor mode allows the design of operating systems that can make it more difficult for a user's program to crash the system.
10. Much faster.
11. 16 megabytes.
12. D0–D7 and A0–A7.
13. The lowest.
14. No, an instruction can be one or more words. The first word is the opcode word.
15. The PC contains the addresses of the instructions as they are executed.
16. A7.
17. None; memory-mapped I/O is used.

CHAPTER 3

ASSEMBLER SOURCE FORMAT

There are many assemblers available for the 68000 family. They differ from each other in minor ways. It would be virtually impossible to present the details of every assembler on the market. Rather, I will present what is a relatively standard core, based on the specifications provided by Motorola for its assemblers. There are many assembler features that are left out. A careful reading of your assembler manual will provide these details. What is presented here is enough information to get you programming in 68000 assembler. You should, however, verify that your assembler is compatible with this core.

The assembler processes the source program line by line. A line of the source program can be translated into a machine instruction, or generate an element or elements of data to be placed in memory; or the line may only provide information to the assembler itself. The lines of the source program are sometimes referred to as *source statements*.

Regardless of the use of a particular line of the source program, the format of each line is relatively standard. The general format of a source line consists of four fields, as follows:

```
[<label>] <operation> [<operand>] [<comment>]
```

Not all of the four fields must appear on all lines; brackets [ ] have been used to indicate fields that are optional. The comment field is always optional, but the label and/or operand fields may be required depending on the contents of the operation field. Unless a source line consists solely of a comment, the operation field is required. If a line is to consist only of a comment, the first character on the line must be an asterisk (*). This must appear in the leftmost position on the line, column 1. The remainder of the line is ignored by the assembler.

A field consists of one or more *tokens*. A token is the smallest meaningful unit of information that the assembler uses. Tokens are identifiers or numeric constants. The symbolic names of the machine instructions are an example of identifiers. The fields of a source line are separated by one or more spaces. All 68000 assemblers recognize the space character as a field separator; most assemblers also recognize the tab character as a field separator, and treat it as a space. Generally, where one space or tab is allowed, you may also use more than one. You must be careful not to insert a space in the middle of a field, as this causes the assembler to treat the next non-blank characters as the next field.

A *delimiter* is a special character that can serve to mark the end of a token, besides having its own special meaning. Punctuation characters such as commas, periods, and colons are examples of delimiters.

Figure 6 is an excerpt from a sample program that we will use to further discuss the format of assembler source lines. As you can see, the program consists mainly of character sequences that look like English language words separated by punctuation. These character sequences are the *identifiers*. The rules for creating identifiers varies slightly from assembler to assembler, but the following rules work with almost every assembler:

1. The first character must be alphabetic (A...Z, a...z).
2. Any additional characters may be alphabetics or digits (0...9).
3. Only the first eight characters are significant; the rest are ignored.

There are a number of variations from these rules. Some assemblers retain significance for more than eight characters. Others treat the upper- and lower-case alphabetic characters as equivalent, or retain uniqueness, or allow only the use of one case. For example, "COUNT" and "count" may be completely different identifiers. Generally, assemblers allow instructions and directives to be in either case. Characters other than the alphanumerics are sometimes allowed. Check your assembler manual to be sure. Throughout this book we will use upper case, and be careful not to mix cases.

The Label Field

The label field always contains a symbol formed with the standard rules for identifiers. If a label is present, it is used to associate the symbol with a value. This value may represent the location of data in memory, a constant, or the location in memory of the instruction in the operation field.

Labels can be used to locate data, such as a variable, stored at particular locations in memory. A variable consists of one or more bytes. Normally variables will be bytes, words, or longwords. It is important to reserve sufficient space for a variable. If an instruction tries to place a longword of data at a memory location only large enough to hold a word, the data will overwrite a part of memory that it shouldn't.

```
*PROGRAM TO ECHO A LINE
        TEXT
*
START:  LEA      BUFFER,A0          INITIALIZE BUFFER POINTER
LOOP:   JSR      GETC               GET A CHARACTER
        MOVE.B   D0,(A0)+           SAVE CHARACTER IN BUFFER
        CMPI.B   #CR,D0             END OF LINE?
        BNE      LOOP               NEXT CHARACTER
        LEA      BUFFER,A0          RESET BUFFER POINTER
        JSR      NEWLINE            GO TO A NEW LINE
LOOP2:  MOVE.B   (A0)+,D0           GET A CHARACTER
        JSR      PUTC               OUTPUT TO SCREEN
        CMPI.B   #CR,D0             END OF LINE?
        BNE      LOOP2              GET NEXT CHARACTER
        JSR      NEWLINE            GO TO NEW LINE
FINI:   MOVE.W   #0,-(SP)           RETURN TO SYSTEM
        TRAP     #1                 "
*
PUTC:   MOVEM.L D0-D7/A0-A6,-(SP) SAVE REGISTERS
        ANDI.L   #$FF,D0            MAKE SURE WE HAVE ONLY A BYTE
        MOVE.W   D0,-(SP)           OUTPUT TO OP. SYS.
        MOVE.W   #2,-(SP)           "
        TRAP     #1                 "
        ADDQ.L   #4,SP              CLEAN UP STACK
        MOVEM.L (SP)+,D0-D7/A0-A6 RESTORE REGISTERS
        RTS                         RETURN
*
GETC:   MOVEM.L D1-D7/A0-A6,-(SP) SAVE REGISTERS
        MOVE.W   #1,-(SP)           GET A CHAR. FROM OP. SYS.
        TRAP     #1                 "
        ANDI.L   #$7F,D0            MASK TO 7 BITS
        ADDQ.L   #2,SP              CLEAN UP STACK
        MOVEM.L (SP)+,D1-D7/A0-A6 RESTORE REGISTERS
        RTS                         RETURN
*
CR:     EQU      $0D                CARRIAGE RETURN
LF:     EQU      $0A                LINE FEED
*
NEWLINE:MOVE.L   D0,-(SP)           SAVE D0
        MOVE.B   #CR,D0             OUTPUT A CR
        JSR      PUTC               "
        MOVE.B   #LF,D0             OUTPUT A LF
        JSR      PUTC               "
        MOVE.L   (SP)+,D0           RESTORE D0
        RTS                         RETURN
*
        DATA
*
BUFFER: DS.B     100                100 CHARACTER BUFFER
        END
```

Figure 6 Sample program.

A symbol in the label field can be made to equal a numeric constant. Anywhere this symbol appears in your program it is interpreted as if you wrote the constant itself. For example, you could define the symbol MAX to represent the constant 1000.

A symbol in the label field can also be used to specify the memory location of an instruction. This is a true label. Although the first field is called the label field, only the symbols that are present in the label field of a source line that translates into a memory location are the true labels of a 68000 assembly language program. Unless a label starts in column 1, it must be delimited with a semicolon. In the latter case, the label can start in any column as long as it is the first thing on the line.

The Operation Field

The operation field contains either a machine instruction or an assembler directive. Each machine instruction has a special symbol or *mnemonic* associated with it. If a particular machine instruction is desired, the proper mnemonic must be placed in the operation field. Assembler directives have symbolic names that are different from the machine instructions. The assembler is thus able to differentiate between a machine instruction and a directive.

If a machine instruction is placed in the operation field, the assembler will generate the appropriate words to be placed in memory corresponding to the translation of the source statement. Assembler directives may or may not generate bytes to be stored in memory. Some directives merely control the format of the assembly listing, or provide other information about the program. Directives are also used to define symbols.

The Operand Field

Many machine instructions as well as assembler directives require one or more *operands*. The operand field is used to provide these operands. Individual operands can consist of constants, variables, or special symbols. Expressions made up of constants, variables, and special symbols are also permitted. The rules for making up expressions vary slightly from assembler to assembler. Standard arithmetic expressions such as

```
COUNT+5
```

are allowed by all assemblers. The characters +, −, *, and / are interpreted as addition, subtraction, multiplication, and division respectively. Most assemblers allow the use of parentheses in arithmetic expressions. Consult your assembler manual for details on expression evaluation.

If more than one operand is required with an instruction or assembler directive, the operands are separated by commas. These commas are delimeters, and you must not insert a space before or after their use. For example,

```
ADD.L   D2,D3
```

results in the two registers, D2 and D3, being added together, with the result placed in register D3.

The 68000 microprocessor uses a variety of *addressing modes*. The addressing mode is the method the CPU uses to locate its operands in memory. In order to specify the particular addressing mode desired, the operands are formed with the use of special delimiters. For example,

```
MOVE.L  D0,(A0)
```

indicates the register indirect mode of addressing used with the AO register. The left and right parenthesis are the special delimeters used to indicate this type of addressing. You will learn more about the 68000 addressing modes in Chapter 6.

The Comment Field

The comment field is used to provide information for the programmer and others who may have occasion to examine the program. Assembly language is not self-documenting. Often, even the programmer may have difficulty in remembering exactly how her program works if she has been away from it for some time. Comments are best used to provide a running description of the program's operation. Comments help those who may have to maintain the program in the future. Comments can also be used to provide information as to how to use a particular program.

A comment can be used on every line of the program. The first space after the operand field starts the comment. The remainder of the line is ignored by the assembler. This is why it is very important not to include any spaces in the operand field. Comments are not interpreted or used in any way by the assembler. When a comment is the only thing on a source line, you must use an asterisk in column 1. You can see the comments in Figure 6.

On Choosing Symbols

When you need to select a new symbol for use as a constant, variable, or label for an instruction, you are free to create arbitrary symbols as long as you adhere to the rules for creating an identifier. However, some assemblers do not allow you to create symbols that are the same as the instruction mnemonics or assembler directives. These reserved symbols are known as the *keywords* of the assembler. Although it may seem clear when a symbol is used as an instruction rather than a variable, some assemblers are not that smart. Even if your assembler can make this distinction, it is a good practice to avoid using keywords. Consult your assembler manual. You can usually find a table of all the keywords that the assembler recognizes.

It is good programming practice to choose symbols that have a meaning related to their use in the program. For example, if you use a variable to keep track of a count, why not name it COUNT? Short symbols like I, J, or N can be used, but don't tell us much. Labels for instructions can indicate the function of a particular portion of the program. The label READDATA clearly indicates the reading of some data. The label L23 does not convey any meaning. Although many assemblers allow extremely long identifiers, keeping them to eight characters or less is standard practice. Most programmers line up the source line fields on tab stops set at every eight columns, and long identifiers make lining up the fields difficult unless a lot of extra space is used to accommodate the longest symbols.

Constants

A constant is a value that doesn't change during program assembly or execution. Two types of constants can be used: *integers* and *character strings*.

Integer constants are numeric quantities that can be represented by 32 bits or less. You will remember from Chapter 1 that numbers can be represented in various number bases. If a constant is specified without indicating this base or radix, it is assumed to be in the decimal number base. To indicate that a constant is written in a number base other than 10, we can prefix the number with a radix indicator. The radix indicators we can use are:

Indicator	Base
%	2
@	8
[none]	10
$	16

A binary constant would naturally consist of a percent sign followed by only 1's and 0's. If we try to write a binary constant with other than 1's and 0's, it is an error. The following are all valid constants:

1234	1234_{10}
$1234	1234_{16}
%1100111001	1100111001_2
$FFFF	$FFFF_{16}$
@377	377_8

Character string constants are ASCII character strings delimited by apostrophes. A character string constant must appear entirely on one line. Any valid "printing" characters from the ASCII character set are allowed. For example,

```
'Hello there.'
```

is a character string of length 12. The two apostrophes are not part of the string. What do we do if we want an apostrophe? We can't just place one in the middle of the string, that would terminate the string. If we want a single apostrophe, we merely write two apostrophes. For example,

```
'Don''t give up the ship.'
```

is actually the string "Don't give up the ship.".

If a string is one to four characters long it can be used as a numeric value. In this case, the characters are right-justified. This means that the ASCII values of the characters are used as the low-order bytes. Any high-order bytes that do not have a corresponding character are filled with zeros. If it is longer than four characters, it is merely the string of bytes with the appropriate ASCII values. Both upper and lower case characters can be used in character strings.

Data-Defining Directives

Before we cover the specific instructions of the 68000, it is important that we discuss the methods used with the assembler for placing specific data values in memory. The *define constant* or DC directive is used for this purpose. The general form of the DC directive is

```
[<label>]          DC[.<size>]       <list>
```

The size specifier indicates the size of the data to be placed into memory. It may be B, W, or L, which stand for byte, word, and longword, respectively. If the size specifier is omitted, the size defaults to word. <list> is a list of one or more data values. If a label is used, it is assigned the address of the data. Without a label it is difficult to refer to the data. Here are some examples of the use of the DC directive:

```
COUNT:   DC.L     100
ARRAY:   DC.B     1,2,3,4,5,6
WORDS:   DC.W     $FF,$1000
WORD:    DC.W     %11111
```

If a value doesn't take up exactly the full number of bits in the memory location, the high-order bits of the byte, word, or longword are padded with zeros. For example, the constant \$FF is placed into a word as \$00FF.

The DC directive is also used to place ASCII character strings into memory. This is the only directive that allows a character string.

```
STR1:    DC.B     'ENTER VALUE:'
```

The above example would place the ASCII character codes for the string "ENTER VALUE:" into successive bytes of memory starting at the location whose address is assigned to the label STR1.

At this point I should mention an important requirement of data that is stored in memory. For word and longword data, the address of the first byte must be on an even boundary. This means that addresses like \$12345 or \$1001 are not legal for word or longword data. Most assemblers will ensure that word or longword data is aligned on these even boundaries by skipping a byte where necessary. This byte is essentially wasted. It is always a good idea to group all word and longword data together to minimize the number of these wasted bytes. For example, the following directives would cause an extra byte to be used.

```
DC.W     0
DC.B     1,2,3
DC.L     100
```

Sometimes we desire to reserve a location in memory for some data whose value is not known at assembly time. Rather than place a meaningless value in the location, we can use another directive. The *define storage* directive or DS is used for this purpose. Its form is

```
[<label>]         DS[[.<size>]     <items>
```

The size is specified just as it is for the DC directive. <items> specifies the number of bytes, words, or longwords we want to reserve space for. It normally has a value starting at one. If zero items are specified, some assemblers merely ensure that the current memory address is even and don't reserve any storage unless a skipped byte is needed for alignment. Here are some examples:

```
COUNT:  DS.L    1       1 LONGWORD
ARRAY:  DS.B    100     100 BYTE ARRAY
BUFFER: DS.W    50      50 WORD BUFFER
```

Symbol Equates

Quite often a programmer desires to assign a specific value to a symbol. The equate directive, EQU, is used for this purpose. This is quite different from letting the assembler assign an address value to a label. Suppose we want to set the value of symbol MAX to the value 100 decimal. Here is how we do it:

```
MAX:    EQU     100
```

Notice that the symbol appears in the label field. You may have been tempted to write MAX=100. This is the way you would do it in a language like BASIC or FORTRAN, but not with 68000 assembler. You must use EQU. We can assign a value to a symbol that involves another symbol just as long as the other symbol is already defined. For example,

```
ALPHA:  EQU     100
BETA:   EQU     ALPHA+100
```

would assign the value 200 to BETA. If we reversed the order, it would not be legal. The general form of EQU is

```
<label> EQU     <exp>
```

<exp> is any legal expression as long as it does not contain any undefined symbols. Symbols that will be defined further along in the program are called *forward references.*

The END Directive

The END directive is an important directive. It is only used once during a program and is the very last source line. This directive informs the assembler that there are no more source lines to follow. The assembler stops processing input lines when it reaches the END directive. Be sure always to include an END, and make sure you don't include any extra ones in the middle of your program. Some assemblers allow a label to be used on the END directive. The value of this symbol will represent the first memory address not used by your program. While few programmers will ever use this feature, there are some applications where it is useful. For example, if the first and last locations of a program are known, it is simple to compute its size. If the first statement contains the label START, and the END directive contains the label FINISH, the program's length is FINISH–START.

Exercises

1. Does every line of the source program have to represent a machine instruction?
2. Is a comment required on every source line?
3. What is the smallest unit of information that the assembler uses?
4. What characters can be used to separate the fields of the source statement?
5. Indicate which of the following are legal identifiers:
   FOO   5ORANGES   F1040   FULL(BYTE
6. What two things can the operation field contain?
7. What special character starts a comment line?
8. What special character is used to separate multiple operands in the operand field?
9. When is it legal to leave out the operation field of a source statement?
10. What are the four fields of a source statement?
11. What is a mnemonic?
12. Are blanks or tabs allowed in the operand field?
13. Can a comment precede an instruction on a source line?
14. Tab stops are normally set up for every how many columns?

15. Indicate which of the following are legal constants:
    12345 $ABCD @F00 %345 @777
16. What is the character string constant for "Let's quote''''"?
17. What is the last statement in a program?
18. Write the assembler directive to place the word constant 123 in memory at location ALPHA.
19. Write the assembler directive to reserve 1000 bytes at location BETA.
20. Write the assembler directive to set the value of SIZE to 8.

Answers

1. No. Source line may be used to create data items or provide information for the assembler.
2. No. Comments are always optional, but it is a good idea to provide as many comments as possible.
3. A token. Tokens are identifiers or numbers.
4. Spaces or tabs.
5. F00 is legal; 5ORANGES is not legal since it starts with a digit; F1040 is legal; FULL(BYTE is not legal since a (is not a legal character in an identifier.
6. A machine instruction or an assembler directive.
7. An asterisk.
8. A comma.
9. When the source line consists solely of a comment.
10. Label, operation, operand, and comment.
11. The symbolic representation of a machine instruction.
12. No, the blank or tab starts a comment.
13. No, the remainder of the line is ignored.
14. 8
15. 12345 is a legal decimal constant; $ABCD is legal; @F00 is not a legal octal (base 8) constant; %345 is not a legal binary constant because only the digits 0 and 1 can be used with binary constants; @777 is a legal octal constant.
16. 'Let''s quote'''''''
17. A statement with the END directive.
18. ALPHA: DC.W 123
19. BETA: DS.B 100
20. SIZE: EQU 8

CHAPTER 4

GETTING STARTED

In order to write a program in assembly language, you must develop a familiarity with the machine instructions of the 68000. These instructions can be grouped together depending on their functions. For example, there are instructions that are used to move data between memory and the registers, and another group of instructions that perform the standard arithmetic operations like addition, subtraction, multiplication, and division. Still others perform only control functions such as looping. Rather than present all the instructions from each group in order, you will learn some key instructions from each group so that you can start to understand complete programs without being overwhelmed with too many instructions.

After you have completed this chapter you will know enough to actually write and execute simple 68000 assembly language programs. It is important that you take the time to experiment with your computer system before going on to the more advanced material. Try running the programs from this chapter as well as some of your own design. Let's get started.

Data Movement

Moving data between registers, and between registers and memory, is a fundamental requirement of all programs. The 68000, like many other microprocessors, provides a variety of machine instructions to perform these operations. The most fundamental instruction is the move instruction, which has the appropriate mnemonic, MOVE. There are actually a number of different move instructions which all have this same mnemonic. The assembler determines which of the actual machine instructions is needed by a combination of an optional suffix or extension to the mnemonic, and the types of the operands used with the MOVE instruction. This means that we can move a constant into a register, the contents of a memory location into a register, or a register into a register, without having to remember different mnemonics for all these instructions.

The general form of the MOVE instruction is

```
[<label>]  MOVE[.<size>]  <source>,<destination>  [<comment>]
```

The <size> following the MOVE indicates the type of operation to be performed. It must be a B, W, or L, standing for byte, word or longword. If the size is omitted, the default value is taken as word. The MOVE instruction takes the value of the source operand and places a *copy* of it into the destination operand. The source operand is not changed. The destination operand may be a data register or a memory location, but not a constant. The source operand may be a data register, memory location, or constant. A number of other instructions have source and destination operands. Always remember that the direction of the data flow is from the left operand to the right operand. You may have used an assembly language for another computer (for example, from the 8080 or 8086 families) in which the flow is reversed. Be careful when you start out programming the 68000 so you don't make a mistake.

Let's assume that the D0 and D1 registers contain the following values:

D0	D1
123	456

We now execute the following instruction:

```
MOVE.L      D0,D1
```

The D0 and D1 registers would contain the following values after execution:

D0	D1
123	123

Notice that the previous value in the D1 register has been lost and that the new value is identical to that contained in the D0 register. Also note that the contents of the D0 register remains unchanged. We must also be careful that the size of the source operand in bytes matches the size of the destination operand in bytes. This is normally not a problem with the registers, since they will always accommodate a full longword. However, specifying a memory location that is actually a byte, when we really want a word or longword, will result in faulty program behavior. Your assembler will not be able to catch this mistake, and it is a common cause of subtle errors that are hard to debug. If you must perform a move between two data elements of different lengths, there are techniques that can be used. We will discuss them as we move along. The following is an example of a MOVE instruction used to move the contents of the byte at memory location ALPHA to the byte at memory location BETA.

```
MOVE.B  ALPHA,BETA
```

A constant value can be moved into a register or into a memory location. A constant as a source operand is specified by preceding it with the special character #. This is known as an *immediate* operand. The following instruction will move the constant 100 into register D0:

```
MOVE.L  #100,D0
```

Although it makes no sense, it is possible to write a MOVE instruction indicating that the contents of a register or a memory location are to be stored into a constant. This is not permitted, but if you forget the order of the source and destination operands it may come out this way.

```
MOVE.L  D0,#100
```

is not legal. Fortunately, your assembler will detect this error and let you know.

If the byte or word form of an instruction is used with a data register as the destination, only the lower byte or word of the register is changed. All the high-order bits remain unchanged. This is important to remember, since we may move a byte into a register and then subsequently use the register as a longword. All those high-order bytes will most likely be meaningless garbage and cause an erroneous value to be used. For example, if register D0 contains the value $12345678,

```
MOVE.B  #$00,D0
```

would result in D0 containing $12345600, and not $00000000. Further along in the book I will discuss ways to handle this problem.

Quite often a programmer desires to swap the contents of two registers. The 68000 provides a special instruction to perform this operation. Before looking at this instruction, let's see how to program a swap operation using only the MOVE instruction. To swap the contents of registers D0 and D1, a programmer may at first be tempted to write:

```
MOVE.L  D0,D1
MOVE.L  D1,D0
```

Unfortunately these two instructions do not accomplish the desired result. The first MOVE instruction has destroyed the contents of register D1. This is the value that must be placed in register D0 by the second MOVE. This second MOVE will erroneously result in the value of register D0 not being changed. To perform the swap correctly, a temporary storage location is needed. This can be a register or a memory variable. The instructions

```
MOVE.L  D0,D2
MOVE.L  D1,D0
MOVE.L  D2,D1
```

will perform the swap correctly. However, register D2 has thus been used as a temporary storage location, and we may not wish to destroy its contents either. The use of a memory location as a temporary frees the registers but will cause the instructions to execute at a slower speed.

The 68000 EXG (exchange registers) is our salvation. We can swap between any of the 16 registers but not between two memory locations or between a memory location and a register. We can write the above program as:

```
EXG.L   D0,D1
```

The EXG instruction will operate on bytes, words, or longwords when the proper instruction extension is specified. Of course, we can't swap two constants or a constant and anything else.

I didn't mention it above, but a value cannot be moved into an address register using the MOVE instruction; the MOVEA instruction must be used. Its general form is

```
MOVEA[.<size>]   <ea>,An

<size> = W or L
```

Any operations involving an address register as a destination can only use the word or longword forms. In the case of a word form, the word is sign-extended to 32 bits before being used. The entire address register is always used.

Addition and Subtraction

While moving values from one register to another is an important part of assembly language programming, arithmetic operations such as addition and subtraction will allow you to start writing programs that actually perform meaningful tasks. The general form of the add and subtract instructions are:

```
[<label>]  ADD[.<size>] <source>,<destination>  [<comment>]
[<label>]  SUB[.<size>] <source>,<destination>  [<comment>]
```

As with the MOVE instruction, <size> may be B, W, or L.

The ADD instruction forms the sum of the source and destination operands, which may be words, bytes, or longwords, and replaces the destination operand with this sum. Both operands may be signed or unsigned numbers. SUB works like ADD except that the source operand is subtracted from the destination operand. Once again, the result replaces the destination operand. The source operand may be any register or memory location, or a constant. The destination operand may be a data register or memory location. For the ADD and SUB instructions, MOVE source and destination operands cannot both be memory locations. At least one operand must be a data register, and the destination operand cannot be an address register.

Here, and in later chapters, we will express instructions in a more proper manner by indicating the allowable type for the source and destination operands. The ADD and SUB instructions have the following forms:

```
ADD[.<size>]     <ea>,Dn
ADD[.<size>]     Dn,<ea>

SUB[.<size>]     <ea>,Dn
SUB[.<size>]     Dn,<ea>
```

<ea> is a general way of expressing an *effective address*. An effective address generally includes the data registers and the contents of memory locations. Each instruction has more complicated limitations on the effective addresses of instructions. You should consult Appendix C for these details. Dn indicates that any of the eight data registers D0 through D7 can be used.

The following are all valid ADD and SUB instructions:

```
ADD.L   D2,D3
SUB.W   #5,D0
ADD.B   D6,COUNT           COUNT IS A BYTE LOCATION
```

As mentioned in the discussion of the MOVE instruction, the size, in bytes, of the source and destination operands must be the same. When a constant is used, it must be capable of being represented by the number of bytes of the destination operand. If a two-byte (word) constant is specified, it cannot be used with a MOVE.B, ADD.B, or SUB.B instruction; in this case the destination operand is only a single byte. However, if a one-byte constant is used with a word or longword destination, the assembler is able to generate the proper machine instruction. The 68000 assembly language includes a mechanism in which numeric constants are automatically sign-extended to 8, 16, or 32 bits as needed. The following instruction is not legal and would be flagged as an error by the assembler:

```
ADD.B   #1000,D0
```

The source and destination operands can be the same.

```
ADD.L   D0,D0
```

results in the D0 register being doubled.

Note that the ADD or SUB instructions do not allow the more general form

```
ADD[.<size>]    <ea>,<ea>
SUB[.<size>]    <ea>,<ea>
```

This would eliminate the possibility of adding a constant to a memory location, or subtracting a constant from an address register. There are a couple of additional forms of the ADD and SUB instructions that help to eliminate some of these restrictions.

```
ADDA[.<size>]   <ea>,An
SUBA[.<size>]   <ea>,An

<size> = W or L
```

allows adding or subtracting to an address register.

```
ADDI[.<size>]   #<data>,<ea>
SUBI[.<size>]   #<data>,<ea>
```

allow adding or subtracting an immediate value to a memory location or data register. This instruction cannot be used to add or subtract an immediate value to an address register. For example, the following instructions are correct:

```
ADDI.L  #1000,COUNT
ADDA.L  #2,A5
```

Many assemblers allow the use of the mnemonics MOVE, ADD, SUB, and so on without qualifying the instruction; the assembler decides what instruction to use. For example, if you write

```
MOVE    D0,A0
```

the assembler would use the MOVEA form of the instruction. Check your assembler manual to be sure you can do this. Even if allowed, it is better to use the correct instruction mnemonic.

Quite often we may want to set a register or memory location equal to zero. We can always move a zero value into the destination operand. Or we can subtract a register from itself. There are other ways to zero a register or memory location, but none is better than the clear instruction (CLR). This instruction is provided for just this purpose. Its general form is

```
[<label>]  CLR[.<size>] <ea>  [<comment>]
```

The size may be B, W, or L. We can clear a data register or memory location, but not an address register. Here are some examples:

```
CLR.L   D0      CLEARS D0
CLR.B   CHAR    CLEARS A BYTE IN MEMORY
CLR.W   D5      CLEARS LOW ORDER WORD IN D5
```

Input and Output

While we can write many programs that do not require data to be entered by the user, we certainly do not want to limit ourselves in this way. Programs can be written that manipulate data that is included in the assembly language source itself. This would be of limited use if the data required frequent modification: each time the program is to be run with different data the source program would have to be edited and then reassembled, a time-consuming and unreasonable requirement for many users. What we seek is the ability to obtain data entered from the user's terminal or keyboard at the time the program is executed.

Similarly, a method is normally required to obtain output from the program during or after its execution. Unless there is some way of displaying the program output on a terminal or a printer, a program's action can only be determined by looking at the contents of variables or registers that may have changed during the program's execution. While this may be possible with programmer utilities, such as a debugger, it is certainly not the best way to start programming in assembly language.

Unfortunately, input and output is always dependent on the particular computer you are using. Not all computer systems using the 68000 processor are equipped with the same input/output devices. Some systems have a built in video display and others may have a separate CRT terminal. Normally, some degree of hardware independence is provided by the operating system being used. But here again we will not all be using the same operating system. Some readers may be using an Apple Macintosh and others may be using an Atari ST or one of many other operating systems that operate with 68000-based systems.

In order to start to write programs without worrying about the system-dependent details, we will use a set of input/output subroutines whose inner workings will be different for different operating systems. These subroutines will assume a standard ASCII terminal or display. Since the interface is through your operating system, the details of your particular hardware are automatically taken care of. It doesn't matter if you have a video display or a printing terminal. Appendix B gives the actual source statements for these subroutines written for the Atari ST, Commodore Amiga, and Apple Macintosh operating systems. (While this does not cover every operating system in use, the majority of readers will probably be accommodated.)

It is possible to write many programs that involve inputting one or more decimal numbers from the keyboard and outputting one or more decimal numbers to the screen. It is also necessary to be able to input and output ASCII characters. We will start by introducing some useful subroutines to perform these tasks. A *procedure,* or *subroutine,* is a portion of a program that can be referenced, or called, from many different places within the program without the necessity of repeating the instructions for this procedure each time it is used. Here are the procedures; read their descriptions carefully so that you will understand their use.

1. INDEC—Input an unsigned decimal number from the keyboard. The number is entered as one or more decimal digits terminated by a character other than 0–9. This terminating character may be a carriage return (RETURN key on most keyboards). The number must be representable by four bytes and must therefore be between 0 and 4,294,967,295. The number is placed in the D0 register.
2. OUTDEC—Output an unsigned decimal number to the screen. The number is taken from the longword in register D0. It is output without a terminating carriage return and line feed (doesn't advance to the next line). The range of the output value is the same as for INDEC.
3. NEWLINE—Terminate the present output line and output the carriage return and line feed characters to advance to the start of the next line.
4. GETC—Input a single character from the keyboard. The ASCII value of the character is returned in the lower eight bits of the register D0. The high-order bits are cleared.

5. PUTC—Output a single character to the screen. The character is taken from the low-order eight bits of register D0.

In order to use these procedures within your program, a special instruction, JSR (jump to subroutine) is provided in the 68000 instruction set. The exact operation of this instruction, and of subroutines in general, will be discussed in Chapter 8. The mnemonic JSR is followed by the symbol representing the subroutine's name. For now, assume that when you use the JSR instruction, the program performs the operations specified by the subroutine that is called, and then continues on to the next instruction. The following program excerpt will obtain two numbers from your keyboard, add them together, and then output the result to your screen:

```
JSR      INDEC
JSR      NEWLINE
MOVE.L   D0,D1
JSR      INDEC
JSR      NEWLINE
ADD.L    D1,D0
JSR      OUTDEC
JSR      NEWLINE
```

Notice that the third instruction is used to save the contents of the D0 register so that the second JSR instruction to INDEC does not destroy the first number to be added. Other than the D0 register that is used with the INDEC procedure, the input/output procedures given above do not destroy the contents of any of the 68000 registers. The JSR to NEWLINE ensures the advance to the beginning of a new line after each number is input and after the result is output. A call to NEWLINE is required even if you terminate the number you enter with a carriage return. A line feed must be output to advance to the beginning of the "next" line. The carriage return only positions you at the beginning of the "current" line.

The Program Shell

For the writing of a complete program, certain assembler directives and standard code sequences are needed for each different assembler and operating system. This *program shell* will enclose each program. So that we don't have to depend on one particular assembler or operating system, we will not include this program code for each program presented. Appendix B shows an appropriate program shell for the Atari ST, Commodore Amiga, and Apple Macintosh.

Note that the shell is terminated by an appropriate mechanism to return control to the operating system. The 68000 does have a halt instruction, STOP, but if this instruction is used to terminate your program, the microprocessor will literally stop and you will have to reboot (start from scratch) your operating system. It is much better to return control such that you can continue to issue system commands.

So that you can actually start to write programs using the input/output procedures presented above, these must be included along with your program and the shell. If you require one or more of these subroutines in your program, just copy the appropriate source statements. You will have to consult your system documentation to adapt these procedures for other operating systems and/or assemblers.

Looping

With the instructions you have learned so far, it is possible to write a few simple programs that perform addition and subtraction of a limited number of values. To form the sum of 20 numbers entered from your keyboard would take 20 lines of assembler source code just to obtain these values. An additional 20 ADD instructions would be required as well. If you desire to add up a larger number of values, you would soon tire of all the typing needed to produce the source program. Consider also that each assembly language instruction will take one or more words of memory space when it is translated into machine language. Often it is important to write a small program as well as an efficient one.

The solution to this problem is the use of a *program loop*. There are many ways to write a program loop for the 68000 microprocessor. The simplest type of program loop is the *infinite program loop*. While it may seem of no value to write an infinite loop, if there is a method for escaping the loop, it is often useful. You might like a program that repeats itself over and over again for an arbitrary number of input data values. This would eliminate the need to reinvoke the program for each new value. The methods of escaping from an infinite loop will be discussed in Chapter 5. For now, let us see how we can write one.

Execution normally passes from one instruction to the next. This is known as *sequential execution*. The 68000 provides a special instruction to alter the normal sequential program flow. The jump instruction, JMP, provides the ability to transfer control to any instruction that has a label. The following is a simple infinite loop:

```
OVER:   .
        .
        .
        .
        JMP     OVER
```

Any number of instructions can be contained within the loop. Here is a simple program that will obtain a number from the terminal, double it, and then output the result. These steps are then repeated over and over.

```
*
*INPUT A VALUE FROM THE TERMINAL, DOUBLE,
*AND THEN OUTPUT THE RESULT
*
NEXT:   JSR     INDEC           OBTAIN AN INPUT VALUE
        JSR     NEWLINE
        ADD.L   D0,D0           DOUBLE THE VALUE
        JSR     OUTDEC          OUTPUT THE NUMBER
        JSR     NEWLINE
        JMP     NEXT
```

If you actually run this program, you may have to stop your computer manually and reboot your operating system (the exact procedures to follow depend on your particular computer; consult your owner's manual for the details). Some systems allow you to abort a program and return to the operating system by typing a "Control C" (character C typed while also holding down the key labeled CTRL).

Another frequently used type of loop is the *counting loop*. This is a loop that repeats a number of instructions a fixed number of times. Unlike most 8-bit microprocessors, the 68000 provides a single instruction to perform a counting loop. This is the test condition, decrement, and branch instruction, with the peculiar mnemonic DBRA. (It is actually a member of a family of instructions with the mnemonics DBcc, where the characters cc are replaced by the appropriate characters to select the particular instruction desired.) The DBRA instruction has the following format:

```
DBRA    Dn,<label>
```

It works somewhat like a JMP instruction except that it uses the value contained in the data register as a loop counter. It does this by first subtracting 1 from the current value in Dn and then checking to see if the result is equal to −1. If the updated value contained in Dn is not equal to −1, the DBRA instruction then performs like a JMP to the label specified as the second operand. If the new value of Dn is −1, the next sequential instruction is executed.

In order to use the DBRA instruction, the Dn register must first be set up with the *total* number of times we wish to go through the loop *minus one*. The instructions between the label of the DBRA and the DBRA instruction itself will be executed. These instructions will always be executed at least once even if Dn is initialized with −1. In fact, initializing Dn to −1 results in repeating the loop the maximum number of times—65,536, to be exact. Only the low-order 16 bits of the register are used as a counter. As a simple example, let's say you want to output 20 blank lines. You could call the newline subroutine 20 times by writing 20 lines of assembler source, or you could write the following three lines:

```
        MOVE.W  #19,D2    INITIAL VALUE IS COUNT-1
NEXT:   JSR     NEWLINE
        DBRA    D2,NEXT
```

You must be careful not to modify the contents of the Dn register within the program loop, since it then would no longer represent the loop count and would not yield the result desired. If you must use the Dn register within the loop, you must save and restore it. You could move the contents to another register or to a memory location. Here's how to do it with a variable:

```
         .
         .
         MOVE.W  #100,D1
NEXT:    MOVE.W  D1,SAVED1
         .
         .
         .   <Use D1>
         .
         MOVE.W  SAVED1,D1
         DBRA    D1,NEXT
         .
         .
SAVED1:  DS.W    1
```

Recall from Chapter 3 that DS.W is not an instruction, but rather a directive to reserve one or more words in memory. In this case one word of uninitialized memory has been reserved at location SAVED1.

There is one restriction with the DBRA instruction that is not found with the JMP instruction. With the JMP instruction the programmer can transfer control to any distant label. In other words, there can be loops of arbitrary size. Unfortunately, the DBRA instruction, and many others you will discover, only allow transfer of control over a limited distance. This distance is approximately plus-or-minus 32,768 bytes from the position of the DBRA instruction itself. This distance can't be represented as a fixed number of instructions, because the number of bytes per instruction varies with the particular instruction. It is a very rare occasion when a loop must contain a greater number of instructions than this maximum. Fortunately, the assembler tells the user if all the instructions do not fit into the loop. In this case there are several methods to get around the problem. You will have to read on to find out how.

```
SPACE:   EQU      $20              ASCII SPACE
*
         MOVE.W   #30,D1           SET UP LOOP COUNT
MLOOP:   MOVE.L   EXP,D0           GET CURRENT EXPONENT
         JSR      OUTDEC           OUTPUT
         ADDQ.L   #1,EXP           INCREMENT EXPONENT
         MOVE.B   #SPACE,D0        OUTPUT A SPACE
         JSR      PUTC             "
         MOVE.L   POWER,D0         GET CURRENT POWER
         JSR      OUTDEC           OUTPUT
         ADD.L    D0,D0            DOUBLE IT
         MOVE.L   D0,POWER         AND SAVE
         JSR      NEWLINE          GO TO A NEW LINE
         DBRA     D1,MLOOP         LOOP UNTIL DONE
         ...                       WE CONTINUE HERE
*
EXP:     DC.L     1
POWER:   DC.L     2
```

Figure 7 Program to output powers of two.

Putting It All Together

Figure 7 shows a complete program that will output a table of the powers of 2 from 2^1 to 2^{31}. As you learned in Chapter 1, 2^{31} is the largest power of 2 that can be represented with a 32-bit unsigned number. The program is written as one counting loop. The D1 register is initialized to 30, which is the number of powers that we wish to output minus one. MLOOP is the label referenced by the DBRA instruction, which is the last instruction of the program prior to the return to the operating system. We also declared two variables, EXP and POWER, to represent the current exponent and the actual power of 2 for the value of EXP. These two variables are initialized prior to entering the main loop. Each successive power is computed by doubling the previous power with the ADD.L D0,D0 instruction. Since the D0 register is used for several functions, POWER and EXP are updated after their new values are computed.

Formatting of the output lines is accomplished by inserting a space after outputting the exponent, and an advance to the next line after outputting the power. The ASCII character value for the space character is 20 in hexadecimal. The standard procedure, PUTC, is called with this value in the D0 register. The output from this program should look like the following:

```
1 2
2 4
3 8
4 16
5 32
6 64
7 128
8 256
9 512
10 1024
11 2048
12 4096
13 8192
14 16384
15 32768
etc.
```

Exercises

1. Write an instruction to move the contents of D0 to D1.
2. Write an instruction to move the low-order byte in register D0 to memory location SAMPLE.
3. Is MOVE.L D0,#10 a legal instruction?
4. Is MOVE.B #2056,D0 a legal instruction?
5. Write an instruction to exchange the contents of registers D5 and D6.
6. Write the instruction to add D0 to the longword at ALPHA.
7. Write the instructions to add memory location INCREMENT to memory location TOTAL. Assume longwords.
8. Write the instruction to add the constant 25 to A0.
9. Write the instruction to add the word at memory location OFFSET to register A5.
10. Write the instruction to move the contents of the longword at INITVAL to register A2.
11. Write the instruction to clear the low-order byte of register D5.
12. Write an instruction to clear register A0.
13. Write the instructions to obtain an input value, add 100, and output the result.
14. Write the instructions to obtain an input character and repeat it on output.
15. Write an infinite loop to output the integers starting at zero.
16. Write a counting loop to output the digits 0 through 9 in that order.
17. Write a program to sum the numbers from 1 through 100.
18. Write a program to output your name.
19. Write a program to evaluate D0−D1+D2+100 and output the result.
20. Write a program to output the letter A 100 times, with 10 A's per line.

Answers

1.
```
MOVE.L D0,D1
```

2.
```
MOVE.B D0,SAMPLE
```

3. No, a constant can't be a destination operand.
4. No, the constant is larger than a byte.

5.
```
EXG D5,D6
```

6.
```
ADD.L D0,ALPHA
```

7.
```
MOVE.L  INCREMENT,D0
ADD.L   D0,TOTAL
```

8.
```
ADDA.L #25,A0
```

9.
```
ADDA.W OFFSET,A5
```

10.
```
MOVEA.L INITVAL,A2
```

11.
```
CLR.B D5
```

12.
```
MOVEA.L  #0,A0
```

13.
```
JSR      INDEC
JSR      NEWLINE
ADD.L    #100,D0
JSR      OUTDEC
JSR      NEWLINE
```

14.
```
JSR      GETC
JSR      PUTC
```

15.
```
       CLR.L    D0
NEXT:  JSR      OUTDEC
       ADD.L    #1,D0
       JMP      NEXT
```

16.
```
       CLR.L    D0
       MOVE.W   #9,D1
NEXT:  JSR      OUTDEC
       JSR      NEWLINE
       ADD.L    #1,D0
       DBRA     D1,NEXT
```

17.

```
        CLR.L   D0          TOTAL
        MOVE.L  #1,D1       NUMBER TO ADD
        MOVE.W  #99,D2      LOOP COUNT
NEXT:   ADD.L   D1,D0       ADD TO TOTAL
        ADD.L   #1,D1       GET NEXT NUMBER TO ADD
        DBRA    D2,NEXT     LOOP TILL DONE
        JSR     OUTDEC      OUTPUT RESULT
        JSR     NEWLINE
```

18.

```
        MOVE.B  #'T',D0
        JSR     PUTC
        MOVE.B  #'O',D0
        JSR     PUTC
        MOVE.B  #'M',D0
        JSR     PUTC
        JSR     NEWLINE
```

19.

```
        SUB.L   D1,D0
        ADD.L   D2,D0
        ADD.L   #100,D0
        JSR     OUTDEC
        JSR     NEWLINE
```

20.

```
        MOVE.W  #9,D1       OUTER LOOP COUNT
        MOVE.B  #'A',D0 GET ASCII "A"
NEXT:   MOVE.W  #9,D2       INNER LOOP COUNT
        JSR     PUTC        OUTPUT CHARACTER
        DBRA    D2,NEXT     INNER LOOP
        JSR     NEWLINE     GO TO NEW LINE
        DBRA    D1,NEXT     OUTER LOOP
```

CHAPTER 5

CONDITIONAL AND ARITHMETIC INSTRUCTIONS

In Chapter 4 you learned a small number of 68000 instructions. These were enough to write some very simple programs. I hope that you have taken the time to actually run some of the programs presented in the chapter, as well as a few programs of your own design. Nothing gives you more confidence that you are successfully mastering assembly language programming than the joy you experience when a program actually performs as it should. By now you should have become familiar with your own computer's procedures for editing, assembling, and executing assembly language programs. If you are having trouble, you should carefully review your computer system's manuals before going on with this chapter.

The remainder of this book is designed to expand your vocabulary of 68000 instructions. Rather than present *all* the remaining instructions at one time, we will present groups of instructions and specific examples of their use. You should not attempt to learn all of the 68000 instructions before practicing with each group. Take the time to actually experiment with the instructions presented in each chapter. Don't limit yourself to the exercises. Be creative.

In this chapter you will learn the very powerful set of conditional instructions. These instructions allow the control flow of your program to vary depending on the results of certain instructions. Among these are the arithmetic instructions you have already learned as well as several others. Crucial to understanding the conditional instructions is a thorough knowledge of certain bits in the condition code register and how they are affected by arithmetic instructions.

Arithmetic and the Condition Code Register

As you learned in Chapter 2, the 68000 has a special register known as the condition code register (CCR). This register is not used in the same way as the other registers. We don't treat the contents of the CCR as a numeric quantity. Instead, we indirectly use the values of *individual* bits in the CCR. Each of these special bits, or condition codes, has a specific meaning when set or reset. If a bit is set it has a value of binary 1. If it is reset it has a value of binary 0. The CCR is an 8-bit register, but not all of the 8 bits are used. It is organized as follows:

CONDITION CODE REGISTER

7			4				0
			X	N	Z	V	C

X(extend)	Transparent to data movement. When affected, it is set the same as the C bit.
N(negative)	Set if the most significant bit of the result is set. Cleared otherwise.
Z(zero)	Set if the result equals zero. Cleared otherwise.
V(overflow)	Set if there was an arithmetic overflow. Cleared otherwise.
C(carry)	Set if a carry is generated out of the most significant bit of the operands for an addition. Also set if a borrow is generated in a subtraction. Cleared otherwise.

After the execution of a 68000 instruction, some of the condition codes may be affected. Not all instructions affect the CCR. The majority of CCR usage is related to arithmetic operations such as addition, subtraction, and the comparison of two numeric quantities.

The representation of numbers in two's complement binary was discussed in Chapter 1. Recall that numbers can be interpreted as signed or unsigned depending on the interpretation of the most significant bit. This bit is referred to as the *sign bit* for signed numbers. Many times we will desire to treat a number as a positive value only. By allowing the use of the most significant bit as a normal bit of the number, and not a sign, we can double the magnitude of the numbers that can be represented. The ADD and SUB instructions operate identically for both signed and unsigned numbers. The interpretation is up to the programmer. However, by the use of particular bits in the CCR we can test the outcome of arithmetic operations for both signed *and* unsigned numbers.

The Carry Bit

One of the most important checks that must be made on an arithmetic operation is whether or not the result has exceeded the size of the destination register. For example, the addition of the following unsigned 8-bit binary numbers results in a sum that will not fit in an 8-bit destination (register or memory byte).

```
  11101001
+ 10110111
---------
 110100000
```

The carry of a bit from the most significant (high-order) bit position has no place to go. Actually, this event causes the carry bit (C) to be set. If there was no carry, the carry bit would be reset.

In order to determine if the result of an unsigned addition is valid, the setting of the carry bit must somehow be tested. Fortunately, the 68000 provides a group of instructions that allow the testing of each of the bits of the CCR individually and in various combinations. These instructions all have the form of a *conditional branch*. A conditional branch is similar to a JMP instruction except that for the former the jump is not taken unless a particular condition is true. This condition corresponds to the value or values of one or more of the bits of the CCR. If the branch is not taken then the next sequential instruction is executed. The branch on carry set instruction, BCS, provides a conditional branch based on the setting of the carry bit. If the carry bit is set (binary one) then the branch is taken. The following program illustrates the use of the BCS instruction to validate the result of an unsigned addition.

```
         MOVE.L  NUM1,D0
         ADD.L   NUM2,D0
         BCS     INVALID
           .             RESULT IS OK
           .
           .
INVALID:   .             RESULT EXCEEDS REGISTER SIZE
           .
           .
```

The label used with the BCS instruction, and with *all* the conditional branches, must be to a location that is within approximately plus-or-minus 32,768 bytes of the location of the instruction itself. As mentioned in Chapter 4, this restriction is also present with the DBRA instruction. It is usually difficult to tell how many instructions will represent 32,768 bytes. It is best to let the assembler do the work for you. But let's suppose that you really must perform a conditional branch to a location that is greater than plus or minus 32,768 bytes. What can you do to get around this problem? One simple solution is to perform the conditional branch to a JMP instruction that is "close" to the conditional branch and then have the JMP instruction actually jump to the target label. Here's how it's done.

```
                  .
                  .
                  .
                 BCS      CLOSE      --------------
                  .                                 |
                  .                    < 32K BYTES  |
                  .                                 |
        CLOSE:   JMP      FARWAY     --------------|
                  .                                 |
                  .                                 |
                  .                    > 32K BYTES  |
                  .                                 |
                  .                                 |
        FARWAY:   .                  --------------
                  .
                  .
```

We can also do this:

```
                  .
                  .
                  .
                 BCS      CLOSE
                 BRA      NEXT
        CLOSE:   JMP      FARWAY
        NEXT:     .
                  .
                  .
```

This second approach has the advantage that we know the JMP is close enough, and we have a definite place for it to go without interfering with other instructions. The BRA instruction is an unconditional branch. It always branches, but it suffers from the same limited range as the conditional branches. The solution to this problem can be made even simpler if the condition for branching is reversed. In other words, if we could perform a conditional branch when the carry bit was *not* set, rather than set, then we could use the conditional branch to go to the next sequential instruction in the program. We are in luck! The 68000 provides complementary instructions for all conditional branches. We can always find an appropriate conditional branch that branches when the condition we wish to test is *not* true. In the case of the BCS instruction, the BCC (branch on carry clear) is the one to use. Our program can now be written:

```
                  .
                  .
                 BCC      NEXT
                 JMP      FARWAY
        NEXT:     .
                  .
```

The Overflow Bit

What if we were adding signed numbers? A carry out of the high-order bit is not necessarily indicative of a result that is too large. Adding two negative numbers will result in the carry bit being set. For example,

```
   11111110   -2
 + 11111111   -1
  ---------
  111111101   -3
```

A result that is too large can be detected when the sign bit (most significant bit) changes when we don't want it to. This condition is known as *overflow*. The overflow bit (V) is set or reset depending on the occurrence of the overflow condition. V is affected by all arithmetic instructions regardless of whether operands are treated as signed or unsigned numbers. The 68000 instructions don't know the difference. Either V or C must be used, for signed or unsigned arithmetic, respectively. The BVS (branch on overflow set) and BVC (branch on overflow clear) instructions are provided for signed arithmetic.

Subtraction also results in similar effects on C and V. If an unsigned subtraction results in a borrow into the most significant bit position, the carry bit is set. Since an unsigned subtraction cannot result in a negative value, this is an error. The overflow bit is set for subtractions as well. If we subtract a positive number from a negative number, and the result is a negative number that is too large, V will be set. Overflow can also result from subtracting a negative number from a positive number. If the positive result is too large, V will be set.

The Zero and Negative Bits

In addition to determining if the result of an arithmetic operation has exceeded the size capacity of the destination, a programmer may also desire to know if the result is positive, negative, or zero. The zero bit (Z) and negative bit (N) are provided for these purposes. The zero bit is set if the numerical result is zero. This means that all bits of the result are zero. The BEQ (branch on equal) and BNE (branch on not equal) instructions will conditionally branch depending on the value of Z.

A zero value can be used as a signal to exit an indefinite loop. The following program outputs the integers from 10 to 1 in reverse order.

```
        MOVE.L  #10,D0
NEXT:   JSR     OUTDEC
        JSR     NEWLINE
        SUB.L   #1,D0
        BNE     NEXT
```

The programmer may also want to determine if an arithmetic operation results in a positive or a negative value. The negative bit (N) will be set to a binary 1 for all negative numbers (note that zero is always a positive number in two's complement). The negative bit is set to the same value as the sign bit of the result of the operation. The BMI (branch on minus) and BPL (branch on plus) instructions will test for negative and positive numbers respectively.

The MOVE instruction always sets the negative and zero bits in the CCR just as the arithmetic instructions do. However, the programmer sometimes desires to determine if a value is zero or negative, but hasn't moved it or used it in arithmetic. A special instruction, TST, is provided for just such a purpose. The general form is

```
TST[.<size>]    <ea>
```

The following instructions test register D5 and memory location COUNT.

```
TST.L   D5
TST.L   COUNT
```

Of course, the TST instruction must be followed with an appropriate conditional branch.

The Extend Bit

The extend bit (X) is normally a copy of the carry bit. It is used for performing multiple precision arithmetic, which will be covered in detail in Chapter 11. However, you should be aware that some instructions do not affect the extend bit. The most notable of these instructions is the MOVE instruction. MOVE conditionally sets or clears N and Z, clears V and C, but doesn't change the current value of X. You won't be using the extend bit at this time, so this fact shouldn't cause concern.

Comparisons

An essential task in any programming language is the comparison of two numbers, or any data items that are being represented by numerical values such as ASCII characters. One way to perform a comparison would be to subtract the two numbers and then test the flags to determine their relationship. If the two values are equal to each other, the zero flag will be set. The carry flag, sign flag, and so on, can also be tested to determine other inequalities. The particular flags that must be tested depends on whether the comparison is between signed or unsigned quantities. In fact, it is important to test for overflow as well. This may result in a requirement to test two or more flags.

A disadvantage in performing a subtraction to compare two numbers is the fact that the destination operand will be changed. Since the destination operand must be one of the values to be compared, its value will be destroyed. We could, of course, make a copy. The following example determines if the contents of register D0 are equal to the contents of register D1.

```
        MOVE.L  D0,D2       MAKE A COPY OF D0
        SUB.L   D1,D2       SUBTRACT D1 FROM D2
        BEQ     EQUAL       BRANCH IF THEY ARE =
          .                 NOT EQUAL
          .
EQUAL:    .                 EQUAL
          .
```

There is a better way to compare numbers. A special compare instruction, CMP, works almost like the SUB instruction except that the result of the subtraction is not actually saved—in other words, the operands remain unchanged. All the flags that would be set or reset by the SUB instruction are also set or reset by the CMP instruction. The destination operand must be a data register, but the source operand can be a register, variable, or constant. In fact, the source operand can use any of the addressing modes that will be discussed in Chapter 6.

The previous example can be rewritten using the CMP instruction.

```
        CMP.L   D1,D0
        BEQ     EQUAL
          .
          .
EQUAL:    .
          .
```

Since we are using the CMP instruction and not an SUB, the value of D0 does not have to be copied.

In general we will desire to compare both signed and unsigned numbers. The standard inequalities all have unique conditional branches that are used with the CMP instruction. For inequalities other than equal or not equal, it is sometimes difficult to remember which value should be the source and which value should be the destination. The CMP instruction compares the destination with the source. Therefore, if we wish to determine if D0 is less than or equal to D1 we would write

```
CMP.L   D1,D0
BLE     LABEL
```

An easy way to remember this is:

```
destination <inequality> source
```

The following table shows the conditional branches for signed numbers.

<	BLT	Branch on less than
<=	BLE	Branch on less or equal
=	BEQ	Branch on equal
>=	BGE	Branch on greater or equal
>	BGT	Branch on greater than
not =	BNE	Branch on not equal

When you compare unsigned numbers you should use the following.

<	BCS*	Branch on carry set
<=	BLS	Branch on lower or same
=	BEQ	Branch on equal
>=	BCC*	Branch on carry clear
>	BHI	Branch on higher
not =	BNE	Branch on not equal

* These mnemonics are not particularly indicative of their function, but they are the ones to use.

The tests for equal and not equal use the same conditional branches for both signed and unsigned numbers. The following program finds the largest unsigned number from an arbitrary number of input values. Entering a zero value terminates input and outputs the result.

```
* FIND LARGEST INPUT VALUE
* ZERO VALUE TERMINATES INPUT
          CLR.L   D1          INITIAL VALUE IS ZERO
NEXT:     JSR     INDEC       GET NEXT INPUT VAL
          TST.L   D0          ZERO?
          BEQ     FINI        YES, ALL DONE
          CMP.L   D1,D0       LARGER?
          BLE     NEXT        NO
```

```
         MOVE.L  D0,D1         YES, SAVE AS NEW VAL
         BRA     NEXT          BACK FOR NEXT VAL
FINI:    MOVE.L  D1,D0         SET UP FOR OUTPUT
         JSR     OUTDEC        OUTPUT THE VALUE
         JSR     NEWLINE       GO TO NEXT LINE
```

Two CMP instructions are used. The first CMP tests for the zero terminating value. The second determines if a new input value is larger than the largest value encountered so far. It is important to remember to initialize this value to something meaningful. In this case, a zero value is smaller than any value we will encounter.

There are several additional versions of the compare instruction. Although any addressing mode, including immediate values, can be used as the source operand, the destination operand can only be a data register. The general form of the CMP instruction is:

```
CMP[.<size>]    <ea>,Dn
```

The CMPA instruction allows the use of an address register as the destination operand. Its form is:

```
CMPA[.<size>]   <ea>,An
```

While we may often desire to compare a data or address register with an immediate value, we sometimes desire to compare a constant with the contents of a memory location. It is not possible to use the CMP or CMPA instruction in such a manner. We would first have to copy the contents of memory to a register and then use the CMP instruction. Fortunately, a special version of the CMP instruction, CMPI, exists to solve our problem. Its general form is:

```
CMPI[.<size>]   #<data>,<ea>
```

The destination operand is restricted in that it can't be an address register (use CMPA in this case), or an immediate value. (This latter restriction really isn't a restriction, because it makes no sense to compare one constant with another, since the outcome is always the same.) Let's assume that we want to see if the contents of memory location COUNT, a byte value, is less than 10. These are the instructions we would use:

```
CMPI.B  #10,COUNT
BLT     LESSTHAN
```

Many assemblers will allow the use of the CMP mnemonic for all variations of the CMP instruction. The assembler figures out what version to use by looking at the type of the operands in use. However, it is somewhat sloppy programming to do this. You should always be aware of what the actual 68000 instructions are. If you issue the following instruction,

```
CMP.L   VAL1,VAL2
```

you will lose out. No version of the CMP instruction will allow the use of two memory operands.

ADDQ and SUBQ Instructions

Many programs require adding or subtracting the constant 1 from a register or variable. Naturally, the ADD or SUB instruction can be used to perform this operation.

```
ADD.L #1,D0
```

increments the value in the D0 register.

```
SUBI.L #1,VAR55
```

decrements memory location VAR55. Many microprocessors provide special instructions to increment or decrement a value. The 68000 instruction set provides a better way to increment or decrement a number. The ADDQ (add quick) and SUBQ (subtract quick) instructions are provided. They can be used to add or subtract a value ranging from 1 to 8. Since they allow small values other than 1, they are more flexible than their counterparts on other CPUs. All arithmetic flags are updated just as they are with the ADDI and SUBI. Here are their general forms:

```
ADDQ[.<size>]    #<data>,<ea>
SUBQ[.<size>]    #<data>,<ea>

<size> = B, W, L
<data> is a value between 1 and 8 inclusive
```

The effective address can be almost any valid addressing mode including an address register. There is no special form of these instructions when referencing an address register. However, only word and longword forms of the instruction can be used with an address register. The following instruction would increment the value of memory location COUNT:

```
ADDQ.W   #1,COUNT          COUNT IS A WORD
```

At first it may seem that these instructions are identical to the ADDI and SUBI instructions. In order to understand why the ADDQ and SUBQ instructions are better, we have to delve into the actual machine instructions generated when these mnemonics are used. The ADDI and SUBI instructions will generate a 16-bit opcode word and one or two additional 16-bit values corresponding to the immediate operand. With the ADDQ and SUBQ instructions, only the 16-bit opcode word is generated. This results not only in a savings in memory locations but also in a significant increase in speed because the programmer doesn't have to perform the memory fetch to obtain the immediate data. In the case of the ADDQ and SUBQ instructions, this data is contained in the 16-bit opcode word.

Along a similar line, a special MOVE instruction, MOVEQ, is provided. This instruction allows an immediate source operand that must be represented in 8 bits or less, giving a signed range between −128 and +127, or an unsigned range between 0 and 255. The destination is always a data register, and the full 32 bits are used. This instruction is only available in the longword form. It should be used whenever possible, since the number of bytes required will be less than the corresponding MOVE instruction. For example,

```
MOVEQ    #100,D0
```

is preferable to

```
MOVE.L   #100,D0
```

Many assemblers will automatically use the MOVEQ version whenever possible, even if it hasn't been specified.

The 68000 provides many instructions that can be functionally duplicated by other instructions. When a programmer uses the more appropriate instructions, programs are more readable and take up less space in memory. This latter consideration is important for large programs, or when you only a small amount of memory is available. We will make extensive use of the ADDQ and SUBQ instructions for a variety of purposes throughout this book.

Exercises

Assume longword operands unless otherwise specified.

1. What CCR bit is used to detect overflow of unsigned arithmetic operations?
2. What CCR bit is used to detect overflow of signed arithmetic operations?
3. Is there a limit as to how far away the label of a conditional branch may be?
4. What CCR bit determines if the result of an arithmetic operation is zero?
5. What CCR bit determines if the result of an arithmetic operation is positive or negative?
6. What is the difference between the CMP instruction and the SUB instruction?
7. Write the instructions necessary to branch to label STOP if the D0 register is equal to 100.
8. Write the instructions to branch to label BIGER if register D0 is larger than variable LIMIT. Assume unsigned values.
9. What CCR bits were discussed in this chapter?
10. Are all the bits of the CCR used?
11. If we add the following unsigned bytes, will the carry bit be set? The values are in decimal.
    55 and 27
    150 and 110
12. If we add the following signed bytes, will the overflow bit be set? The values are in decimal.
    −100 and +50
    −100 and −50
13. Write the instructions necessary to add the signed values in the D0 and D1 register and branch to label OK if there is no overflow.
14. Repeat the above problem for unsigned values.
15. Write the instructions necessary to test if register D0 is zero and, if so, to branch to label ZERO.
16. Write the instructions necessary to compare variables NUM1 and NUM2, branching to label EQUAL if they are equal, to label LESS if NUM1 is less than NUM2. Assume signed values.
17. Write the equivalent of the DBRA instruction using instructions introduced in this chapter.
18. What is the purpose of the extend bit?
19. What is the advantage of using ADDQ and SUBQ rather than ADD AND SUB?

20. Can MOVEQ be used to load only the low-order byte of a data register?

Answers

1. The carry bit, C.
2. The overflow bit, V.
3. Yes, approximately plus or minus 32,768 bytes.
4. The zero bit, Z.
5. The negative bit, N.
6. The CMP instruction does not store the result in the destination operand.

7.
```
        CMP.L   #100,D0
        BEQ     STOP
```

8.
```
        CMP.L   LIMIT,D0
        BHI     BIGER
```

9. The carry, overflow, negative, zero, and extend bits.
10. No, only five out of the eight.
11. 55+27=82, which is within the range of an unsigned byte; the carry bit will not be set. 150+110=260, which is larger than the range of an unsigned byte; the carry bit will be set.
12. (−100) + (+50) −50. The overflow bit will not be set. (−100) + (−50) = −150. The largest signed negative byte is −128. In this case the overflow bit will be set.

13.
```
        ADD.L   D0,D1
        BVC     OK
```

14.
```
        ADD.L   D0,D1
        BCC     OK
```

15.
```
        TST.L   D0
        BEQ     ZERO
```

16.
```
        MOVE.L  NUM1,D0
        CMP.L   NUM2,D0
        BEQ     EQUAL
        BLT     LESS
```

17.
```
        SUB.W   #1,D0           ASSUME COUNT IN D0
        BGE     LABEL
```

18. The extend bit is used for multiple precision arithmetic.
19. The ADDQ and SUBQ take up less memory and execute faster.
20. No, MOVEQ is always a full longword operation.

CHAPTER 6

ADDRESSING MODES

The majority of 68000 instructions have one or more operands. An operand is used either as a source operand or a destination operand. A source operand is always a data value that is only read by the instruction and never modified. A destination operand may be read as well as written. In other words, its value can be modified by the action of the instruction.

The programmer normally explicitly specifies the operand or operands of an instruction. A small number of instructions have implicit operands. This means that a register is used as an operand without being so specified. The JSR instruction is an example of this. As you will see in the next two chapters, address register A7 is implicitly used by this instruction.

Operands always ultimately specify a register or location in memory where the data for the instruction is found. It is quite clear in

```
MOVE.L  D0,D1
```

that the source operand is to be found in data register D0 and the destination operand is in data register D1. If we write

```
MOVE.L  (A0)+,D0
```

what does (A0) +mean? In order to answer this and many other questions concerning operands, it is necessary to introduce the concept of an *addressing mode.* The addressing mode is the method we specify for the instruction to find a particular operand. The *effective address* of an instruction is the actual location of the data. When a simple data register is specified, the effective address is the data register itself. When an instruction such as

```
ADD.L   COUNT,D0
```

is specified, the effective address of the source operand is the location in memory that contains the variable COUNT.

The 68000 has a total of 12 different addressing modes. This may seem like a lot, but not all of these modes are commonly used, and some are automatically selected by many assemblers to allow more efficient execution of instructions. You have actually learned several of these modes already.

At this point I should mention something about the limitations on the use of these 12 addressing modes with all instructions. Life would indeed be nice if we could use any of these 12 addressing modes as the source and/or destination of each and every instruction. Computer scientists refer to the *orthoganality* of a machine architecture as to the degree to which all addressing modes can be used with all instructions. A fully orthoganal architecture would allow all combinations. Unfortunately, the 68000 is not fully orthoganal, although it comes remarkably close. We do have to be careful. Appendix C should be used as a reference as to what is legal and what is not.

We will now go over the details of each of the addressing modes. I will show some simple examples of how each mode is used. First, let's review the addressing modes that we have already covered in previous chapters.

Register Direct Modes

These are actually the simplest of the modes. The effective address is the specified register itself. There are two register direct modes:

1. Dn—Data register direct
2. An—Address register direct

Any of the seven address or seven data registers can be used. Don't forget that some instructions will not allow an address register to be specified. We must use a MOVEA instruction instead of MOVE, and an ADDA or SUBA instead of ADD or SUB.

Immediate Data

We have used immediate data addressing to place a constant in a register or memory location. This value must be a constant value that is known at the time of assembly. The general form of this addressing mode is #<data>, where <data>can be a byte, word, or longword value.

Where is this constant located? It is actually located right along with the instructor's opcode word. You may recall that each instruction consists of at least one word of memory. If we have an immediate operand, this immediate constant data is placed in one or two successive words of memory, right along with the instruction—a byte or word constant takes up a word of memory, while a longword constant takes up the next two words.

The data may be a numeric constant, a symbol, or an expression. Here are some examples of valid immediate addresses:

```
        MOVE.B  #$FF,BDATA
        ADDI.L  #1000,D5
MAX:    EQU     200
        SUBI.W  #MAX*3,COUNT
```

Note that ADDI and SUBI were used instead of ADD and SUB.

Absolute Addressing

This is the third addressing mode that you have already used. In order to understand the operation of this addressing mode, you will first have to recall the structure of memory. Remember that each byte of memory has an associated address or location. These addresses start at zero and continue up to the maximum size of allowable memory. A byte, word, or longword can be stored in memory. Words or longwords must be located at even-numbered memory addresses. So, we can specify a particular piece of data by its address in memory. There are actually two different absolute addressing modes: absolute short and absolute long. The normal one is absolute long. This allows a full 32-bit address to be specified.

When we want to directly access the contents of a location in memory, we can use absolute addressing. The instruction

```
MOVE.B  5000,D0
```

moves the byte of data at location 5000_{10} in memory into register D0. We normally don't use a numeric address, but a symbolic one.

```
MOVE.B  DATA,D0
```

would be more common. Don't get confused by the first example. This not the same thing as immediate mode; without the # character it is taken as absolute addressing. In the second example, the assembler substitutes the correct value for the memory address of symbol DATA. For absolute long addressing, the address is held in two words that follow the opcode word. This is similar to the technique used with immediate addressing, but these words are an address and not the data itself.

The absolute short mode only provides a single extension word to the instruction. This word has a range of from 0 to FFFF in hexadecimal. The 68000 takes this word and sign-extends it to 32 bits. This means that the sign bit is copied into the high-order 16 bits. Therefore the range of an absolute short address is

$$00000000_{16} - 00007FFF_{16} \text{ and}$$

$$FFFF8000_{16} - FFFFFFFF_{16}$$

An address between 00008000_{16} and $FFFF7FFF_{16}$ does not lie in this range and can not be accommodated by the absolute short addressing mode.

If you have a smart assembler and are specifying an address in the short range, the assembler can use this mode and save a word of memory. Some assemblers always use the long absolute mode. I should mention that on the majority of systems, even with a smart assembler, absolute short mode may never be used. This is because you will normally be specifying addresses by their symbolic names. These addresses are not really absolute in the sense that they are pinned down to specific memory locations. Most programming environments use some form of program relocation. This can be accomplished at the time of linking, or at the time the program is loaded for execution, or at both times. Therefore, the assembler can't guarantee that the final address will be in range of the short addressing mode. Your only chance to use this mode is if you specify a numeric address explicitly such as

```
MOVE.L  $100,D0
```

If your assembler is smart, it will use absolute short. One way to find out is to look at the assembly listing and count the total number of words generated for that instruction. If there are two, then absolute short was used.

Address Register Indirect

This is an addressing mode that has not been introduced in earlier chapters. When we write an assembly language program, we normally use a symbol to specify the location of data in memory. It is the job of the assembler to assign memory locations to each of these symbols. The 68000 CPU doesn't operate with symbolic addresses; rather, it requires the actual memory address. If we somehow had a method of obtaining this memory address at program execution time, we could reference data using this address value rather than a symbol. This is the essence of address register indirect addressing.

To use this addressing mode, an address must be placed into one of the address registers. An address used in this manner is often called a *pointer*. If we assume that the address of our data is in register A0, we can reference the data by specifying the operand as (A0). In other words, all we do is put parenthesis around the register designator. The general form of this addressing mode is (An). Let's assume that a word of data is at location $10000. If we place the value $10000 into register A0, we can reference this data. The following instructions will move this data to register D0:

```
MOVEA.L #$10000,A0
MOVE.W  (A0),D0
```

In this case we used the MOVEA.L instruction to place the value $10000 into register A0. Note that we used a MOVEA.L and not a MOVEA.W for this instruction. Even though we are going to obtain a word of data, an address is *always* a 32-bit longword value.

It is rare that we know the actual memory address for a particular piece of data. How, then, can we find the address of a location represented only by a symbolic name? This is actually quite simple. There are two methods we can use. The first method simply moves the address value in as an immediate value. The following program excerpt will move the address of COUNT into A0 and then move the data value at COUNT into register D0.

```
        MOVEA.L #COUNT,A0
        MOVE.W  (A0),D0
        .
        .
COUNT:  DC.W    1234
```

The second method is to use a special instruction specifically designed for this purpose, the load effective address instruction, LEA. Its general form is:

```
LEA     <ea>,An
```

It has the advantage that it determines the effective address at execution time and can therefore be used with a number of different addressing modes. The above instructions would be rewritten as

```
LEA     COUNT,A0
MOVE.W  (A0),D0
```

The LEA instruction takes the address of COUNT, not the value at location COUNT, and places it in register A0. The LEA instruction always has a longword size, since it specifies an address value.

You might be wondering, why not just use absolute addressing? The answer to this is best shown by example, but there are a couple of reasons. Unlike in absolute addressing, the address can be modified if it is in a register. This helps with data structures like arrays. Another real power of the address register indirect mode is that it avoids the necessity of knowing the symbolic name for the location of a data value in order to reference it. This will start to have a greater meaning when subroutines are discussed in Chapter 8.

Address register indirect can be of great help in managing data in arrays. You are no doubt somewhat familiar with the use of arrays from your experience in a high-level language. An array is a type of data structure created by grouping together many similar data elements of the same type in successive locations in memory. For example, we can create an array of word-sized data items with the DC.W directive.

```
ARRAY:  DC.W    345,862,10000,-26,473
```

This example is an array composed of arbitrary values. Suppose we wanted to print out these five values—how could it be done using address register indirect addressing? First, we observe that the label ARRAY specifies the first address in the array. If we place this address in register A0, we should be able to access the first data element using address register indirect addresssing. How do we then get to the next value? We merely add the proper constant to A0. In this case it will be a 2, since word data requires two consecutive memory bytes. The following is a program that does just this:

```
        LEA     ARRAY,A0        GET ADDRESS OF ARRAY
        CLR.L   D0              CLEARS HIGH ORDER WORD
        MOVE.W  #4,D1           INIT FOR LOOP
NEXT:   MOVE.W  (A0),D0         GET ARRAY ELEMENT
        JSR     OUTDEC          OUTPUT
        JSR     NEWLINE         GO TO NEXT LINE
        ADDQ.L  #2,A0           BUMP FOR NEXT ELEMENT
        DBRA    D1,NEXT         BACK FOR MORE
```

Wouldn't it be nice if we didn't have to increment the value of A0 by 2 each time through the loop, if it could be done automatically? The 68000 has granted our wish. The next addressing mode we will discuss, address register indirect with postincrement, does just that.

Address Register Indirect With Postincrement

This addressing mode works exactly the same way as address register indirect except that the value contained in the address register specified is automatically incremented by 1, 2, or 4, depending on whether the instruction was a byte, word, or longword operation. The general form of the addressing mode is (An)+. The plus sign follows the register as a reminder that the incrementing is performed *after* the operand is used. The previous example can be rewritten as:

```
        LEA     ARRAY,A0        GET ADDRESS OF ARRAY
        CLR.L   D0              CLEARS HIGH ORDER WORD
        MOVE.W  #4,D1           INIT FOR LOOP
NEXT:   MOVE.W  (A0)+,D0        GET ARRAY ELEMENT AND INCREMENT
        JSR     OUTDEC          OUTPUT
        JSR     NEWLINE         GO TO NEXT LINE
        DBRA    D1,NEXT         BACK FOR MORE
```

As an interesting example of the use of address register indirect with postincrement addressing, I would like to introduce the concept of a character string. You will recall from Chapter 3 that the DC.B directive can be used to place character strings into memory. It will generate memory bytes that are equivalent to the ASCII character codes. One problem exists with these character strings: How do we determine the size? Unless we keep the size of each string along with the string, we can't really tell its length. There is another approach that has been widely adopted by the C language. A null character, or zero byte, is used as a terminator for the string. This acts as a special mark that indicates the end of the string. The space occupied by the string will be one longer than the actual length of the string. We could declare some strings as follows:

```
STR1:   DC.B    'This is string 1',0
STR2:   DC.B    'Line 1',13,10,'Line 2',13,10,0
STR3    DC.B    0
```

The second string would be output on two lines. ASCII 13 is a carriage return and ASCII 10 is a line feed. The third string is a null- or zero-length string.

The first thing we might want to do with a string is to output it to the terminal. A simple program will accomplish this. Assuming that a string is located at location STR, the following will output all the characters except the null:

```
        LEA     STR,A0          GET ADDRESS OF STRING
LOOP:   MOVE.B  (A0)+,D0        GET NEXT CHARACTER
        BEQ     FINI            DONE?
        JSR     PUTC            NO, OUTPUT THE CHARACTER
        BRA     LOOP            BACK FOR MORE
FINI:   .                       DONE
        .
```

Another useful example is in moving a string from one place to another. This same technique can be used to move one area of memory to another. Here, address register indirect with postincrement addressing is used for both the source and destination operands. We will move string S1 to string S2. S2 must be large enough to contain S1.

```
        LEA     S1,A0           A0 -> SOURCE
        LEA     S2,A0           A1 -> DESTINATION
LOOP:   MOVE.B  (A0)+,(A1)+     MOVE A BYTE
        BNE     LOOP            LOOP TILL ZERO BYTE
```

It may come as a shock that the loop consists of just one instruction, but that is all it takes. One nice feature of the 68000 instruction set is that all condition codes except X are set for a MOVE instruction. This allows us to perform the conditional branch immediately following the MOVE.

As a final example of the use of this addressing mode, here is a simple program to compare two strings.

```
        LEA     S1,A0           A0 -> S1
        LEA     S2,A1           A1 -> S2
LOOP:   TST.B   (A0)            NULL?
        BEQ     LAST            YES
        CMPM.B  (A0)+,(A1)+     NO, COMPARE BYTES
        BEQ     LOOP            CONTINUE WHILE =
        BRA     DIFF            NOT =
LAST:   TST.B   (A1)            NULL?
        BEQ     SAME
DIFF:   .                       HERE WHEN STRINGS DIFFERENT
        .
SAME:   .                       HERE WHEN STRINGS MATCH
        .
```

The CMPM instruction is a special version of the compare instruction that must be used when *both* the operands are register indirect with postincrement addressing. We end up at label DIFF if the strings are different and at label SAME if they are the same. The first TST.B is needed to ensure that we don't continue to compare memory locations beyond the strings. The TST.B at LAST is needed to make sure that the

the second string is the same length as the first. If it is not, then the first string would be a substring of the second and the two are therefore not identical. If the second string were a substring of the first, the CMPM.B instruction would fail. I will leave it as an exercise to rewrite this program to allow matching substrings.

Address Register Indirect With Predecrement

This addressing mode is very similar to address register indirect with postincrement. Its general form is −(An). Notice that the minus sign must precede the register number. There are two major differences. First, the value in the specified address register is decremented by the data size rather than incremented. The other difference is in when this decrementing takes place. With address register indirect with postincrement, the address register was incremented *after* the effective address was computed. With address register indirect with predecrement, the decrementing takes place *before* the effective address is computed.

At first, you might be tempted to think of this addressing mode as a way to access memory in decreasing address order. You might want to move a chunk of memory starting with the highest memory location. This can be done with some care. You have to remember that predecrementing will occur. This means that the initial address value you place in the address register will not be the address of the first piece of data. It will be off by data-size bytes. You can certainly take this into consideration by adjusting the value in the address register. This can be done in two ways. You can generate a label that is on the next higher memory location:

```
         DS.W    100      WORD ARRAY
BLOCK:   EQU     *
```

The asterisk is used to obtain the current value of the assembler's location counter. In this case, its value will be equal to the memory location immediately following the last word of the data. You would then be able to access this array in reverse order with the following instructions:

```
LEA      BLOCK,A0
MOVE.W   -(A0),D0         GETS DATA ELEMENT INTO D0
```

The other method would involve placing a pointer to the last data element in the address register and then adjusting it before use. Here is how you would do it:

```
        LEA      BLOCK,A0
        ADDQ.L   #2,A0                ADJUST BY ONE WORD
        MOVE.W   -(A0),D0             GETS DATA ELEMENT INTO D0
        .
        .
        .
        DS.W     99                   FIRST 99 WORDS OF ARRAY
BLOCK:  DS.W     1                    THE LAST WORD OF ARRAY
```

In the next couple of chapters you will learn some additional uses for this addressing mode. Before going on to the next addressing mode I should mention one minor detail that you must keep in mind. When you use register A7 with either predecrement or postincrement modes, it will always be adjusted by a multiple of two bytes. This means that byte operations cause the value 2 to be added or subtracted. This is due to the special significance of register A7 as a stack pointer, the topic of the next chapter. Another thing you may be tempted to do is to use the CMPM instruction with this addressing mode. You cannot do this. CMPM can only be used with the address register indirect with postdecrement mode.

Address Register Indirect With Displacement

This addressing mode is also a variant of address register indirect. However, in this case there is no predecrement or postincrement. Rather, this mode provides the ability to include a constant displacement to be added to the value in the address register before it is used to form the effective address. This value is not used to modify the contents of the address register, but only in forming the effective address. The general form is d_{16}(An), where d_{16} indicates a displacement value which is 16 bits long. It is a signed value; therefore, it can represent both a positive and a negative offset given by the contents of An. Let's say that A0 contains the value $10000. The instruction

```
        MOVE.L   4(A0),D0
```

will move the word at location $10004 to register D0. Using a symbol for the displacement, the above example could be written as

```
DISP:   EQU      4
        MOVE.L   DISP(A0),D0
```

If a symbol is used for the displacement, it must be a constant value and not a label used on a memory location. Although some assemblers may allow you to assemble the following:

```
          MOVE.L  ARRAY(A0),D0
          .
          .
          .
ARRAY:    DS.L    100
```

you will most likely run into trouble. The label ARRAY can ultimately be located anywhere in memory and therefore should be represented by a 32-bit value. The displacement must be a signed 16-bit value.

Address register indirect with displacement is extremely useful for data structures that contain records. A record can contain almost anything. All records must be the same size if a simple array access technique is to be used. Let's say that we want a simple data structure containing the names and ages of various people. We will restrict a name to be 10 characters, plus a byte for the terminating null character. An age can be represented by a single byte. This gives us a total record size of 12 bytes. We can declare an array of names as follows:

```
NAMLST: DC.B    'TOM       ',0
        DC.B    43
        DC.B    'ERIN      ',0
        DC.B    3
        DC.B    'KRISTIN   ',0
        DC.B    5
        DC.B    0
```

Here a null name has been used to mark the end of the list. We can access the name and age of a particular record by defining constants to represent the displacements into the record for each component.

```
NAME:    EQU    0
AGE:     EQU    11
RECSIZ:  EQU    12
```

Here is a program that will add up the ages of the names in this array:

```
        CLR.L   D0              D0 HAS SUM
        LEA     NAMLST,A0       A0 -> ARRAY
LOOP:   TST.B   NAME(A0)        FINISHED?
        BEQ     FINI            YES
        CLR.L   D1              NO, CLEAR HIGH ORDER BYTES
        MOVE.B  AGE(A0),D1      GET AGE
        ADD.L   D1,D0           ADD IN AGE
```

```
        ADDA.L  #RECSIZ,A0        GET NEXT RECORD
        BRA     LOOP              BACK FOR MORE
FINI:   .
        .
```

Notice that the age is not added directly to the sum in D0. This is because the age is a byte value, and adding a byte to D0 would only allow a sum as large as a byte. To get around this, we clear the high-order bytes of D1 and then move the age byte into the low-order byte of D1. Then we can perform a full longword addition.

We can also take advantage of this addressing mode to rewrite the string compare previously presented.

```
        LEA     S1,A0             A0 -> S1
        LEA     S2,A1             A1 -> S2
LOOP:   CMPM.B  (A0)+,(A1)+       COMPARE BYTES
        BNE     DIFF              DIFFERENT
        TST.B   -1(A0)            FINISHED?
        BEQ     SAME              YES, THEY MATCH
        BRA     LOOP              LOOP FOR NEXT CHAR.
DIFF:   .                         HERE WHEN STRINGS DIFFERENT
        .
SAME:   .                         HERE WHEN STRINGS MATCH
        .
```

Address Register Indirect With Index

This mode is very similar to address register indirect with displacement. In fact, it is address register indirect with displacement plus the addition of a value contained in any one of the address or data registers. The general form is d_8(An,Rn.W) or d_8(An,Rn.L). d_8 is an 8-bit displacement. Its range is −128 to +127. This is not as great a range as with address register indirect with displacement mode. Rn is any one of the address or data registers. Either the sign-extended word or the complete longword is taken from the index register, depending on the suffix the programmer specifies. The effective address is formed by adding the displacement, the contents of the address register, and the contents of the index register. This can be expressed as <ea> = (An)+(Ri)+d, where Ri is the appropriate value from Rn.

This addressing mode is especially useful for two-dimensional arrays. For a simple two-dimensional array of bytes, words, or longwords, the address of the appropriate row can be placed in the address register and the index of the column in the index register. In this case the displacement would be set to zero. The effective operand would then be the location of the data item. In order to determine the address of the row, a value must be added to the address of the array that is equal to the row number (assume rows start at 0) × the number of data elements in each row × the size of each element. A two-dimensional array stored this way is referred to as being in *row major* form.

We haven't discussed multiplications just yet, so as an example I will assume we want to access a particular element that we know in advance—this way we can just use a constant. Let's assume the size of each element in the array is a longword and that the array is 100 by 100 elements. Furthermore, let's say we want the 25th element in the 10th row. The following instructions will move the longword from this array element to register D1.

```
RO:     EQU      10*100*4          ;ROW OFFSET
        LEA      ARRAY,A0          ;GET PTR. TO ARRAY
        ADDA.L   #RO,A0            ;ADD IN ROW OFFSET
        MOVE.W   #25,D0            ;COLUMN NUM. TO D0
        MOVE.L   0(A0,D0.W),D1     ;MOVE ELEMENT TO D1
```

If we have a two-dimensional array of records, we can use the displacement to access the particular field of the record. There are many ways to use this addressing mode. Just remember that the displacement must be a constant value that is known at assembly time. The two register values can be computed at execution time.

Program Counter Relative Modes

There are two program counter relative addressing modes. These modes function similarly: the effective address is formed as a relative displacement to the value of the program counter at the time the instruction is executed. Since this is a multi-word instruction, the programmer must be a bit more specific as to exactly what value the program counter will have. The value is the address of the extension word of the instruction. This is the word following the opcode word. The general forms of the program counter with displacement addressing modes are d_{16}(PC), where d_{16} is the sign extension of a 16-bit value, and d_{16}(PC,Ri), where Ri is either Rn.W or Rn.L. This is similar to the use of the index register with address register indirect with index mode. The effective addresses for these addressing modes are (PC) +d and (PC) +(Ri) +d respectively.

At first, these addressing modes may seem utterly useless, since we don't know what the value of the PC will be at the time the program is executed. However, we do know where some things will be located relative to the position of an instruction using this addressing mode. In fact, we can let the assembler do the work for us. By specifying a label for the displacement, the assembler will automatically compute the proper offset value. If we wish to access the data at location COUNT, we can use PC with displacement addressing:

```
         MOVE.L  COUNT(PC),D0
         .
         .
         .
COUNT:   DC.L    1000
```

There are a couple of advantages in using this addressing mode. First, the length of the instruction will be shorter than if the long absolute mode is used, and a full word of memory will be saved. Second, when we use PC relative addressing modes, the program code becomes *position-independent*. This means that we can move the program around in memory without modifying it and it will still work. Of course, this is assuming that no absolute addressing is used anywhere in memory, which, with great care, can be done. It is a help that all the branch instructions use this mode at all times. Only with JMP and JSR do you have a choice. This technique is useful for dynamically loaded programs that will be loaded into various locations in memory. It is somewhat beyond the level of this book to discuss all the applications of these techniques; however, one application is that of dynamically loaded device drivers in an operating system. If you program the Apple Macintosh, you will always have to write position independent code—this is a drawback of the Macintosh programming environment.

A couple of restrictions apply. PC relative modes can never be used for the destination operand of an instruction. Additionally, many assemblers and systems support the concept of a *program section*. Normally, PC relative modes cannot be used with a label that is in another program section. The specific restrictions on the use of these modes is somewhat system-dependent. Consult the manuals for your assembler and system. Additionally, some assemblers will generate this addressing mode automatically for references to labels that are not *forward references*. A forward reference is a reference to a label that has not yet been defined. You should take a good look at your assembly listings to determine the addressing modes that your assembler uses. Just look at the extension words to the instruction. If there is only one, then PC relative mode is used.

Addressing Mode Summary

Here is a table of all the possible addressing modes and their assembler syntax:

Data Register Direct	Dn
Address Register Direct	An
Address Register Indirect	(An)
Address Register Indirect with Postincrement	(An)+
Address Register Indirect with Predecrement	−(An)
Address Register Indirect with Displacement	d(An)
Address Register Indirect with Index	d(An, Ri)
Absolute Short	xxx.W
Absolute Long	xxx.L
Program Counter with Displacement	d(PC)
Program Counter with Index	d(PC, Ri)
Immediate	#xxx

Exercises

1. Are source operands ever modified by an instruction?
2. What is an "effective address"?
3. Is the 68000 a fully orthoganal machine?
4. What is the effective address for register direct mode?
5. Where is immediate data located?
6. What is the range of absolute short addressing?
7. What is a pointer?
8. How is address register indirect mode specified?
9. Use address register indirect mode to add the first 10 longwords starting at absolute location $2000. Leave the result in D0.
10. Repeat the above problem using address register indirect with postincrement addressing.
11. Write the instructions necessary to determine the length of a null terminated string found at MYSTR. Leave the length value in register D0.
12. With address register indirect with predecrementing or postincrementing, is the value in the address register always modified by plus or minus one?
13. What addressing modes are allowed with the CMPM instruction?
14. What is the range of the displacement for address register indirect with displacement addressing?
15. Set up equates to define a record consisting of a 12-character (including the null) employee name, a longword employee number, and a word salary.
16. For the above record definition, assume a pointer to the record is in A4. Write the instruction that will place the salary data into D0.

17. What are the general forms of the address register with index addressing mode?
18. What restrictions do we have with the PC relative modes?
19. What do you think the instruction MOVE.W 0(PC), D0 would do?
20. What is a forward reference?

Answers

1. No, only destination operands are.
2. The ultimate location where the operand data is found. This may be a register or memory location.
3. Unfortunately no.
4. The register itself.
5. In one or more extension words found with the instruction.
6. 00000000_{16} to $00007FFFF_{16}$ and $FFFF8000_{16}$ to $FFFFFFFF_{16}$.
7. An value used to represent an address in memory.
8. (An)

9.

```
        MOVE.L  #$2000,A0
        MOVE.W  #9,D1
        CLR.L   D0
NEXT:   ADD.L   (A0),D0
        ADDQ.L  #4,A0
        DBRA    D1,NEXT
```

10.

```
        MOVE.L  #$2000,A0
        MOVE.W  #9,D1
        CLR.L   D0
NEXT:   ADD.L   (A0)+,D0
        DBRA    D1,NEXT
```

11.

```
        CLR.L   D0
        LEA     MYSTR,A0
NEXT:   TST.B   (A0)+
        BEQ     FINI
        ADDQ.L  #1,D0
        BRA     NEXT
FINI:   .
```

12. No, it is incremented or decremented by 1, 2, or 4, depending on whether the size was byte, word, or longword.
13. Only address register indirect with postincrementing for both the source and destination operands.

14. A 16-bit signed number. This is −65,536 to +65,535.

15.
```
NAME:           EQU     0
EMPNUM:         EQU     12
SALARY:         EQU     16
RECSIZ:         EQU     18
```

16.
```
MOVE.W SALARY(A4),D0
```

17. d_8(An,Rn.W) and d_8(An,Rn.L)
18. PC relative modes can not be used for destination operands. Some assemblers will not allow these modes for references to other program sections.
19. It copies the value in the instructions extension word to register D0. This contains a zero.
20. A reference to a symbol that has not yet been defined.

CHAPTER 7

THE STACK

In this chapter we will examine the hardware stack implementation on the 68000. A stack is a type of data structure. Computer scientists refer to data structures like stacks as abstract data types. This is because we manipulate the data items contained on the stack by indirect means. In other words, we do not have to know the exact details of the particular abstract data structure in order to use it. The 68000 provides a number of addressing modes and instructions that can be used to manipulate data on a stack. Additionally, a number of other instructions use the stack to support their main functions. The JSR instruction that we have already used is a good example.

A stack is just about what its name implies: a stack of data elements. As with a stack of dishes or books, items are normally added to or removed from the top of the stack. While it is possible to add or remove an element from the middle of a stack, it is not a proper use. The data elements that form a 68000 stack may be bytes, words, or longwords. A stack may be placed anywhere in memory. It can be of any size. Normally, one of the eight address registers, A0 through A7, is used to reference the contents of a stack. However, register A7 is the register that is used by many instructions, such as JSR, to implicitly reference a stack. This register also has the symbolic representation SP (stack pointer). The diagram on the following page shows what an empty stack looks like. Each position in the stack is capable of holding a different value. The initial contents of the stack are of no significance. Whatever values are in the respective memory addresses are indicated by the question marks in the diagram. The actual length of the stack is up to the programmer as long as the total length fits within an area the programmer has reserved.

Stack Instructions

While it might seem a bit confusing, the 68000 hardware stack is upside down. That is, when we add something to the stack, the elements are added to progressively lower memory addresses. For each data element

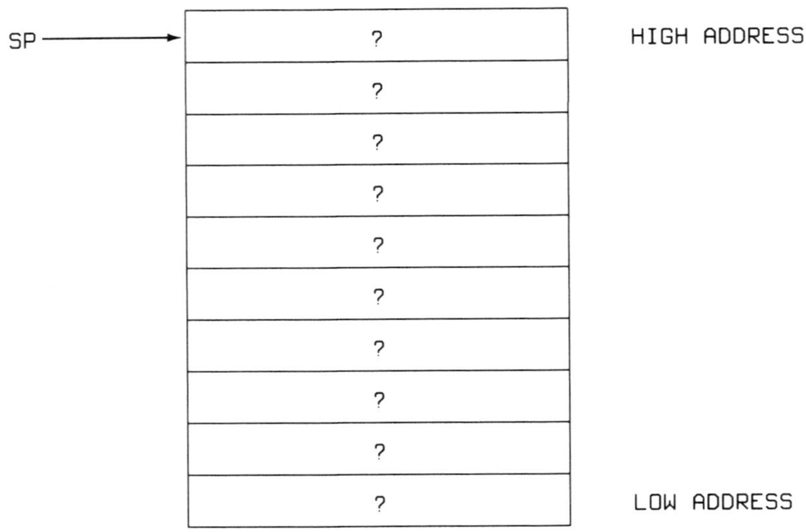

added to the stack, the value of the stack pointer, SP, is decremented by 2 or 4. Remember, memory addresses are byte addresses and not word or longword addresses. Even if we place a byte of data on the stack, the SP register is always changed by 2, to allow a mixture of byte, word, and longword data on the stack. Data on the stack should always be aligned at even byte boundaries. This is necessary for word and longword data. This is only true of register A7, and not when one of the other registers is used as a stack pointer. If you use a register other than A7 as a stack pointer, you will have to avoid placing byte data on the stack, or be sure to keep things aligned properly.

The two main operations that are performed on a stack are *push* and *pop:* we push data onto the stack, and later we pop it off. These are descriptive terms, but are not the actual instruction names, although some microprocessors actually use PUSH and POP. The 68000 uses two of its addressing modes instead of special instructions. This allows us to push and pop values onto and off of the stack with a variety of instructions.

To push a value onto the stack, the register indirect with predecrement addressing mode is used. The general form is −(An), or −(SP) when we use register A7 (of course, we could write −(A7), but the use of the alternate symbolic name for address register 7 is more appropriate). The instruction

```
MOVE.W  #1234,-(SP)
```

would result in the following stack:

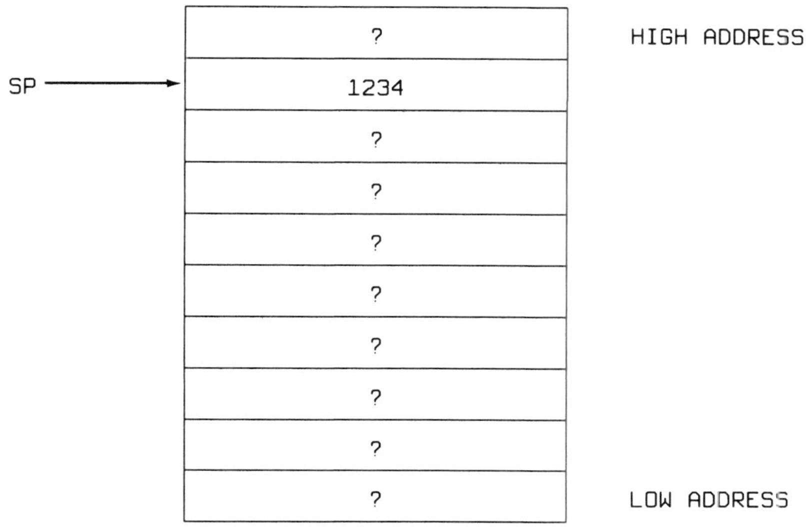

The stack pointer always points to the top element on the stack. This is our push operation. If we push another value on the stack, let's say 5555, the stack would look like this:

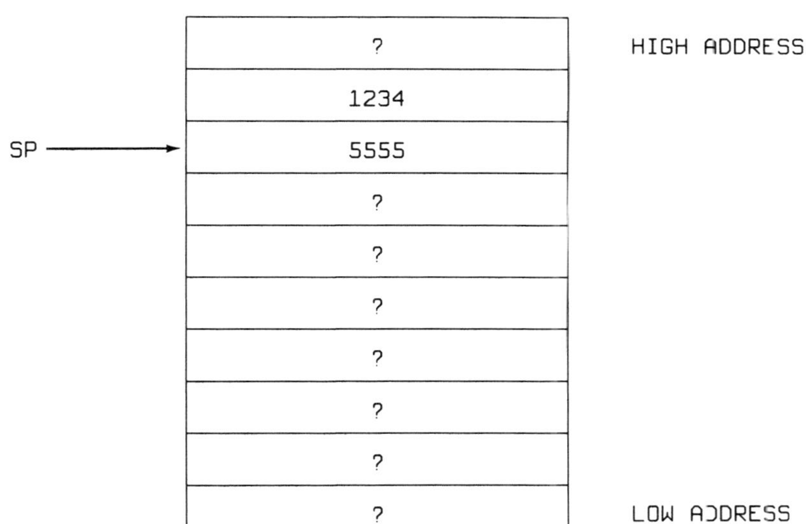

To retrieve elements from the stack, we use a MOVE instruction with address register indirect with postincrement addressing. The general form of this addressing mode is (An)+ and (SP)+ for the stack pointer. The use of this addressing mode is the reverse of register indirect with predecrement addressing and results in popping the topmost value off the stack. The data element pointed to by the stack pointer, SP, is obtained from the stack and placed into the destination operand of the MOVE instruction. The stack pointer is then incremented by 2 or 4. If we perform a

```
MOVE.W   (SP)+,D0
```

on the above stack, the value 5555 is placed in the D0 register. The stack then looks like this:

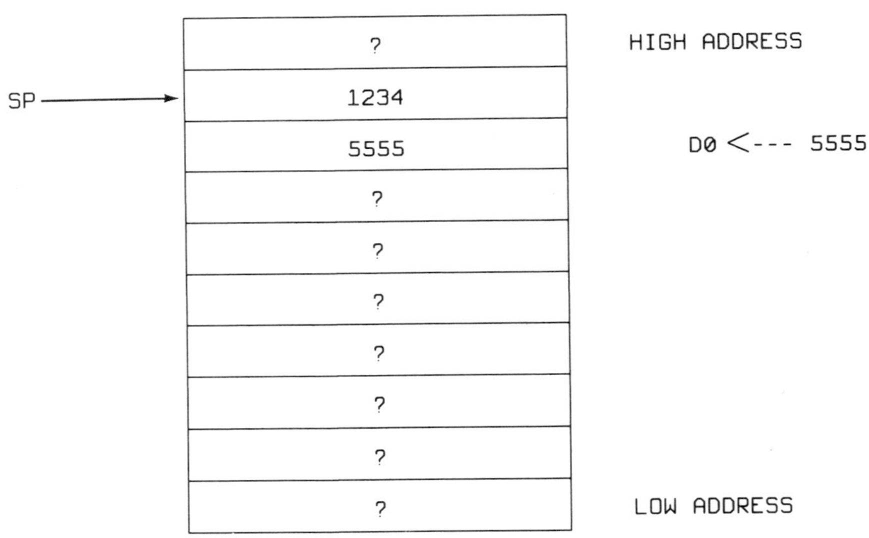

Notice that the value 5555 has not been changed on the stack. However, it is below the stack pointer and is therefore no longer relevant. You might be tempted to try to access this value by modifying the stack pointer directly, perhaps with a SUB instruction. This is not a good idea. In fact, if hardware interrupts are enabled, it might be changed without your being able to predict just when (hardware interrupts will be covered in Chapter 12). Always regard data below the stack pointer as lost forever.

What happens if we pop one too many elements from the stack? Since the 68000 has no way of knowing how many valid elements are on the stack, it just obtains the element pointed to by the stack pointer. If this points to an invalid stack element, then the value obtained is garbage. For this reason, all stack operations must be performed in pairs. A pop is matched with a previous push. Due to the last-in first-out (LIFO) action of the stack, you must be careful to pop things in the reverse order they were pushed.

Before we go on to discuss stack applications, there is one other instruction that should be mentioned. The push effective address instruction, PEA, will compute the effective address of the source operand and then push it on the stack. The general form of this instruction is

```
PEA     <ea>
```

It always pushes a full 32-bit value onto the stack. It is equivalent to executing the two instructions

```
LEA     <ea>,A0
MOVE.L  A0,-(SP)
```

except that the address register is not used. Its main application, for passing address values to subroutines, will be covered in more detail in the next chapter. As a curiosity, the following two instructions are equivalent

```
PEA     (An)

MOVE.L  An,-(sp)
```

Stack Applications

A stack can have many uses. In addition to its usage for subroutine calls, which will be discussed in Chapter 8, the stack can be used by a programmer as a versatile temporary storage area. The only restriction is that the information stored on the stack must be saved and restored in reverse order.

Quite often a programmer may need one or more registers for an operation, and these registers currently contain values that may be needed later. The registers could be moved to other registers, if available, or saved in variable storage. This latter approach has the disadvantage that unless we define specific variable names for each such operation, we run the risk of accidentally using the same temporary storage location more than once, which would wipe out the previous value before it was restored. This problem does not exist with the stack, because the stack can continue to grow and thus create new temporary storage locations.

The following instructions save the D0, D1, D2, and D3 registers and then restore them after performing some arbitrary operations.

```
MOVE.L  D0,-(SP)
MOVE.L  D1,-(SP)
MOVE.L  D2,-(SP)
MOVE.L  D3,-(SP)
...
...
...
MOVE.L  (SP)+,D3
MOVE.L  (SP)+,D2
MOVE.L  (SP)+,D1
MOVE.L  (SP)+,D0
```

Note that the number of pushes matches the number of pops and that the order of the registers is reversed when the pops are performed.

If we want to push and pop a large number of registers, it can get very tiresome to type all these MOVE instructions. The 68000 includes a special version of the MOVE instruction, MOVEM (move multiple registers). This instruction will push or pop any or all of the data or address registers. The general forms of this instruction are:

```
MOVEM[.<size>]  <register list>,<ea>
MOVEM[.<size>]  <ea>,<register list>

<size> = W, L
```

A register list is the list of registers to be pushed or popped. It consists of:

1. Rn—a single register.
2. Rn-Rm—a range of registers (m > n).
3. Any combination of 1. and 2. separated by a slash.

The effective addresses that are normally used with this instruction are the address register indirect with predecrement or postincrement. With these two modes, the MOVEM operates just like a single MOVE except that multiple registers are pushed or popped. To push registers D0 through D5 and registers A3 through A6, the following instruction would be used:

```
MOVEM.L D0-D5/A3-A6,-(SP)
```

They can be popped with:

```
MOVEM.L (SP)+,D0-D5/A3-A6
```

Just remember to make sure that the register lists match for the push and pop. If the wrong number of registers are used for the pop operation, the stack will be left in an improper state.

The MOVEM can also be used to move a set of register contents to an area of memory rather than on the stack. All that is needed is an array large enough to hold the contents of the register list. Here is how a set of registers would be saved and restored to an area of memory:

```
                MOVEM.L D0-D7/A0-A7,SAVEREGS
                .
                .
                .
                MOVEM.L SAVEREGS,D0-D7/A0-A7
                .
                .
                .
SAVEREGS:DS.L   16
```

A stack can be used to reverse the order of a list of data items. The following program reverses a character string entered from the keyboard:

```
*PROGRAM TO REVERSE A CHARACTER STRING
CR:     EQU     13              ASCII CARRIAGE RETURN
        MOVE.B  CR,-(SP)        PLACE A RETURN ON THE STACK
NEXT:   JSR     GETC            GET A CHARACTER
        CMP.B   #CR,D0          IS IT A RETURN?
        BNE     REV             YES, NOW REVERSE
        MOVE.B  D0,-(SP)        NO, SAVE ON STACK
        BRA     NEXT            LOOP FOR MORE
REV:    JSR     NEWLINE         GO TO A NEW LINE
RNEXT:  MOVE.B  (SP)+,D0        GET A CHAR FROM THE STACK
        CMP.B   #CR,D0          FINISHED?
        BEQ     FINI            YES, EXIT
        JSR     PUTC            NO, OUTPUT THE CHAR
        BRA     RNEXT           LOOP FOR MORE
FINI:   JSR     NEWLINE         GO TO A NEW LINE
```

This program does not keep a count of the number of characters stored on the stack. Instead, the ASCII value of the carriage return is placed on the stack as a marker to indicate when we have reached the start of the string. As we reverse the string, we will be moving from the end of the string to the start. The carriage return tells us to stop popping the stack. Any character code could be used, as long as it does not appear in the string itself.

What happens if we do use a character code that appears in the string? When we try to reverse the string, we will terminate the reverse loop prematurely. This will leave data on the stack that should have been removed. The consequences of this bad stack depend on the rest of the program. The very next pop that is performed will result in the wrong value. Since returns from procedures also use the stack, we can have disastrous results.

In the next chapter we will discuss subroutines. The stack will be an extremely important element in the implementation and use of subroutines.

Exercises

1. Which register is used as the hardware stack pointer?
2. Do some instructions implicitly reference the stack?
3. Does the 68000 stack grow upward or downward in memory?
4. What addressing mode is used to push data onto the stack?
5. What addressing mode is used to pop data from the stack?
6. Write the instructions necessary to push the value 100 onto the stack.
7. Write the instructions necessary to push the D0 register onto the stack and pop it into the D1 register.
8. Can you access data below the stack pointer?
9. Write the instruction to place the address of variable COUNT onto the stack.
10. Write the instructions necessary to push the values 1 to 10 onto the stack.

Answers

1. A7.
2. Yes, the JSR is one example.
3. Downward.
4. Address register indirect with predecrement.
5. Address register indirect with postincrement.

6.

```
        MOVE.L #100,-(SP)
```

7.

```
        MOVE.L  D0,-(SP)
        MOVE.L  (SP)+,D1
```

8. Yes, but you can't be sure of what it is.

9.
```
PEA COUNT
```

10.
```
        MOVE.W  #9,D0           LOOP COUNT
        MOVE.L  #1,D1           INITIAL DATA VALUE
NEXT:   MOVE.L  D1,-(SP)        PUSH DATA ONTO STACK
        ADDQ.L  #1,D1           INCREMENT DATA VALUE
        DBRA    D0,NEXT         LOOP TILL DONE
```

CHAPTER 8

SUBROUTINES

We often find that we are repeating the same sequence of instructions in several different parts of the program we are writing. Unlike the instructions that are repeated in a loop, these sequences of instructions must be repeated at different places in the program. Without the facility of using subroutines, we would be forced to repeat these sequences of instructions in our source code, and the machine instructions generated by the assembler would be repeated in memory as well. This results in a larger program—not to mention extra typing.

Fortunately, we do have the ability to write subroutines and use the 68000 instructions that support them. Any sequence of instructions that we wish can be defined as a subroutine. The early high-level programming languages like FORTRAN used the term *subroutine,* while newer languages like PASCAL use the term *procedure*. However, you should not regard a procedure and a subroutine in a high-level language as *exactly* the same thing in assembler.

JSR, BSR, and RTS Instructions

As a simple example, let us say that we have a need to select the largest of three numbers. Assuming that these numbers are contained in the D0, D1, and D2 registers, and that we wanted the largest value to be placed in the D0 register, we might do it with the following instructions:

```
        CMP.L   D1,D0
        BGE     L1
        MOVE.L  D1,D0
L1:     CMP.L   D2,D0
        BGE     L2
        MOVE.L  D2,D0
L2:     .
        .
```

Each time we wished to perform this operation, we would have to repeat the above six instructions. We would also have to change the labels to make sure they were different for each repetition.

If we define these six instructions as a subroutine, we can call the subroutine each time we want to execute these six instructions. We use the JSR (jump to subroutine) instruction for this purpose. You have already used JSR for performing input/output. You have been calling the appropriate input/output subroutines all along. Here is how we would define a subroutine:

```
BIGEST: CMP.L   D1,D0
        BGE     L1
        MOVE.L  D1,D0
L1:     CMP.L   D2,D0
        BGE     L2
        MOVE.L  D2,D0
L2:     RTS
```

The general form of a subroutine is:

```
<name>: .
        .
        .
        .
        RTS
```

The subroutine's name and the RTS instruction bracket the instructions that constitute the subroutine. One or more RTS instructions must appear in the subroutine. Otherwise, execution will "fall out" the bottom. The RTS instruction can be the last instruction of the subroutine, but it doesn't have to be. This will become a bit clearer when we examine the exact mechanism by which subroutines work.

Subroutines can be defined at any convenient place in your program, but keep in mind that the instructions of the subroutine appear in memory in exactly the position they appear in the source program. This means that you can't just stick a subroutine in the middle of your main program. When the subroutine's instructions are encountered, they will be executed in line. Normally, subroutines are placed after your main program.

The subroutine name is defined as a normal instruction label and corresponds to the address of the first instruction of the subroutine. Your subroutine BIGEST can be invoked from several places in your program just by using a JSR instruction with the name of the subroutine. For example:

```
•
•
JSR     BIGEST
•
•
JSR     BIGEST
•
•
```

Each time the JSR instruction is executed, the instructions of the subroutine BIGEST are executed. How does the program find these instructions? The label BIGEST is used to tell the JSR instruction where to find the subroutine. This can be thought of as equivalent to a simple JMP BIGEST instruction. So far this is easy. But now consider what happens after the steps of BIGEST are executed. How do we get back to the instruction after the JSR? Which JSR? There may be quite a few. The answer lies with the use of the stack and the RTS instruction.

Prior to transferring control to the subroutine, the JSR instruction places the address of the instruction that immediately follows the JSR instruction itself on the stack. This is the instruction that should be executed when the instructions of the subroutine are completed. When the RTS instruction is executed in the subroutine, this return address is popped from the stack and placed in the program counter (PC). This acts like another JMP instruction. Now control returns to the part of the program that called the subroutine, with execution continuing at the proper instruction. Figure 8 shows the sequence of events for a typical subroutine call.

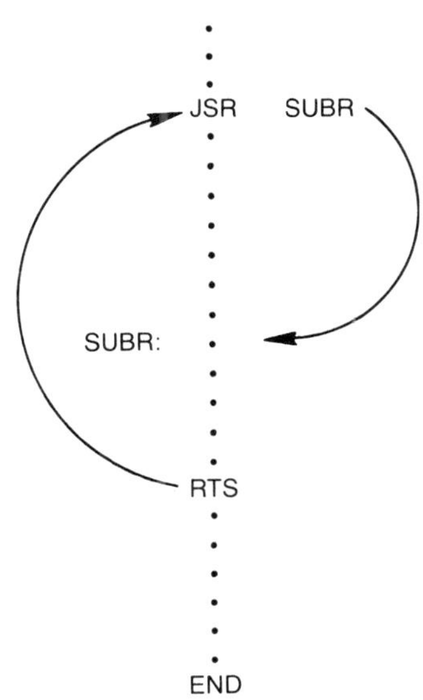

Figure 8 Subroutine call.

The BSR instruction operates identically to the JSR instruction except that it has the same limited addressing range as the conditional branch instructions discussed in Chapter 5. The target address of the BSR instruction must be a label. The JSR instruction allows the use of a wider range of addressing modes. For example, we can place the address of the subroutine in an address register and then use register indirect addressing. The instructions

```
        LEA     SUBR,A0
        JSR     (A0)
```

have the same effect as the single instruction

```
        JSR     SUBR
```

You should use the BSR instruction whenever possible, since it takes up less space in memory for subroutine calls that are relatively close to the address of the BSR itself.

Passing Parameters

An assembly language subroutine is normally free to access any variables within a program. You might want a subroutine to use specific variables of your program as data for its operation. Some variables might only be examined and not modified by the subroutine. Others might be modified. An important point is that if a subroutine specifically references variables other than ones it uses for its own internal purposes, the programmer is stuck with always using these variables to pass data to and from the subroutine. From your programming in a high-level language, you are most likely wondering if parameters or arguments can be passed to subroutines in assembly language. The answer is yes. By allowing parameters, we can make a subroutine more general by not always requiring the same specific variables to be used to pass data to or from the subroutine.

Parameters or arguments can be passed to subroutines in a great variety of ways. There are no standard methods as would be used by high-level languages. The choice is up to the programmer. In fact, it is common practice for several different methods to be used in the same program. The simplest method is to place the parameters to be passed *to* the subroutine in one or more of the registers. We did this with the BIGEST subroutine. Under normal circumstances one or more values are returned by the subroutine. These values can be placed in the same or different registers. This was also the case with BIGEST. For subroutines with a small number of parameters, the use of the registers is simple and efficient. Unfortunately, the number of registers is limited. Additionally, the use of registers may require copying data values to and from variables. We might also have to save values already in the registers before we use them for parameters.

An alternative to the exclusive use of registers is to pass the address of a list of parameters to the subroutine. The address can be passed in one of the address registers. This allows a parameter list of arbitrary length, just as long as all the parameters can be placed in memory at the same place. Using the register indirect addressing mode (introduced in Chapter 6), an address register contains the address of the operand rather than the operand itself. Recall that to use an address register in this way we must enclose it in parenthesis. Here is BIGEST rewritten to have parameters passed by the use of an argument list:

```
BIGEST: MOVE.L   (A0),D0          GET 1ST. ARG.
        ADDQ.L   #4,A0            SET A0 TO 2ND. ARG.
        CMP.L    (A0),D0          COMPARE
        BGE      L1
        MOVE.L   (A0),D0
L1:     ADDQ.L   #4,A0            SET A0 TO 3RD. ARG.
        CMP.L    (A0),D0          COMPARE
        BGE      L2
        MOVE.L   (A0),D0
L2:     RTS
```

We are still using the D0 register to return the largest value. This actually has the advantage that none of the parameters passed to the subroutine are modified. A fourth parameter, or return argument, could be used to return this value. Here is how we set up a call to BIGEST:

```
        .
        .
        LEA      ARG1,A0
        JSR      BIGEST
        .                  D0 NOW CONTAINS THE LARGEST VALUE
        .
ARG1:   DS.L     1
ARG2    DS.L     1
ARG3    DS.L     1
```

The three arguments, ARG1, ARG2, and ARG3, would have values placed in them before the subroutine call.

You might be asking whether it is possible to use the address register indirect with postincrement mode rather than simple address register indirect. It would be, except that we require up to two references through

A0, one for the compare and possibly one for the move. If we postincrement on the compare, we will not have A0 pointing to the proper place for the move. If we use a postincrement on the move, we may not always execute this instruction. Give a lot of thought to those cases where you may be tempted to use address register indirect with postincrement.

The above technique works quite well if we can always group the parameters to a subroutine in one list. If, however, some variables are used as parameters to several subroutines and the argument lists are not the same, we are in trouble. Unless each subroutine is written such that it knows which parameters to skip in the argument list, we can't use just one list. It would be poor programming practice to write subroutines in this manner. A solution does exist. Instead of passing the actual parameters in the argument list, we can pass the addresses of the actual parameters. Just as we passed the address of the argument list in the A0 register, we can pass the parameter addresses as longword constants in the argument list. These values will correspond to the address of each parameter in memory. It is a bit more work to get to the actual parameter. This is how BIGEST would be written:

```
BIGEST: MOVEA.L (A0),A1          GET 1ST. ARG. PTR.
        MOVE.L  (A1),D0          GET 1ST. ARG.
        ADDQ.L  #4,A0            SET A0 TO 2ND. ARG. PTR.
        MOVEA.L (A0),A1          GET 2ND. ARG. PTR.
        CMP.L   (A1),D0          COMPARE
        BGE     L1
        MOVE.L  (A1),D0          NEW LARGEST
L1:     ADDQ.L  #4,A0            SET A0 TO 3RD. ARG. PTR.
        MOVEA.L (A0),A1          GET 3RD. ARG. PTR.
        CMP.L   (A1),D0          COMPARE
        BGE     L2
        MOVE.L  (A1),D0          NEW LARGEST
L2:     ADDQ.L  #4,A0            SET A0 TO 4TH. ARG. PTR.
        MOVEA.L (A0),A1          GET 4TH. ARG. PTR.
        MOVE.L  D0,(A1)          RETURN RESULT
        RTS
*
        .
        .
        LEA     ARGLST,A0
        JSR     BIGEST
        .
        .
;
ARGLST: DC.L    ARG1
        DC.L    ARG2
        DC.L    ARG3
        DC.L    ARG4
        .
ARG1:   DS.L    1
        .
ARG2:   DS.L    1
```

```
         .
ARG3:    DS.L    1
         .
ARG4:    DS.L    1
         .
```

The MOVEA.L (A0),A1 instruction obtains each argument pointer in turn. Note also that the parameters ARG1 through ARG4 do not have to be adjacent or in any order, but can be anywhere in memory.

Saving and Restoring the Registers

Most subroutines will no doubt require the use of one or more of the registers. If these registers are used to pass parameters, the programmer is well aware of the use of these registers by the subroutine. However, a register may be used by the subroutine that is not used for a parameter. The programmer who uses the subroutine must be aware of which of these registers are used if the contents are not preserved by the subroutine. If the programmer is not careful, a bug is introduced. It is important to be sure that either the caller or the subroutine saves and restores the appropriate registers.

The saving and restoring of the registers can be done by the caller or the called subroutine. Both have their advantages and disadvantages. The caller who saves and restores the registers may be doing extra work. Let's say he is using most of the registers. The subroutine he is calling may only use one or two. Unless the caller knows which registers are used by the subroutine he must save and restore all those he is using. The assumption that only certain registers are used by the subroutine is a common source of bugs in assembly language programming. If the subroutine is modified in the future to use an additional register, all calls must be checked to make sure a bug has not been introduced. On the other hand, if the called subroutine is responsible for saving and restoring the registers it uses, the caller will never be doing extra work and the probability of errors is sharply reduced. However, if the subroutine uses a large number of registers, it may save and restore some of them that are not being used by a particular caller.

The technique of saving and restoring the registers is normally handled by using the stack. If the caller is saving and restoring the registers, he must push the desired registers prior to the call and then pop these same registers after control returns from the subroutine. Remember, the registers must be popped in the reverse order from the pushes. The caller would save and restore D0, D1, and D3 as follows:

```
MOVE.L  D0,-(SP)
MOVE.L  D1,-(SP)
MOVE.L  D3,-(SP)
JSR     MYPROC
MOVE.L  (SP)+,D3
MOVE.L  (SP)+,D1
MOVE.L  (SP)+,D0
```

You may recall from Chapter 7 that the MOVEM instruction can be used in place of a sequence of moves. The above instructions could also be written

```
MOVEM.L D0-D1/D3,-(sp)
JSR     MYPROC
MOVEM.L (sp)+,D0-D1/D3
```

Passing Parameters on the Stack

A technique of passing parameters to a subroutine that is often overlooked by assembly language programmers is that of using the stack. This is the most common technique that is used by high-level languages. If parameters are pushed onto the stack by the caller, the subroutine can access them. How does this work, considering that the return address is also pushed onto the stack by the JSR instruction? If the subroutine were to pop values from the stack, the first value would be the return address. Unless this value is saved, and later pushed back onto the stack, the subroutine will not have the ability to return to its caller. A better method is possible.

Let us say that you, as caller, want to pass three longword parameters to a subroutine. You would use the following instructions:

```
MOVE.L  PARM3,-(SP)
MOVE.L  PARM2,-(SP)
MOVE.L  PARM1,-(SP)
JSR     MYPROC
```

The execution of these instructions would result in the stack at the top of the following page. If you could access the stack without changing the stack pointer, SP, you could obtain the parameters. A push or pop can't be used, since they automatically modify, the stack pointer. However, you can use register indirect with displacement addressing. The appropriate register is,

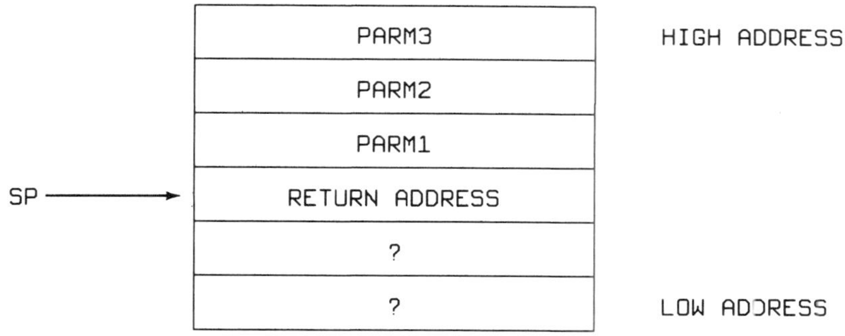

of course, SP. After the call, SP is pointing at the 32-bit return address value. The first parameter is located at 4(SP) (assuming that the parameters were pushed onto the stack in reverse order). Where would the second parameter be? Well, that depends on the size of the first parameter. If the first parameter is a longword, as in this example, then the second parameter is at 8(SP). Each of the other parameters can be found in a similar manner.

I should refresh your memory concerning register A7 (SP), the stack pointer. When postincrement or predecrement addressing are used with a byte-sized operand, SP is always modified by 2, even though the operand is a byte. This is so the stack can always be aligned on an even-word boundary. You should remember this fact if you pass a byte parameter on the stack—always count it as two bytes. If you use a byte-sized instruction for both the push and the pop, everything will work out okay.

The following instructions will obtain the three parameters from the above example and place them into registers D0, D1, and D2:

```
MOVE.L  4(SP),D0       PARM1
MOVE.L  8(SP),D1       PARM2
MOVE.L  12(SP),D2      PARM3
```

Of course, the parameters do not have to be moved to registers to be used; they can be referenced directly.

This very common and simple method of passing parameters is referred to as *call by value.* The actual value of the parameter is placed on the stack. There are some limitations to this technique. First, it is only practical to pass byte, word, or longword arguments on the stack. What if we want to pass an entire array? Second, the subroutine has no way to change the actual parameter; it can only change the *copy* it has on the stack. Both of these limitations can be overcome by the use of a *call by reference*. With call by reference, the *address* of the parameter is passed on the stack. This allows the subroutine not only to access the parameter in the caller's domain, but actually to change its value—in other words, the subroutine can have both input *and* output parameters. Call by value only allows input parameters.

The PEA instruction discussed in Chapter 7 is used to pass the address of each parameter that is to be a call by reference. Note that it is certainly possible to have a mix of call by value and call by reference in the same subroutine call. The only restriction is that both the caller and the callee agree on the order and type of the parameters. Let's say we want to call subroutine ALPHA with the single parameter COUNT, using call by reference. We would call ALPHA as follows:

```
PEA     COUNT
JSR     ALPHA
```

Furthermore, assume that subroutine ALPHA does something simple, like adding 10 to its only parameter. Here's how we can do it:

```
ALPHA:  MOVEA.L 4(SP),A0          GETS ADDRESS OF COUNT IN A0
        ADD.L   #10,(A0)          ADD 10
        RTS
```

Keep in mind that the data object to which the parameter points can be as simple as a single integer or as complicated as the programmer desires—an array of records, or even a record consisting of several arrays. Anything that can be located by a single address can be passed as a parameter using call by reference.

One problem still remains: the parameters are still on the stack when the subroutine returns. The subroutine can't pop the parameters, since the return address is at the top of the stack. One method is to have the caller clean up the stack. The caller has several choices as to what to do. The caller can pop the parameters:

```
MOVE.L  (SP)+,D0          PARM1
MOVE.L  (SP)+,D0          PARM2
MOVE.L  (SP)+,D0          PARM3
```

This technique is most useful when one or more parameters are return values. The caller can also modify SP directly:

```
ADDA.L  #12,SP
```

A unique method that you might come across is to use the LEA instruction:

```
        LEA     12(SP),SP
```

This method is reported to execute somewhat faster than the ADDA.

An alternate approach is to have the subroutine clean up the stack. This is complicated by the fact that the return address is on the stack. You can't just add a value to SP. You must first move the return address to a safe place, adjust SP, and finally return the return address to the stack in preparation for the RTS. For the above example, this can be done as follows:

```
        MOVEA.L (SP)+,A0        GET RETURN ADDRESS
        ADDA.L  #12,SP          ADJUST SP
        MOVE.L  A0,-(SP)        PUT RETURN ADDRESS BACK
        RTS
```

A subtle method would be to substitute a JMP instruction for the RTS.

```
        MOVEA.L (SP)+,A0        GET RETURN ADDRESS
        ADDA.L  #12,SP          ADJUST STACK
        JMP     (A0)            RETURN
```

These last two methods have the disadvantage in that they use an address register that can't be restored to its prior value before the return.

Stack Frames

There are a number of problems introduced when parameters are passed on the stack. Unless the subroutine keeps track of the value of SP when it was called, it will not be able to find its parameters. For example, if a subroutine needs to push one or more values on the stack during its operation, the value of SP will change and the parameters will not be located at the same relative offsets that they were originally. Also, high-level languages use the concept of *local* or *automatic* variables. These are special storage locations that only exist during the time interval that the subroutine, or a subroutine that it calls, is executing. These local variables are normally allocated from the stack. This allows such nice features as recursive subroutine calls. Each time a subroutine is called it will create a new and distinct set of local variables.

All of this greatly increases the difficulty in keeping track of where things are on the stack. Each time the stack pointer SP changes, all the offsets will also change. What is needed is a method of anchoring our position in the stack and making all references relative to this fixed point. This fixed reference is called the *frame pointer*. Every subroutine that is called in a sequence of subroutine calls uses its own stack frame. It is a simple matter to allocate a specific address register, other than A7, to serve this purpose. Quite often register A6 is used as a frame pointer. All we have to do is to move the particular value of SP that is our anchor point into A6. SP can then change and we will still be able to access parameters and local variables relative to our anchor point. The logical choice of such an anchor point is the value of SP just after the subroutine is called. This would always allow us to access parameters as a positive offset from the frame pointer. If we want local variable storage, we can subtract a fixed number from SP and use this area, referenced as a negative offset from the frame pointer, for our locals. If we execute the following instructions

```
ALPHA:  MOVEA.L SP,A6          SET UP FRAME POINTER
        ADDA.L  #m,SP          RESERVE m BYTES OF LOCALS
```

for subroutine BETA we will have a stack that looks like this:

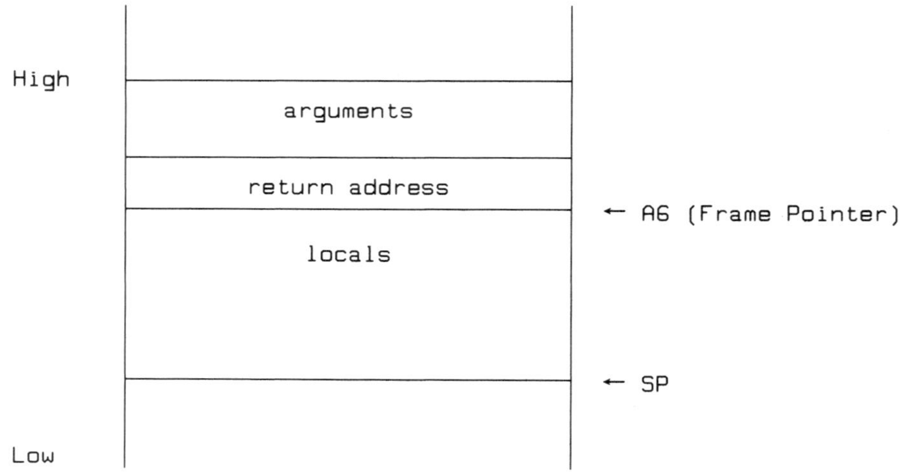

We can then access parameters using address mode 4n(A6), where n is the parameter number. We have to remember to account for the four bytes occupied by the return address when computing this offset. Local variables are addressed as −m(A6), where m is the byte offset into the local area. To return from our subroutine, we can quickly clean up the stack of all locals by merely resetting SP to the value of the frame pointer A6 and then performing the RTS.

8. Write a subroutine called SUM that adds D0 and D1 and returns the result in D0.
9. Write a subroutine and its call that adds word variables A and B. Assume that A and B can be located next to each other in memory. Return the sum in D0.
10. Repeat the above problem, now assuming that A and B cannot be located next to each other in memory.
11. When a JSR is executed, what actions take place?
12. What actions take place when a RTS is executed?
13. What is wrong with the following?

```
CRAZY: MOVE.L  D0,-(SP)
       ADD.L   D0,D1
       RTS
```

14. The following subroutine is designed to double the D0 register and return the result in D1. What is a possible danger with the following procedure if the caller assumes that no registers are changed?

```
DOUBLE:ADD.L   D0,D0
       MOVE.L  D0,D1
       RTS
```

15. Write a subroutine named SKIPLINES that outputs blank lines specified by a count contained in register D0.
16. If we pass parameters on the stack, what method can be used to "clean up" the stack?
17. Write a subroutine named PAIRS that outputs two values on a line. VAL1 is output first, and then VAL2, followed by a new line. These values are passed on the stack by the following instructions:

```
MOVE.L  VAL1,-(SP)
MOVE.L  VAL2,-(SP)
JSR     PAIRS
```

    It might help to draw the stack.
18. What is the difference between call by reference and call by value?
19. Write an instruction to place the address of variable ALPHA on the stack.
20. What is a stack frame?

Answers

1. Yes, but they are not exactly the same as the subroutines and procedures of high-level languages.
2. By a JSR instruction.
3. By a RTS instruction.
4. Anywhere, as long as they are not in the middle of code that is designed for sequential execution.
5. A BSR is similar to the conditional branches in that it only allows a label as an operand; a JSR can use a number of addressing modes, including register indirect.

6.

```
CLEAR: CLR.L   D0
       CLR.L   D1
       CLR.L   D2
       CLR.L   D3
       CLR.L   D4
       CLR.L   D5
       CLR.L   D6
       CLR.L   D7
       RTS
```

7. There are a limited number of them, and data may have to be copied to and from the registers.

8.

```
SUM:    ADD.L   D1,D0
        RTS
```

9.

```
        .
        .
        LEA      A,A0
        JSR      SUM
        .
        .
SUM:    MOVE.W   (A0),D0
        ADDQ.L   #2,A0
        ADD.L    (A0),D0
        RTS
A:      DS.W     1
B:      DS.W     1
```

10.

```
        .
        .
        .
        LEA      ARGLST,A0
        JSR      SUM
        .
        .
SUM:    MOVEM.L A0-A1,-(SP)                SAVE REGS
        MOVEA.L (A0),A1                    -> 1ST. ARG.
        MOVE.W  (A1),D0
```

```
            ADDQ.L   #4,A0
            MOVEA.L  (A0),A1                        -> 2ND. ARG
            ADD.W    (A1),D0
            MOVEM.L  (SP)+,A0-A1                    RESTORE REGS
            RTS
            .
            .
    ARGLST:DC.L      A
            DC.L     B
            .
    A:      DC.W     1
            .
            .
    B;      DC.W     1
```

11. The return address is pushed onto the stack, and control transfers to the location specified by the operand of the JSR.
12. The return address is popped from the stack, and control transfers to the return address.
13. There is no matching pop to the push of D0 onto the stack, and therefore the RTS instruction will not obtain the correct return address.
14. The D0 register is not saved and restored by the procedure.

15.

```
SKIPLINES:     MOVE.L   D0,-(SP)         SAVE D0
NEXT:          JSR      NEWLINE          OUTPUT NEWLINE
               SUBQ.L   #1,D0            DECREMENT COUNT
               BNE      NEXT             BRANCH IF MORE
               MOVE.L   (SP)+,D0         RESTORE D0
               RTS
```

16. The caller can use an ADD instruction to register SP.

17.

```
PAIRS: MOVE.L   D0,-(SP)        SAVE D0
       MOVE.L   12(SP),D0       GET VAL1
       JSR      OUTDEC          OUTPUT
       MOVE.B   #' '            BLANK
       JSR      PUTC            OUTPUT BLANK
       MOVE.L   8(SP),D0        GET VAL2
       JSR      OUTDEC          OUTPUT
       JSR      NEWLINE
       MOVE.L   (SP)+,D0        RESTORE D0
       RTS
```

Note that VAL2 is at 8(SP) because of the extra 4 bytes used when we saved D0 on the stack. VAL1 is at 12(SP) because it was pushed first.

18. With call by value, a copy of the data is placed on the stack. With call by reference, the address of the data is placed on the stack.

19.

```
PEA ALPHA
```

20. A stack frame is an area of the stack used to pass parameters to a subroutine, save the return address, and provide temporary storage or local variables for a subroutine. Each subroutine has an associated stack frame for each active call.

CHAPTER 9

LINKED LISTS—A PROGRAMMING EXAMPLE

You now have a considerable number of useful 68000 instructions in your repertoire, it would be nice to see how a larger program can be constructed. Since a linked list is a very popular type of data structure, I have chosen this as the vehicle for our discussion. We will set out to write out a complete program to form a linked list of words that is organized in alphabetical order. This program will allow you to add to, print, and delete entries in this linked list. In the course of the chapter we will build up a set of subroutines that will prove useful beyond their application to linked lists. To some extent these subroutines look like some of those found in the standard C language library.

A linked list consists of a chain of *nodes*. A node consists of some amount of data and a pointer. The data is arbitrary and the amount can be as large or small as the user desires. The pointer which is just a 32-bit address in memory, is the address of the next node in the chain. As many nodes as we want can be chained together. If we know the address of the first node in the list and have some method of determining when we have reached the last node in the list,we can reach any particular node by progressively chaining down the list from the first node. This will be demonstrated shortly. Figure 9 shows the structure of a single node and a linked list of nodes. HEADER is not a node but merely a pointer to the first node.

When we build a linked list of data items, we must obtain the storage space for a node, fill in the correct data, and finally link it into the list

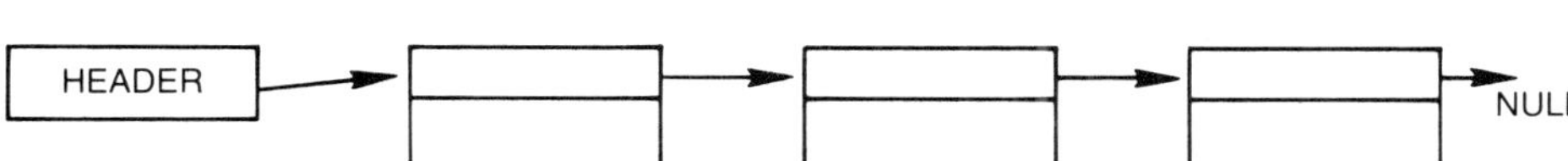

Figure 9 Linked list.

in the correct location. There are many ways to obtain the storage for a node. One way is to maintain a linked list of free nodes. All we have to do is to initialize this linked list by chaining the nodes together. For our example we will have nodes of size NDATA. This represents a node of size NDATA+4, where NDATA is the size of the data in the node. A header, FLIST, will be maintained that will point to the pool of free nodes. Assuming the total number of nodes is equal to the value of symbol NNODES the following subroutine, INIT, will initialize a free list of nodes:

```
NDATA:  EQU      10                 10 BYTES OF DATA (MUST BE EVEN NO.)
NSIZE:  EQU      NDATA+4            DATA + POINTER
NNODES: EQU      100                NUMBER OF NODES
****************************************************************
* INIT - INITIALIZE THE FREE LIST
****************************************************************
INIT:   MOVEM.L D1/A0-A1,-(SP)     SAVE REGS
        LEA      NODES,A0           A0 -> NODE POOL
        LEA      FLIST,A1           A1 -> HEADER OF FREE LIST
        MOVE.W   #NNODES-1,D1       SET UP FOR LOOP
INIT1:  MOVE.L   A0,(A1)            SET -> TO NEXT NODE
        MOVEA.L A0,A1               SET UP FOR NEXT NDOE
        ADDA.L   #NSIZE,A0          A0 -> NEXT NODE
        DBRA     D1,INIT1           LOOP UNTIL DONE
        CLR.L    (A1)               PLACE NULL PTR IN LAST NODE
        MOVEM.L (SP)+,D0/A0-A1     RESTORE REGS
        RTS
*
        DATA
FLIST:  DS.L     1                  -> FREE LIST
NODES:  DS.B     NSIZE*NNODES       NODE POOL
```

The CLR.L instruction places a zero value in the very last pointer. A value of zero is used to represent the NULL pointer. We can never have a node at address zero for reasons that will be covered in Chapter 12. Locations starting at zero are special reserved locations on the 68000.

Our next step is to write a subroutine that will obtain a free node from this free list. Here is how we do it:

```
******************************************************
* GETFREE - RETURNS PTR TO FREE NODE IN A0.
*           IF NO NODES LEFT, NULL IS RETURNED
******************************************************
GETFREE:
        MOVEA.L FLIST,A0            GET HEAD PTR
        CMPA.L   #0,A0              NULL?
        BEQ      GETFRET            YES, JUST RETURN
        MOVE.L   (A0),FLIST         NO, SET NEW HEAD
GETFRET:RTS
```

This subroutine merely uses the address contained in the head pointer FLIST as a pointer to the the node to obtain. If it is NULL, it means our free list is empty. If the pointer in FLIST is not NULL, then it gives the address of a free node. If the free list is not empty then the head pointer FLIST is set to point to the next node in the free list. Either a valid node pointer or a NULL is returned by the subroutine.

Before we can start to build some linked lists that contain actual data, we will have to take time out from our linked lists and develop some other important subroutines.

In Chapter 6 I introduced the concept of a character string. You may recall that a character string can be specified as a list of successive bytes followed by a terminating or null byte. One important subroutine determines a string's length:

```
****************************************************************
* STRLEN - RETURNS LENGTH OF NULL TERMINATED STRING IN D0
*              A0 -> STRING
****************************************************************
STRLEN: MOVE.L  A0,-(SP)         SAVE REG
        CLR.L   D0               INITIALIZE
STRLEN1:TST.B   (A0)+            NULL?
        BEQ     STRLENR          YES, RETURN
        ADDQ.L  #1,D0            BUMB COUNT
        BRA     STRLEN1          LOOP
STRLENR:MOVE.L  (SP)+,A0         RESTORE REG
        RTS
```

We might also want to copy a string:

```
************************************************************
* STRCPY - COPY A NULL TERMINATED STRING
*              A0 -> SOURCE STRING
*              A1 -> DESTINATION STRING
************************************************************
STRCPY: MOVEM.L A0-A1,-(SP)      SAVE REGS
STRCPY1:MOVE.B  (A0)+,(A1)+      MOVE A BYTE
        BNE     STRCPY1          GET ANOTHER IF NOT NULL
        MOVEM.L (SP)+,A0-A1      RESTORE REGS
        RTS
```

Next, we will want to compare two strings:

```
************************************************************
* STRCMP - COMPARE TWO NULL TERMINATED STRINGS
*              A0 -> STRING 1
*              A1 -> STRING 2
************************************************************
STRCMP: MOVEM.L A0-A1,-(SP)      SAVE REGS
STRCMP1:CMPM.B  (A0)+,(A1)+      COMPARE BYTES
        BNE     STRRET           RETURN IF DIFFERENT
```

```
        TST.B    -1(A0)           HAVE WE HIT A NULL?
        BNE      STRCMP1          NOW MORE BYTES LEFT
STRRET: MOVEM.L  (SP)+,A0-A1      RESTORE REGS
        RTS
```

This subroutine sets the condition code register according to the last two bytes compared, if they were unequal; the zero condition is set if the strings match. We can then determine not only the equality or inequality of the strings, but also their alphabetical order. Fortunately, the ASCII character set is ordered properly from A to Z. These last two subroutines are minor variations of the techniques used in Chapter 6.

The standard I/O subroutines introduced in Chapter 4 only provide a mechanism to input or output a single character. We must be able to input and output a complete character string. Two subroutines, INS and OUTS, will be used to input and output null-terminated strings. OUTS merely calls PUTC for each character in the string until the null is found.

```
*************************************************************
* OUTS - OUTPUT A NULL TERMINATED STRING TO THE SCREEN
*              a0 -> STRING
*************************************************************
OUTS:    MOVEM.L A0/D0,-(SP)      SAVE REGISTERS
OUTS1:   CLR.L   D0               CLEAR HIGH ORDER BYTES OF D0
         MOVE.B  (A0)+,D0         MOVE A CHARACTER INTO D0
         BEQ     OUTSRET          QUIT IF NULL
         JSR     PUTC             OUTPUT THE CHARACTER
         BRA     OUTS1            LOOP FOR ANOTHER
OUTSRET:MOVEM.L  (SP)+,A0/D0      RESTORE REGISTERS
         RTS
```

Inputting a character string is almost as simple. There is one minor detail to keep in mind: the size of the array that we are reading the string into is of a certain size. For this example, the maximum size data string is a total of NDATA characters long. Since the string must be terminated with a null, we must reserve one of these characters for the null byte. Therefore, we can only read a total of NDATA-1 characters from the keyboard. The INS subroutine will read characters using GETC until a carriage return is entered or NDATA-1 characters have been entered.

```
**************************************************************
* INS - INPUT A STRING UNTIL CR OR NDATA-1 CHARACTERS
*        A0 -> STRING
**************************************************************
INS:     MOVEM.L A0/D0-D1,-(SP)   SAVE REGISTERS
         MOVE.W  #NDATA-2,D1      SET UP LOOP COUNT
INS1:    JSR     GETC             GET A CHARACTER
         MOVE.B  D0,(A0)+         STORE IT IN STRING
         CMP.B   #CR,D0           CR?
         DBEQ    D1,INS1          LOOP UNTIL COUNT RUNS OUT OR CR
```

```
INSR:    JSR      NEWLINE         OUTPUT A NEWLINE
         CLR.B    (A0)            ADD A NULL TO STRING
         CMP.B    #CR,D0          LAST CHAR A CR?
         BNE      INSR1           NO
         CLR.B    -1(A0)          YES, PUT NULL THERE TOO
INSR1:   MOVEM.L  (SP)+,A0/D0-D1  RESTORE REGISTERS
         RTS
```

Note that the method used to handle an overflow count is different from that used to handle a string terminated with a carriage return. If the carriage return is entered, it must not appear in the string. The second CMP.B instruction handles this check. If the last character entered was a carriage return, it is overwritten with a null byte.

At this point we have enough basic subroutines to start manipulating the linked lists themselves. We will need two types of list insertions; one that inserts a node at the head of a list, and one that inserts a node in alphabetical order. To insert at the head of the list is very simple. We merely obtain the pointer to the first node from the header. You can think of the header as a special node that has no data and is always located in a known place. For example, the header for the free list is always located at the memory location FLIST. We set the forward pointer in the node we are inserting to point to the node that was pointed to by the header. This may be a null pointer, but we don't care. The only other piece of business is to set the header to point to the node we are inserting. Here is how it's done:

```
****************************************************************
* INSERT - INSERT A NODE AT THE HEAD OF A LIST.
*          A0 -> NODE
*          A1 -> HEADER OF LIST
****************************************************************
INSERT: MOVE.L  (A1),(A0)       SET UP LINK IN NEW NODE
        MOVE.L  A0,(A1)         SET HEADER TO -> NEW NODE
        RTS
```

Figure 10 shows this operation.

Insertion of a node in alphabetical order is considerably more difficult. We must chain down the linked list until we find the proper insertion point. This is determined by a string comparison using STRCMP. We then have to link this node into the list by breaking the previous link and setting the proper pointers. Refer to Figure 11.

```
****************************************************************
* INSERTA - INSERT A NODE ALPHABETICALLY.
*       A0 -> NODE
*       A1 -> HEADER OF LIST
****************************************************************
INSERTA:MOVEM.L A0-A2,-(SP)     SAVE REGISTERS
        ADDQ.L  #4,A0           A0 -> NEW NODE DATA
```

```
INSA0:  MOVEA.L A1,A2          A2 -> PREVIOUS NODE LINK
        MOVE.L  (A1),A1        A1 -> NEXT NODE LINK
        CMPA.L  #0,A1          NULL?
        BEQ     INSAI          YES, END OF LIST
        ADDQ.L  #4,A1          A1 -> NEXT NODE DATA
        JSR     STRCMP         COMPARE STRINGS
        BLT     INSA1          KEEP LOOKING
        SUBQ.L  #4,A1          A1 -> NEXT NODE LINK
INSAI:  SUBQ.L  #4,A0          A0 -> NEW NODE LINK
        MOVE.L  A1,(A0)        SET LINK IN NEW NODE
        MOVE.L  A0,(A2)        SET LINK IN PREVIOUS NODE
INSAR:  MOVEM.L (SP)+,A0-A2    RESTORE REGISTERS
        RTS
INSA1:  SUBQ.L  #4,A1          A1 -> LINK
        BRA     INSA0          CONTINUE SEARCH
```

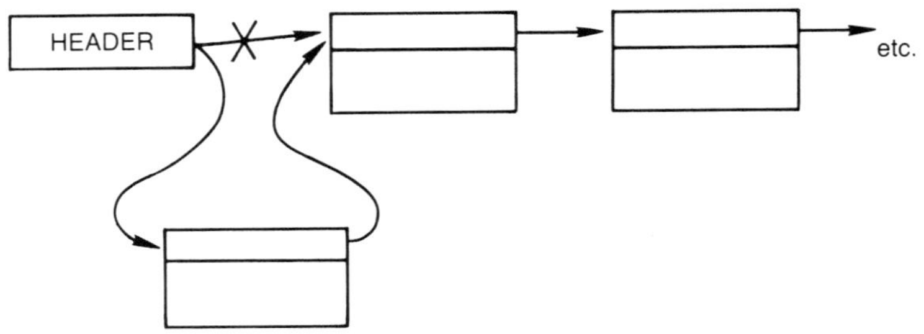

Figure 10 Insertion at head of list.

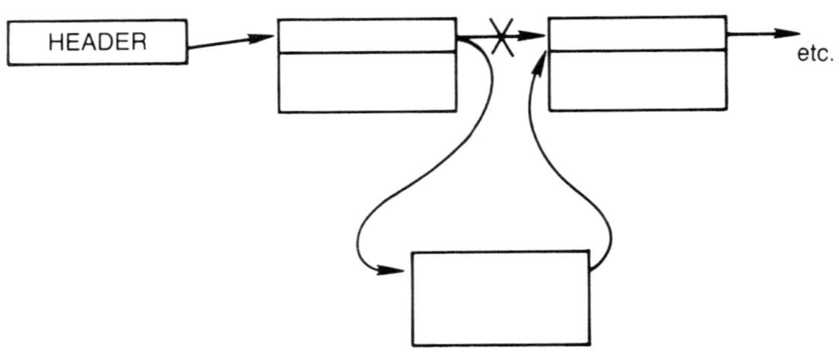

Figure 11 Insertion into middle of list.

By using more registers and/or other addressing modes it may be possible to reduce the size of this subroutine. Can you do it? Is there a way to eliminate the additions and subtractions used to obtain pointers to the data?

To delete a node, we must know its position in the linked list. If we are given the data string for a particular node, we can find the actual node location by searching the string to see if we can find the node. The subroutine SEARCH will search a given list. If a node matches our search string, then a pointer to the node is returned.

```
*****************************************************************
* SEARCH - SEARCH FOR A NODE WITH MATCHING STRING.
*              A0 -> HEADER NODE
*              A1 -> SEARCH STRING
*              oN RETURN A0 -> MATCHING NODE OR IS NULL
*              IF NOT FOUND.
*****************************************************************
SEARCH: MOVEA.L (A0),A0         GET -> NEXT NODE
        CMPA.L  #0,A0           NULL?
        BEQ     SEARCHR         YES, NO MATCH
        ADDQ.L  #4,A0           A0 -> STRING
        JSR     STRCMP          COMPARE STRINGS
        BNE     SEARCH1         DOESN'T MATCH
        SUBQ.L  #4,A0           RESET PTR TO LINK
SEARCHR:RTS
SEARCH1:SUBQ.L  #4,A0           RESET PTR TO LINK
        BRA     SEARCH
```

To complete our deletion, we must unlink the deleted node from the linked list and return it to the free list. The latter operation can be accomplished by the INSERT subroutine already discussed. The former operation is accomplished as follows:

```
*****************************************************************
* DELETE - DELETE A NODE.
*          A0 -> NODE
*          A1 -> HEADER OF LIST
*****************************************************************
DELETE: MOVEM.L A0-A1,-(SP)     SAVE REGISTERS
DELETE0:CMPA.L  (A1),A0         DO NODE PTRS. MATCH?
        BEQ     DELETE1         YES, COMPLETE OPERATION
        MOVEA.L (A1),A1         NO, CHANIN DOWN LIST
        CMPA.L  #0,A1           NULL?
        BEQ     DELETER         YES, NODE NOT FOUND
        BRA     DELETE0         NO, LOOP TO NEXT NODE
DELETE1:MOVE.L  (A0),(A1)       UNLINK THE NODE
DELETER:MOVEM.L (SP)+,A0-A1     RESTORE REGISTERS
        RTS
```

This operation is shown in Figure 12.

One more subroutine is needed before we can write the main program: we must have a way of outputting the list to the terminal or screen.

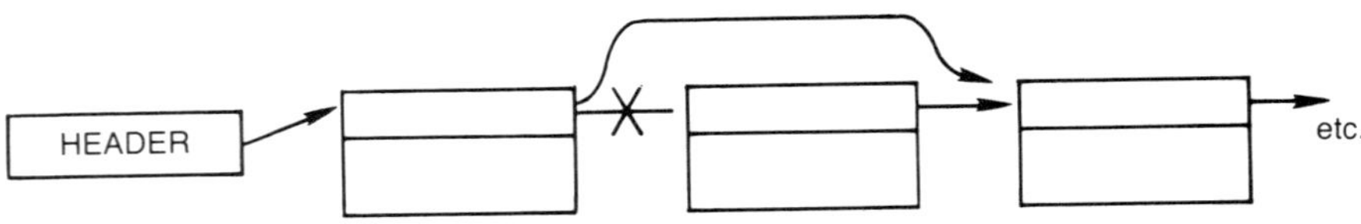

Figure 12 Deletion of a node.

This is accomplished by the subroutine PLIST:

```
*****************************************************************
* PLIST - PRINT A LIST
*         A0 -> HEADER NODE
*****************************************************************
PLIST:  MOVE.L  A0,-(SP)          SAVE REGISTER
        MOVEA.L (A0),A0           GET -> FIRST NODE
PLIST1: CMPA.L  #0,A0             NULL?
        BEQ     PLISTR            YES, RETURN
        ADDQ.L  #4,A0             A0 -> STRING
        JSR     OUTS              OUTPUT THE STRING
        JSR     NEWLINE           OUTPUT A NEWLINE
        SUBQ.L  #4,A0             A0 -> LINK
        MOVEA.L (A0),A0           CHAIN DOWN THE LIST
        BRA     PLIST1            LOOP FOR NEXT
PLISTR: MOVE.L  (SP)+,A0          RESTORE REGISTER
        RTS                       RETURN
```

The main program is very straightforward. A menu is displayed and the user is expected to enter a single character corresponding to one of the valid commands, I (insert), D (delete), P (print), or Q (quit). The character entered is compared with the valid commands and if one is found to match, the appropriate instructions are executed by branching to specific command routines. Each of these command routines branches to the common loop at OVER. Other than to display input prompts or output messages, these routines merely call the proper list-manipulating subroutines and string primitives. Their operation should be clear if you refer back to the descriptions of the subroutines.

```
*************************************************************
* MAIN PROGRAM - EXECUTION STARTS HERE
*************************************************************
        JSR     INIT              INITIALIZE THE FREE LIST
OVER:   LEA     MENU,A0           DISPLAY THE MENU
        JSR     OUTS              "
        JSR     GETC              GET INPUT CHARACTER
        JSR     NEWLINE           OUTPUT A NEWLINE
```

```
*************************************************************
* COMPARE THE INPUT CHARACTER WITH ALL POSSIBLE SINGLE
* CHARACTER COMMANDS AND BRANCH TO THE PROPER COMMAND
* IF FOUND.
*************************************************************
        CMP.B   #'I',D0
        BEQ     COMI
        CMP.B   #'D',D0
        BEQ     COMD
        CMP.B   #'P',D0
        BEQ     COMP
        CMP.B   #'Q',D0
        BEQ     COMQ
        BRA     OVER            NOT FOUND, TRY AGAIN
*************************************************************
* D - DELETE AN ENTRY
*************************************************************
COMD:   LEA     MESS1,A0        PROMPT FOR STRING
        JSR     OUTS            "
        LEA     S1,A0           GET INPUT STRING
        JSR     INS             "
        MOVEA.L A0,A1           A1 -> STRING
        LEA     NLIST,A0        A0 -> NLIST
        JSR     SEARCH          SEARCH FOR ENTRY
        CMPA.L  #0,A0           FOUND?
        BEQ     COMDNF          NO
        LEA     NLIST,A1        YES, CALL DELETE
        JSR     DELETE          "
        LEA     FLIST,A1        A1 -> FREE LIST
        JSR     INSERT          INSERT DELETED NODE ONTO FREE LIST
        LEA     MESS2,A0        OUTPUT MESSAGE
        JSR     OUTS            "
        BRA     OVER            GET ANOTHER COMMAND
COMDNF: LEA     MESS3,A0        OUTPUT MESSAGE
        JSR     OUTS            "
        BRA     OVER            GET ANOTHER COMMAND
*************************************************************
* I - INSERT AN ENTRY
*************************************************************
COMI:   LEA     MESS1,A0        OUTPUT PROMPT
        JSR     OUTS            "
        JSR     GETFREE         GET A FREE NODE
        CMPA.L  #0,A0           NULL?
        BEQ     COMIERR         YES, NO MORE NODES
        ADDQ.L  #4,A0           A0 -> DATA IN NODE
        JSR     INS             GET AN INPUT STRING
        SUBQ.L  #4,A0           A0 -> LINK IN NODE
        LEA     NLIST,A1        A1 -> LIST
        JSR     INSERTA         INSERT ENTRY ALPHABETICALLY
        BRA     OVER            GET NEXT COMMAND
COMIERR:LEA     MESS4,A0        OUTPUT ERROR MESSAGE
        JSR OUTS                "
        BRA OVER                GET ANOTHER COMMAND
*************************************************************
* P - PRINT THE LINKED LIST
*************************************************************
COMP:   LEA     NLIST,A0        A0 -> LIST
        JSR     PLIST           PRINT OUT
        BRA     OVER            GET NEXT COMMAND
*************************************************************
* Q - RETURN TO YOUR OPERATING SYSTEM
*************************************************************
COMQ:   .......                 SYSTEM DEPENDANT
*
```

```
************************************************************
* PROGRAM DATA
************************************************************
* NOTE - CR AND LF ARE DEFINED IN THE STANDARD I/O SUBROUTINES
MENU:    DC.B     'INSERT, PRINT, DELETE, QUIT? ',0
MESS1:   DC.B     'ENTER: ',0
MESS2:   DC.B     'NODE DELETED.',CR,LF,0
MESS3:   DC.B     'NODE NOT FOUND.',CR,LF,0
MESS4:   DC.B     'NO MORE FREE NODES.',CR,LF,0
S1:      DS.B     80                BUFFER FOR INPUT STRING
NLIST:   DS.L     1                 -> LIST
FLIST:   DS.L     1                 -> FREE LIST
NODES:   DS.B     NSIZE*NNODES      NODE POOL
         END
```

To conclude this chapter, I have included a sample dialog that was formed by running this program. It demonstrates all of the features.

```
INSERT, PRINT, DELETE, QUIT? I
ENTER: ALPHA
INSERT, PRINT, DELETE, QUIT? I
ENTER: BETA
INSERT, PRINT, DELETE, QUIT? P
ALPHA
BETA
INSERT, PRINT, DELETE, QUIT? I
ENTER: AAA
INSERT, PRINT, DELETE, QUIT? P
AAA
ALPHA
BETA
INSERT, PRINT, DELETE, QUIT? I
ENTER: ZZZ
INSERT, PRINT, DELETE, QUIT? P
AAA
ALPHA
BETA
ZZZ
INSERT, PRINT, DELETE, QUIT? I
ENTER: GAMMA
INSERT, PRINT, DELETE, QUIT? P
AAA
ALPHA
BETA
GAMMA
ZZZ
INSERT, PRINT, DELETE, QUIT? D
ENTER: BETA
NODE DELETED.
INSERT, PRINT, DELETE, QUIT? P
AAA
ALPHA
GAMMA
ZZZ
INSERT, PRINT, DELETE, QUIT? I
ENTER: A
INSERT, PRINT, DELETE, QUIT? I
ENTER: B
```

```
INSERT, PRINT, DELETE, QUIT? I
ENTER: C
INSERT, PRINT, DELETE, QUIT? I
ENTER: D
INSERT, PRINT, DELETE, QUIT? I
ENTER: E
INSERT, PRINT, DELETE, QUIT? I
ENTER: F
INSERT, PRINT, DELETE, QUIT? P
A
AAA
ALPHA
B
C
D
E
F
GAMMA
ZZZ
INSERT, PRINT, DELETE, QUIT? I
ENTER: NO MORE FREE NODES.
INSERT, PRINT, DELETE, QUIT? D
ENTER: AAA
NODE DELETED.
INSERT, PRINT, DELETE, QUIT? I
ENTER: LASTONE
INSERT, PRINT, DELETE, QUIT? P
A
ALPHA
B
C
D
E
F
GAMMA
LASTONE
ZZZ
INSERT, PRINT, DELETE, QUIT? Q
```

CHAPTER 10

LOGICAL, SHIFT AND ROTATE INSTRUCTIONS

In this chapter we will examine a group of instructions that can manipulate the individual bits of a byte, word, or longword by performing logical operations such as AND and OR. We will also see how shift and rotate instructions can change the positions of all the bits in a byte or word in interesting ways.

Truth Tables

There are four logical operations that have corresponding 68000 instructions: NOT, AND, OR, and EOR (exclusive or). These four logical operations can be described by the use of a truth table. AND, OR, and EOR are operations that require two operands, while NOT only requires one. When used as 68000 instructions, these logical operations act on *all* the bits of the operands in parallel. However, the action on individual bits or bit pairs is the same. We can therefore describe each operation with a truth table consisting of at most a pair of bits.

The NOT logical operation essentially reverses ones and zeros. In other words, a 1 becomes a 0 and a 0 becomes a 1. The truth table looks like this:

	Operand	
	0	1
Result	1	0

NOT

The AND operation takes two operands. The resulting bit is a 1 only if both the operand bits are 1.

Operand 2 \ Operand 1	0	1
0	0	0
1	0	1

AND

OR results in a 1 if either of the operand bits are a 1.

Operand 2 \ Operand 1	0	1
0	0	1
1	1	1

OR

EOR is just like OR except that the result is a 0 if *both* operands are 1.

Operand 2 \ Operand 1	0	1
0	0	1
1	1	0

EOR

Logical Operations

With the exception of NOT, the general form of the logical instructions is exactly the same as for ADD and ADDI. Both a source and destination must be specified. The corresponding bits of the source and destination operands are used to form the result, which is stored in the destination. NOT requires only a destination operand. Here are the general forms:

```
AND[.<size>]      <ea>,Dn
AND[.<size>]      Dn,<ea>
ANDI[.<size>]     #<data>,<ea>
OR[.<size>]       <ea>,Dn
OR[.<size>]       Dn,<ea>
ORI[.<size>]      #<data>,<ea>
EOR[.<size>]      <ea>,Dn
EOR[.<size>]      Dn,<ea>
EORI[.<size>]     #<data>,<ea>
NOT[.<size>]      <ea>

<size> = B, W, or L
```

For example, we can execute the following instructions:

```
MOVE.B   #$55,D0
ANDI.B   #$64,D0
```

The following logical operation is thus performed:

```
          01010101
AND       01100100
          --------
          01000100
```

The result, 44_{16}, would be left in the D0 register. The operation has been shown in binary to make clearer what is happening. The bits in each column are operated on separately. Notice that the result only contains a 1 in bit positions that have both the source and destination bits set to 1.

The source operand of an AND, OR, or EOR instruction is quite often called a *mask*. A mask has the property of changing a certain group of bits in the destination operand while leaving others alone. For example, the AND instruction can be used to zero a group of bits while leaving the others unmodified. We merely form a mask with the bits of the mask set to ones that correspond to bits in the destination that we wish to leave unchanged. Let's say that we want to zero the high-order four bits of a byte in D0. The mask value we would use would be $0F_{16}$.

```
ANDI.B   #$0F,D0
```

We can also make sure that certain bits are set to 1. Those bits will correspond to ones placed in a mask used with the OR instruction. The following instruction would ensure that the high-order two bits of a longword in register D5 are set to 1:

```
ORI.L    #$C0000000,D5
```

EOR has the most interesting property in its use with a mask. Each bit set to 1 in the mask corresponds to a bit in the destination that we desire to complement. In other words, 1 flips to 0 or 0 flips to 1.

Shifts

The logical instructions can be used to manipulate individual bits or groups of bits within a byte, word, or longword. However, the positions of the bits that are manipulated remain the same. We sometimes desire to treat all of the bits of a byte or word as a group and change their positions. One can imagine a virtually unlimited number of possible operations. Since it would not be practical to implement a machine instruction for every possible reorganization of the bits of a word or byte, two of the most useful operations are implemented, shifts and rotates.

The bits of a word or byte are normally numbered as follows:

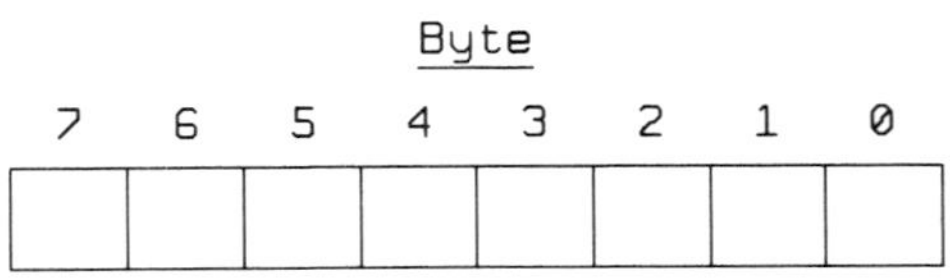

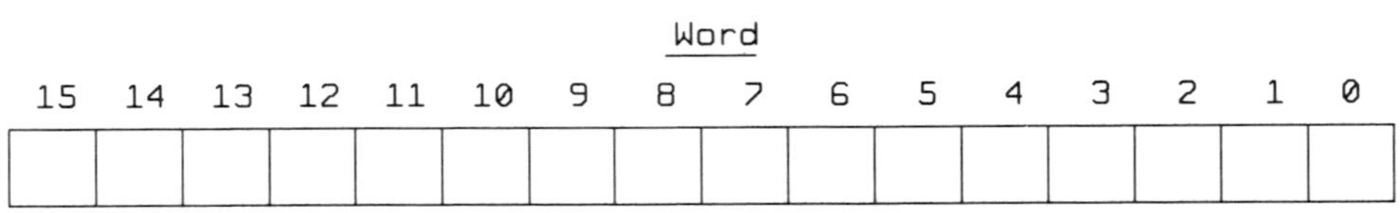

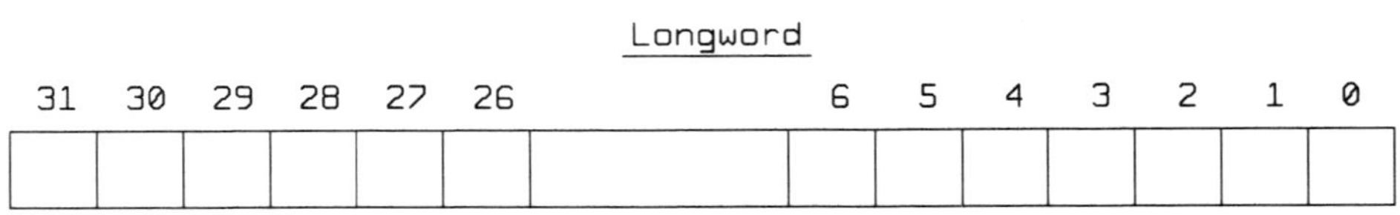

The bits of a word or byte can be shifted either to the left or to the right. For each shift of one position, all the bits move to the left or right, each bit replacing the bit that was previously occupying that position. This looks like the following:

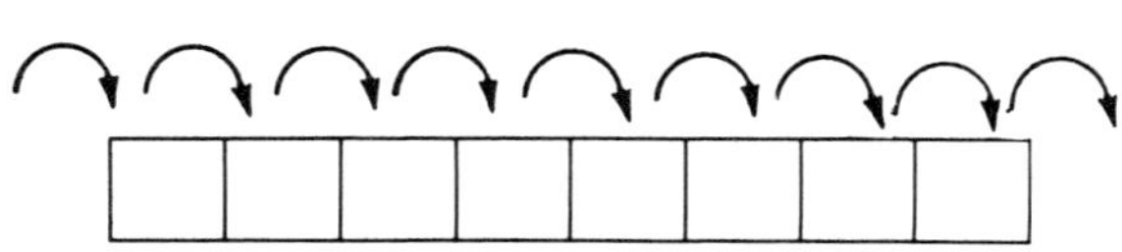

for a right shift, or

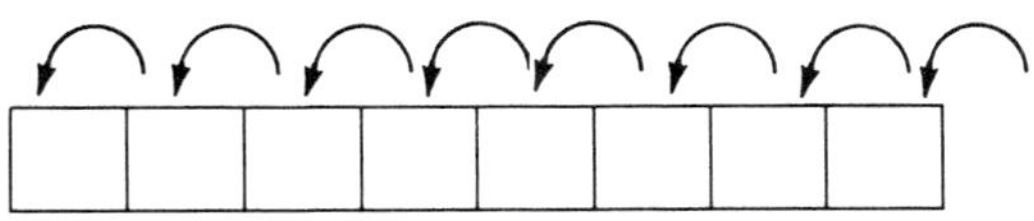

for a left shift.

You are probably wondering what happens to the bit that falls off the end of a left or right shift. You are also probably wondering if a 1 or 0 bit is shifted into the high-order bit position of a right shift or the low-order position of a left shift. The answer to the first question is quite simple. If we shift left or right, the bit that falls off the end is saved in both the carry bit, C, and the extend bit, X. This is either bit 7 for a byte shift, bit 15 for a word shift, or bit 31 for a longword shift, for left shifts, and bit 0 for all right shifts.

If we shift left, a bit with a zero value is *always* shifted into the low-order bit position of the byte or word. This is the bit 0 position. When we shift right, two results are possible. If we use the logical shift right instruction, LSR, a zero bit is shifted into the high-order bit position. If we use the arithmetic shift right instruction, ASR, the value of the high-order bit is shifted into itself. In other words, the value of the high-order bit is not changed. This is what these shifts look like:

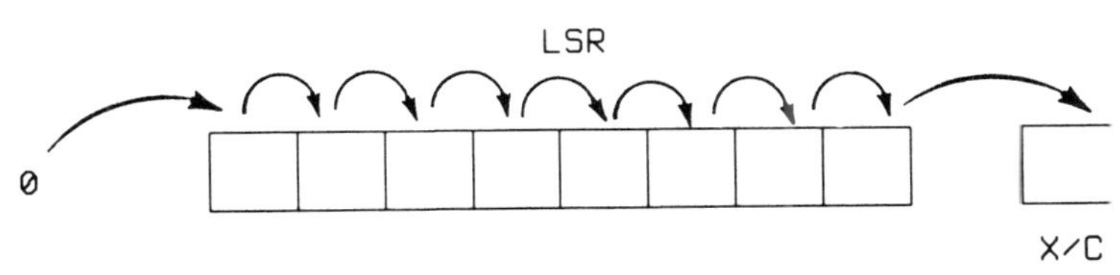

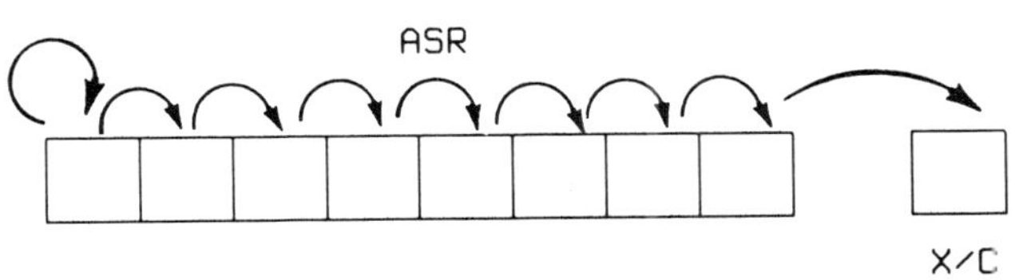

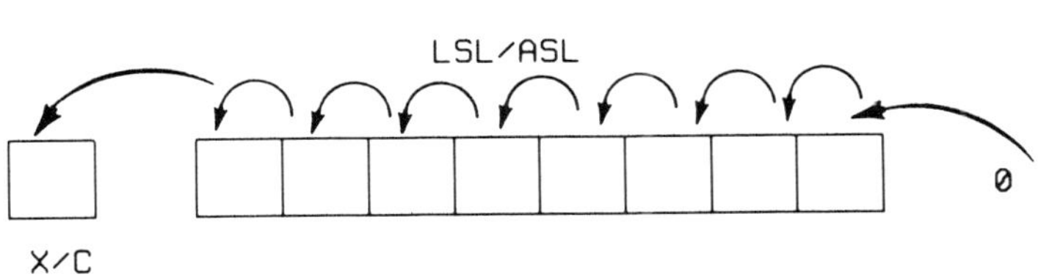

The purpose of the arithmetic shift is to preserve the sign bit. You will recall that the sign bit is the high-order bit when using two's complement representation. One use of the shift instructions is to multiply or divide a number by a power of two. Without the arithmetic forms of the shift instructions, incorrect values would result. The corresponding mnemonics for the left shifts are ASL and LSL. Even though it would at first appear that these are the same instructions, they actually differ slightly. While it is true that the result in the destination of an ASL and an LSL will be identical, the two instructions differ in how they affect the condition code register. The arithmetic versions of the instructions will conditionally set the overflow bit depending upon whether the most significant bit is changed at any time during the shift operation. The remaining bits of the CCR are conditionally set for both versions of the instructions.

There are three forms for the shift instructions:

```
<shift>[.<size>]        Dx,Dy
<shift>[.<size>]        #<data>,Dy
<shift>[.W]             <ea>

<shift> = ASL, ASR, LSL, LSR
<size> = B, W, or L
<data> = 1-8
```

The first form specifies a shift count in register Dx and the destination in register Dy. The second form allows an immediate shift count between 1 and 8. For counts larger than 8, two or more sequential shifts with immediate operands can be used. Naturally, if the shift count is to be variable, the first form is most useful. The third form shifts the contents of a memory location by one bit only. Furthermore, the data width is restricted to one word. If you need to manipulate a byte or longword from memory, you will have to move it into a register first, shift it, and then move it back to memory. Additionally, anything but a shift of a few bits would also require moving the data to a register.

If the D0 register contains 5432_{16}, the shift

```
LSL.W   #1,D0
```

results in $A864_{16}$ in D0. Likewise,

```
LSR.W   #1,D0
```

results in $2A19_{16}$. And

```
MOVEQ.L #10,D1
LSL.W   D1,D0
```

will shift D0 left by 10 bits. This will shift in 10 zeros, and the value in D0 after the shift will be $C000_{16}$. Note that we are performing word operations on the register. The bits shifted out of the low-order word are not shifted into the high-order word.

Even though the 68000 has a number of multiply and divided instructions, it is sometimes easier and faster to use a shift for these operations. This only works for multiplication or division by a power of two. A left shift will multiply by 2^n, where n is the number of bits to shift. A right shift (be sure to use ASR for a signed divide) will divide by 2^n. Since the bits shifted off the end are lost, there will not be a remainder. Also, be aware that no rounding of the result is performed. This means that positive numbers are truncated towards zero, and negative numbers are truncated towards negative infinity. In other words, 5/2 will result in 2, while −5/2 will result in −3. You can verify this for yourself by writing the binary values for 5 and −5 and then shifting.

An interesting application of this use of the shift instructions is a multiplication which is not a power of two. A simple *unsigned* multiplication can be performed using the left shift, LSL. Simply check each bit position in the multiplier to determine if it is a 1 or 0. If it is a 1, add the multiplicand shifted left by the number of bits corresponding to the bit position in the multiplier. Sum these partial products as we go along. Here is a simple routine to perform this multiplication:

```
*
* UNSIGNED MULTIPLY
*   D0 = MULTIPLIER
*   D1 = MULTIPLICAND
*   D2 = PRODUCT
*   D3 = TEMP FOR MULTIPLICAND
*   D4 = SHIFT COUNT
*
         CLR.L    D2        CLEAR PRODUCT
         MOVEQ.L  #-1,D4    SET UP SHIFT COUNT
NEXT:    TST.L    D0        FINISHED?
         BEQ      FINI      YES
         ADDQ.L   #1,D4     SET UP COUNT FOR NEXT SHIFT
         LSR.L    #1,D0     GET NEXT BIT OF MULTIPLIER
         BCC      NEXT      ZERO, CONTINUE
         MOVE.L   D1,D3     COPY MULTIPLICAND
         LSL.L    D4,D3     GET PARTIAL PRODUCT
         ADD.L    D3,D2     SUM TO PRODUCT
         BRA      NEXT
FINI:    .
         .
```

Notice that the shift count is initialized to −1. This is to ensure that the first time it is used it will be zero. We drop out of the loop as soon as the multiplier is zero. This allows the algorithm to operate faster than if we always went through the loop 32 times. Also note that this routine does not check for overflow. The 68000 has a multiply instruction, so this routine should never be required.

Rotates

Rotates are very similar to shifts. We can rotate to the left or right. The difference is that rather than shift in zeros, as for left shifts and logical right shifts, the bit that would normally fall off the end is shifted back into the longword, word, or byte at the opposite end. The ROL (rotate left) and ROR (rotate right) instructions work as follows:

ROL

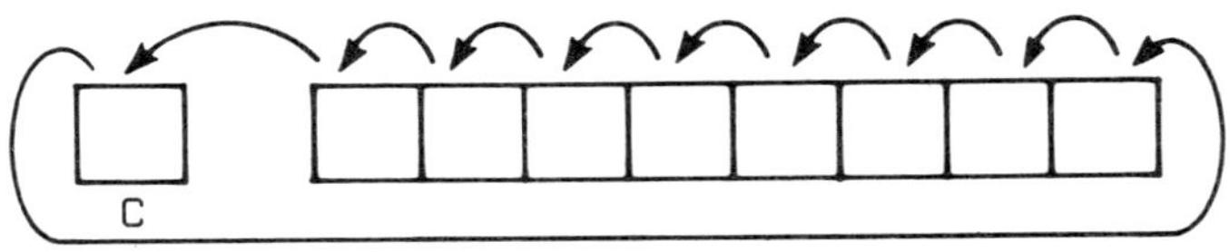

ROR

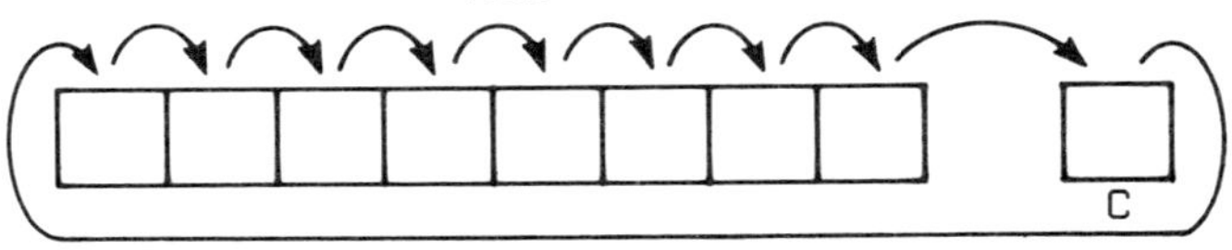

A corresponding pair or rotates, ROXL and ROXR, work in the same way as ROL and ROR except that the extend bit is included as an extra bit to be included in the rotate. Here is how they work:

ROXL

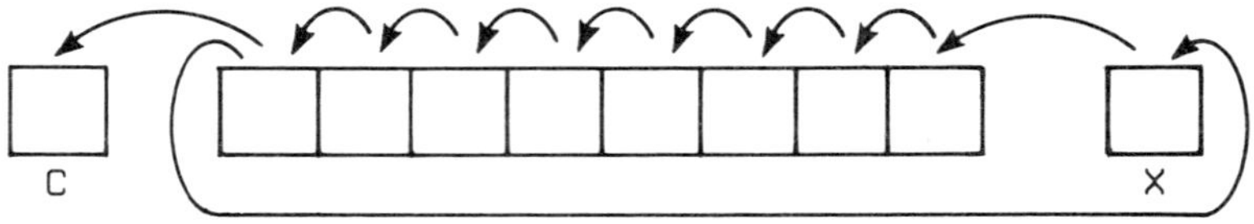

ROXR

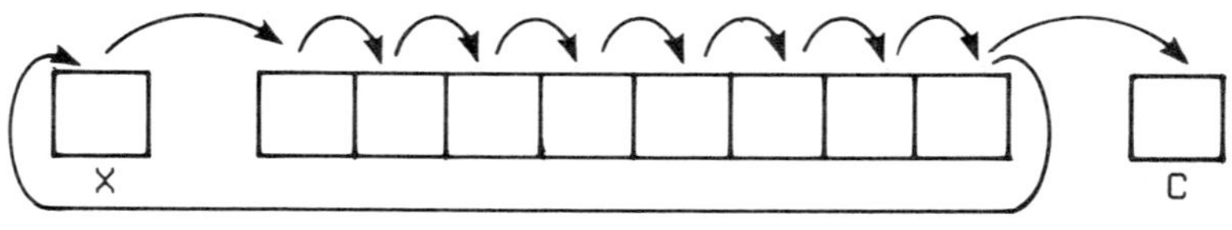

The rotate instructions have the same format as the shift instructions.

```
<rotate>[.<size>]        Dx,Dy
<rotate>[.<size>]        #<data>,Dy
<rotate>[.W]             <ea>

<rotate> = ROL, ROR, ROXL, ROXR
<size> = B, W, L
<data> = 1-8
```

The following subroutine, OUTHEX, demonstrates the use of a rotate instruction and a logical instruction to output the contents of the D0 register as a hexadecimal number.

```
OUTHEX: MOVE.L  D0,-(SP)          SAVE REG. VALUES
        MOVE.L  D1,-(SP)          "
        MOVEQ   #7,D1             8 NIBBLES
OUTL1:  ROL.L   #4,D0             ROTATE NIBBLE INTO PLACE
        JSR     OUTDIG            OUTPUT NIBBLE
        DBRA    D1,OUTL1          LOOP UNTIL DONE
        MOVE.L  (SP)+,D1          RESTORE REGS.
        MOVE.L  (SP)+,D0          "
        RTS                       RETURN
*
OUTDIG: MOVE.L  D0,-(SP)          SAVE D0
        ANDI.L  #$F,D0            ISOLATE NIBBLE
        CMPI.B  #9,D0             >9?
        BLS     OUTD1             NO
        ADDI.B  #'A'-'0'-10,D0    YES, MAKE A-F
OUTD1:  ADDI.B  #'0',D0           MAKE DIG. INTO ASCII
        JSR     PUTC              OUTPUT DIGIT
        RTS                       RETURN
```

The subroutine OUTDIG is used to convert a 4-bit hexadecimal digit to its ASCII character value. Since a hexadecimal digit can range from 0 to 9 and A to F, a check must be made to ensure that the proper ASCII character value is selected for digits with decimal values between 10 and 15. In OUTHEX, a rotate instruction rather than a shift instruction is used, since the digits must be output starting with the high-order digit The left rotate accomplishes this quite nicely.

Bit Manipulation

Sometimes we desire to manipulate only one bit in a byte, word, or longword. While it is possible to use the logical instructions for this purpose, it is much easier to use a special group of instructions known as the *bit manipulation* instructions. There are four of them: BTST, BSET, BCLR, and BCHG. They all have the same general form:

```
<bitop> Dn,<ea>
<bitop> #<data>,<ea>

<bitop> = BTST, BSET, BCLR, BCHG
```

The effective address can be a data register or memory location, but not an address register. For each of these instructions, you specify the number of the particular bit that you want to manipulate. The bits are numbered starting with the low-order bit as bit 0. The bit number may be placed in a register for the first form of the instruction, or specified as an immediate value for the second form of the instruction. If the effective address is a data register, then the instruction operates on any of the 32 bits of the data register. If the effective address is a memory location, then the instruction operates only on the byte at the specified address. In other words, the range of the bit number must be between 0 and 7.

BSET and BCLR will set the specified bit to a 1 or a 0 respectively. BCHG will complement the specified bit—in other words, a 1 becomes a 0, and vice versa. BTST will test the specified bit to determine if it is a 1 or a 0. It does not change it. The Z-condition bit is set accordingly. If the bit is zero, then Z will be set. It doesn't matter what the values of the other bits are in the data item.

Exercises

1. What is NOT $55AA_{16}$?
2. What is $AAAA_{16}$ or 5555_{16}?
3. Write a logical instruction that will clear register D0.
4. Write a logical instruction that will ensure that the high-order three bits of register D0 are ones.
5. Write a logical instruction that will ensure that the low-order four bits of register D0 are zeros.
6. Write a logical instruction that will set the bits of register D1 such that a bit is set to one if it differs from the corresponding bit in register D0.
7. Give the bit number of the high-order bit for
   a) a byte
   b) a word
   c) a longword
8. Where does the bit go that is shifted off the end in a left or right shift?
9. What is the difference between a logical shift right and an arithmetic right?
10. Is there a difference between the ASL and LSL instructions?
11. What register can be used to specify a shift count?

12. Write an instruction to perform a logical shift right by one bit of the D0 register.
13. Write the instruction necessary to divide register D0 by 16 using a shift.
14. There are two types of left and right rotates. What is the difference?
15. Write the instruction necessary to rotate register D0 left by one bit, including the extend bit.
16. Write the instructions necessary to rotate register D0 right by 16 bits, not including the extend bit.
17. There are many more logical operations than the four that are implemented by the 68000. For example, the NOR operation has the following truth table:

		Operand 1	
		0	1
Operand 2	0	1	0
	1	0	0

Write the instructions necessary to form the NOR operation of the D0 and D1 registers.
18. Is LSR.L #10,D0 a legal instruction?
19. Can you think of a way to perform NOT D0 using another logical instruction?
20. Write an instruction to test if bit 12 of register D0 is a 1.

Answers

1. $AA55_{16}$

2. $FFFF_{16}$

3. `EOR.L D0,D0` `ANDI.L #0,D0`

4. `ORI.L #$E0000000,D0`

5. `ANDI.B #$F0,D0`

6. `EOR.L D0,D1`

7. a) 7 b) 15 c) 31
8. Into the carry bit.
9. The logical shift right shifts a zero into the high order bit. The arithmetic shift right shifts the sign bit into itself.
10. Yes, the ASL conditionally sets the overflow bit.
11. Any data register.

12.
```
        LSR.L #1,D0
```

13.
```
        ASR.L #4,D0
```

14. One type includes the extend bit and the other type doesn't.

15.
```
        ROXL.L #1,D0
```

16.
```
        MOVE.L  #16,D1
        ROR.L   D1,D0
```

17.
```
        OR.L    D0,D1
        NOT.L   D1
```

18. No, a count greater than 1 must be specified in a register.

19.
```
        EORI.L #$FFFFFFFF,D0
```

20.
```
        BTST #12,D0
```

CHAPTER 11

ADVANCED ARITHMETIC

In Chapters 4 and 5 you learned the ADD, SUB, ADDQ, and SUBQ instructions. These instructions, along with the condition code register, give you the capability to perform other arithmetic operations such as multiplication and division. For example, you can perform multiplication by repeated addition, and division by repeated subtraction. These are not the best methods to use, but they are simple. By using the shift instructions shown in Chapter 10, more efficient algorithms can be implemented. Fortunately, the 68000 has a set of powerful arithmetic instructions that include multiplication and division as well as some other rather interesting instructions. In this chapter we will take a look at the complete set of arithmetic instructions and introduce some new concepts such as decimal arithmetic. Yes, I did say "decimal" arithmetic. Up to this point we have been dealing strictly with binary arithmetic operations.

Multiple Precision Addition and Subtraction

Before discussing the multiplication and division instructions, I want to introduce the concept of arithmetic *precision*. Basically, the precision of a calculation is proportional to the number of bits used in the calculation. The more bits used, the greater the precision. Even though we are confined to integer arithmetic, we can use a larger number of bits to represent larger numbers which, in turn, can represent *scaled* values. For example, we can represent time intervals in thousandths of seconds rather than seconds. This would require the ability to represent numbers 1,000 times larger for the equivalent times in seconds. However, the precision would be greater, since times would be stored with accuracy down to a thousandth of a second.

The 68000 performs additions and subtractions on bytes, words, or longwords. Therefore, there are actually three built-in precisions available. But what if 32 bits is not a great enough precision for our calculations? Is there anything we can do? The answer is yes, but not with a single instruction. We can perform *multiple precision* operations by representing our numbers as multiple numbers of bytes. Normally it would make no sense to represent numbers as two bytes rather than a word. However, three bytes, two longwords, or other higher multiples of bytes, words, or longwords are logical.

How do we store multiple precision values in memory? You may recall that single words or longwords are stored in memory such that the high-order (most significant) byte comes first. We can adhere to this convention and require multiple precision numbers to be stored with the highest order bytes coming first. This is not absolutely necessary, but it makes things consistent; and some of the new instructions you will learn in this chapter will operate more efficiently if this is the case. For example, if we have a double longword value, $123456789ABCDEF0, it can be stored as:

```
        DC.L      $12345678
        DC.L      $9ABCDEF0
```

This number would be a *double-precision* longword. We can set up values of any precision in a similar manner.

Suppose we want to add two double-precision integers, A and B, and store the result in variable C. We will assume that all three variables are stored high-order bytes first. The following directives might be used to reserve storage:

```
A:      DS.L    2
B:      DS.L    2
C:      DS.L    2
```

Adding the two low-order bytes is straightforward:

```
        MOVE.L  A+4,D0
        ADD.L   B+4,D0
```

Notice that A+4 and B+4 are used as the operands. These are the addresses of the two low-order longwords. Remember, a longword is four bytes. The labels A and B are the addresses of the two high-order longwords. The result is now in register D0. We can store this result as the low-order word of C:

```
        MOVE.L  D0,C+4
```

You might be tempted to say that all we have to do is repeat the above instructions for the two high-order words of A and B. This is almost correct except for the fact that we might have had a carry from the low-order addition. This carry must be added to the calculation for the high-order longwords. The carry condition, C, is set/reset as a result of our first addition. All we have to do is somehow add the carry bit to our high-order addition. But wait, the MOVE instruction used to save the low-order result will clear the carry bit. In fact, we can't even get a hold of the high-order longword without destroying the carry bit. The 68000 designers anticipated this problem. They provided the *extend condition* or X bit in the condition code register. This bit is always a copy of the carry bit for arithmetic operations. However, it is not cleared, or modified in any way, as a result of a MOVE instruction.

The ADDX, SUBX and NEGX instructions are provided to utilize the value in the extend bit. Their general forms are:

```
ADDX[.<size>]    Dy,Dx
ADDX[.<size>]    -(Ay),-(Ax)
SUBX[.<size>]    Dy,Dx
SUBX[.<size>]    -(Ay),-(Ax)
NEGX[.<size>]    <ea>

<size> = B, W, L
```

They work like ADD, SUB and NEG, except that the extend bit is factored into the calculation, and the addressing modes are restricted to those shown. For ADDX, the extend bit is added to the result; for SUBX and NEGX it is subtracted—this is equivalent to a borrow for a subtraction. The ADDX, SUBX, and NEGX instructions all set the C and X bits after a calculation. The remaining instructions needed to complete the calculation are:

```
MOVE.L  A,D0
MOVE.L  B,D1
ADDX.L  D1,D0
MOVE.L  D0,C
```

The above procedure can be used to add numbers of any precision. An ADD instruction is used for the lowest order byte, word, or longword, and all other additions are performed with the ADDX instruction.

Multiple precision subtraction can be performed in a similar manner, using the SUB instruction and the subtract-with-extend instruction, SUBX. The following instructions will subtract the three-byte variable A from B and store the result in C:

```
MOVE.B  B+2,D0
SUB.B   A+2,D0
MOVE.B  D0,C+2
MOVE.B  B+1,D0
MOVE.B  A+1,D1
SUBX.B  D1,D0
MOVE.B  D0,C+1
MOVE.B  B,D0
```

```
        MOVE.B  A,D1
        SUBX.B  D1,D0
        MOVE.B  D0,C
        .
        .
A:      DC.B    3
B:      DC.B    3
C:      DC.B    3
```

The use of a three-byte value is questionable. The complexity in calculation would most likely outweigh the small savings in memory unless there was a very large number of three-byte values. The use of a longword would eliminate this complexity. I presented this only as an example of the flexibility of the 68000 instructions.

One disadvantage to the above technique is that there must always be both operands in data registers before the ADDX or SUBX instructions are performed. If address register indirect with predecrement addressing is used, the multiple precision addition from above can be made completely general. Before showing some specific examples of the use of these instructions, I will have to introduce a new instruction, the MOVE to CCR instruction. This is actually just a version of the MOVE instruction, with the destination operand being the condition code register, CCR. It allows the setting or clearing of any of the bits in the CCR. Its general form is:

```
MOVE[.W] <ea>,CCR
```

Even though the source operand must be a word, only the low-order byte is used to load the condition code register. Recall from Chapter 5 that the CCR bits are:

BIT #	CONDITION
0	C
1	V
2	Z
3	N
4	X

The reason for this sudden interest in the CCR is that the extend bit is *always* included in the calculation. Therefore, we must make sure that it is clear *before* we start a calculation.

The following is a subroutine to do a double-precision addition. The subroutine will add the double-precision values pointed to by registers A0 and A1, and place the result in the location pointed to by register A1.

```
DBADD:  ADDQ.L  #8,A0
        ADDQ.L  #8,A1
        MOVE.W  #4,CCR
        ADDX.L  -(A0),-(A1)
```

```
ADDX.L   -(A0),-(A1)
RTS
```

Moving the constant 4 into the CCR will clear all the bits except for the Z condition. Remember, when the Z bit is set, there is a zero value. I will get back to this point shortly. Notice that the subroutine first adjusts the addresses to point to the longword just beyond the number, and then uses address register indirect with predecrement addressing for the additions. The values in A0 and A1 will be restored to their original values when the subroutine returns. This subroutine could be called as follows:

```
LEA      A,A0
LEA      B,A1
JSR      DBADD
```

This call would result in adding double-precision value A to double-precision value B.

I mentioned that there is a reason to make sure the Z condition is set in the CCR before starting a multiple precision calculation. The reason is that we may want to test the result of our calculation to determine if it is zero. Since this is a multiple precision calculation, what we really require is that *all* the intermediate results are zero, as well as the final addition or subtraction. ADDX, SUBX, and NEGX all have an interesting property when it comes to the Z condition: the Z condition is cleared if a result is non-zero, and *unchanged* otherwise. This means that once it is cleared it will remain cleared. This indicates a non-zero result for our calculation. A BEQ or BNE instruction can then be used to conditionally branch, depending on the state of the Z bit.

The NEGX instruction is used to negate (subtract from zero) a multiple precision value. The following instructions will negate the double-precision longword in location COUNT:

```
MOVE.W   #4,CCR
NEGX.L   COUNT+4
NEGX.L   COUNT
```

Notice that the Z bit must be set prior to execution of the first NEGX. Address register indirect with predecrement addressing can also be used:

```
LEA      COUNT+8,A0
MOVE.W   #4,CCR
NEGX.L   -(A0)
NEGX.L   -(A0)
```

Multiplication and Division

The 68000 has two multiply and two divide instructions. One pair of multiply and divide instructions is used for unsigned values and the other pair is used for signed values. Unlike addition and subtraction, signed and unsigned multiplies and divides require different instructions. The four instructions are:

```
MULU    -unsigned multiply
MULS    -signed multiply
DIVU    -unsigned divide
DIVS    -signed divide
```

A property of the multiplication of two numbers of a given precision is that the result of the multiplication can have a precision equal to the sum of the precisions of the two numbers. This means that the multiplication of two bytes yields a result up to two bytes or one word in length; and the multiplication of two words, a result up to four bytes or one longword in length.

The general form of the multiplication instructions is:

```
MULU    <ea>,Dn
MULS    <ea>,Dn
```

The size of the source and destination operands is *always* a word. If the operand comes from a register, only the low-order 16 bits are used. The remainder of the bits are ignored. The product is stored in all 32 bits of the destination register.

Unlike addition and subtraction in two's complement representation, the result of a multiplication or division will be different for signed and unsigned numbers. A simple example will illustrate. We will assume 4-bit numbers. If we multiply -1 by -1, the signed result should be $+1$. In binary this is:

```
    1111
X   1111
    ----
00000001
```

Notice that I have shown the 8-bit result. Now, an unsigned value of 1111_2 is actually 15_{10}, so this multiplication would be $15 \times 15 = 225$. Our answer should be:

```
    1111
X   1111
    ----
11100001
```

A similar situation exists for division. Therefore, the proper instruction, signed or unsigned, must be used.

The following instruction multiplies the two signed words contained in registers D0 and D1:

```
MULS    D0,D1
```

The result is in D1. The following instructions multiply word variables X and Y:

```
MOVE.W  X,D0
MULS    Y,D0
```

The result is in register D0. The following instruction multiplies register D0 by 100:

```
MULS    #100,D0
```

The general form of the divide instructions are:

```
DIVU    <ea>,Dn
DIVS    <ea>,Dn
```

The destination operand is divided by the source operand, and the quotient is left in the destination operand. The integer part of the quotient is in the lower 16 bits, and the remainder, in the upper 16 bits, of the destination register. The dividend is the full longword in the destination register, but the divisor is only a single word operand. If the source operand comes from a register, only the low-order 16 bits are used.

The following instruction will divide the unsigned longword in register D0 by the constant 10:

```
DIVU    #10,D0
```

The integer part of the result is in the lower 16 bits of the D0 register. Any remainder is in the upper 16 bits of D0. There are a few things to be careful of. First, if you plan to use a word dividend, you must make sure that the high-order bits of the register are zero for an unsigned divide, and equal to the sign extension of the low-order 16 bits for a signed divide. For an unsigned divide, you can merely use a CLR.L instruction before moving the word into the register. Second, you must remember that the remainder is in the upper 16 bits of the destination register. If you want to save the integer part of the quotient as a longword, you must zero the upper 16 bits for an unsigned divide, and sign-extend the lower 16 bits for a signed divide. One way to do this for an unsigned divide is with an AND.L instruction. The following instructions will divide longword B by word A and place the result in longword C:

```
        MOVE.L  B,D0
        DIVU    A,D0
        AND.L   #$FFFF,D0
        MOVE.L  D0,C
        .
        .
A:      DS.L    1
B:      DS.W    1
C:      DS.L    1
```

We can sign-extend a byte to a word, or a word to a longword, using the EXT instruction. The general form is:

```
EXT[.<size>]    Dn

<size> = W, L
```

So, if we want to divide two signed words, we can use the following instructions:

```
         MOVE.W  VAL1,D0
         EXT.L   D0
         DIVS    VAL2,D0
         MOVE.W  D0,RESULT
         .
         .
VAL1:    DS.W    1
VAL2:    DS.W    1
RESULT:  DS.W    1
```

Before leaving division, there are a few more loose ends to clear up. In signed division, the sign of the remainder is always the same as that of the dividend. This means that if a negative number is divided by another negative number, even though the quotient is positive, any remainder will be negative. If we divide -23 by -10, the execution of the DIVS instruction will yield a quotient of $+2$ and a remainder of -3.

In division, signed or unsigned, it is possible for the quotient to be larger than the destination register can hold. This *overflow* condition, always the case when we try to divide by zero, can occur for divisors other than zero. The overflow bit, V, is used to detect this situation. The result of such a division leaves the operands unchanged. A divide by zero is a special case: a special *exception condition* is generated by an attempt to divide by zero. This causes a trap to exception vector number 5. The discussion of traps in the next chapter will show how this capability can be utilized.

Decimal Arithmetic

Up to this point, all our numerical values have been represented as binary data consisting of one or more bytes. Decimal numbers that are input to a program must be converted to binary. Likewise, a decimal number that is output must be converted from the internal binary representation. The INDEC and OUTDEC subroutines introduced in Chapter 4 perform these operations. As it turns out, the 68000 has a number of instructions that allow the represention of decimal numbers internally in a special way that makes the input and output conversions much simpler. This representation is called *binary coded decimal* or BCD.

Four bits are required to represent the digits 0 to 9. As you may recall, we can actually count up to 15 with four bits. That, of course, allows us hexadecimal representation. If, however, we restrict the values of a group of four bits to range from 0 to 9, we can represent a decimal number as a set of these four-bit groups. There are two half bytes, sometimes called "nibbles," per byte. This allows us to represent two decimal digits per byte. The decimal number 35 can be written in BCD form as 00110101_2. The two decimal digits are contained in one byte. Note that this number would be 53_{10} if the "binary" value were converted to decimal.

So far so good, but how are BCD values used in performing arithmetic? If they have to be converted to pure binary, nothing has been gained. The answer lies in examining what happens when we perform additions and subtractions of BCD numbers. Suppose we add the BCD numbers 2 and 7. In the binary representation these numbers are 00000010_2 and 00000111_2. Adding them using the ADD instruction would yield 00001001_2, or 9_{10}. This is just what we want. However, suppose we add 5 and 7. Our result will now be 00001100_2. This is not a valid BCD number, since the low-order nibble is greater than 9. The problem gets worse if we add 8 and 9—this gives us 00010001_2, which we might interpret as 11_{10} if we were using BCD. This is still not right. What we really want is the low-order nibble to be set to the correct BCD value, with some way of determining if there is a carry to the high-order nibble. In other words, we really wanted 00010010_2 when we added 5 and 7 and 00010111_2 when we added 8 and 9. In both these cases there is a carry corresponding to 10_{10}.

The above problem is solved by the use of a number of instructions specifically designed for BCD arithmetic. These instructions fix up the low-order nibble, propagate a carry to the high-order nibble, and set the carry/extend bits as appropriate for a carry out of the high-order nibble. These instructions and their general forms are:

```
ABCD[.B]        Dy,Dx
ABCD[.B]        -(Ay),-(Ax)
SBCD[.B]        Dy,Dx
SBCD[.B]        -(Ay),-(Ax)
NBCD[.B]        <ea>
```

Note that they always operate on bytes. This is the only valid size to use.

Here is how two BCD values can be added, assuming that they are in registers D0 and D1:

```
MOVE.W  #4,CCR
ABCD    D0,D1
```

A subtraction can be performed similarly:

```
MOVE.W  #4,CCR
SBCD    D0,D1
```

Notice that I cleared the extend bit and set the zero bit in the CCR prior to executing the BCD instructions. The BCD instructions will always use the extend bit just as the ADDX, SUBX, and NEGX instructions did.

Now that we know how to perform additions and subtractions of two BCD values, we can extend these operations to multidigit decimal numbers. The address register indirect with predecrement addressing mode is designed for this operation. This works in a similar manner to the multiple precision operations for addition and subtraction. Suppose we are storing 10-digit decimal numbers as arrays of five bytes. If the first entry in the array corresponds to the high order-byte, two of these numbers, VAL1 and VAL2, can be added with the following instructions:

```
          LEA       VAL1+5,A0
          LEA       VAL2+5,A1
          MOVE.W    #4,D0
          MOVE.W    #4,CCR
LOOP:     ABCD      -(A0),-(A1)
          DBRA      D0,LOOP
          .
          .
VAL1:     DS.B      5
VAL2:     DS.B      5
```

In this example, the two decimal numbers VAL1 and VAL2 are added together, with the result stored in VAL2. The MOVE to CCR instruction is used to clear the extend bit prior to the first add. If we don't make sure the extend bit is initially clear, we might get an erroneous result. Subtraction of multidigit BCD numbers can be performed in a similar manner. The SBCD instruction must be used.

Input and output of BCD numbers are really not too difficult. It is important to remember that there are two decimal digits in each byte and they are not in ASCII character codes. A single-byte BCD number in register D0 can be output with the following:

```
MOVE.L   D0,-(SP)          SAVE D0
LSR.B    #4,D0             GET HIGH ORDER NIBBLE
AND.L    #$F,D0            MASK TO 4 BITS
ADD.B    #'0',D0           MAKE INTO ASCII
JSR      PUTC              OUTPUT THE CHARACTER
MOVE.L   (SP)+,D0          GET D0 BACK
AND.L    #$F,D0            MASK TO 4 BITS
ADD.B    #'0',D0           MAKE INTO ASCII
JSR      PUTC              OUTPUT THE CHARACTER
```

To perform additions and subtractions on BCD numbers, the high-order digit must be in the high-order four bits of the byte. The above instructions output the byte with the high-order digit first.

The following instructions are necessary to input a single BCD byte into D0:

```
JSR      GETC          GET A CHARCTER
SUB.B    #'0',D0       MAKE INTO DECIMAL
LSL.B    #4,D0         SHIFT INTO HIGH NIBBLE
MOVE.L   D0,-(SP)      SAVE D0
JSR      GETC          GET A CHARACTER
SUB.B    #'0',D0       MAKE INTO DECIMAL
ADD.L    (SP)+,D0      ADD HIGH NIBBLE
```

This routine does not have any error checking, so if a character other than 0 through 9 is entered, an error will result. It is straightforward to add instructions to test the range of each digit as it enters to ensure that it is valid.

BCD numbers are *unsigned*. The high-order bit of the high-order byte is *not* interpreted as a sign bit. How then can we represent signed BCD numbers? One method is to reserve a single byte as the *sign byte*. We can store the ASCII character + or − in this sign byte and the absolute value of the BCD number in the remaining bytes. Unfortunately we can't just add or subtract these numbers. The sign byte can't enter into the actual arithmetic. Before using a signed BCD number, the sign byte must first be checked. If the BCD number is negative, *ten's complement* must first be taken prior to its use in a calculation. The ten's complement is used in a manner very similar to the two's complement of binary numbers. The ten's complement is the nine's complement plus one. To compute the nine's complement, simply subtract each BCD digit from the number nine, then add in the one. For example: the nine's complement of the four-digit BCD number 1234 is 8765. The ten's complement is then 8766. This *adjusted* number used in a calculation will now give a correct result. From the above example, the number 8766 can be thought of as a negative 1234. If we add a positive 1234, we should get a result of zero. This is true if we ignore the carry.

```
 8766    -1234
 1234    +1234
 ----    -----
10000     0000
```

The same rules apply as for two's complement binary numbers. Unfortunately, we must keep track of the signs separately, or use more complicated schemes. One such scheme would be to use the high-order digit for the sign, with a positive number being represented by a 0 and a negative number by a 9. This is equivalent to the use of the high-order bit as a sign bit with two's complement binary numbers.

The NBCD instruction is used to compute the ten's complement. The action of this instruction is to perform the ten's complement of a pair of BCD bytes and then subtract the extend bit. If the extend bit is 0, then the result is truly the ten's complement. If the extend bit is a 1, then the result is the nine's complement. This instruction can also be thought of as subtracting the two-digit number in a byte from zero. Unless the number is zero, a borrow will be needed. This results in the number being subtracted from 100 if we include the borrow from the next higher digit, the hundreds position. Therefore, unless the two-digit number in a byte is zero, a borrow will be required. This property allows us to take the ten's complement of a multi-byte BCD number by performing the NBCD instruction on each byte, starting with the low order. The extend bit must be cleared prior to the first operation. Here is the code required to take the ten's complement from a four-byte BCD number:

```
MOVE.W  #4,CCR        CLEAR X AND SET Z
LEA     VAL,A0        A0 -> NUMBER
ADDQ.L  #4,A0         ADJUST TO BYTE BEYOND NUMBER
NBCD    -(A0)
NBCD    -(A0)
NBCD    -(A0)
NBCD    -(A0)
```

You might have noticed that I didn't use a loop, but rather used four in-line NBCD instructions. While it might look like we could save space by replacing three of the NBCD's with two instructions for the loop, this is actually not true. The NBCD instruction is only a single word instruction if address register indirect with predecrement addressing is used. The savings would have to be at least one word to be worthwhile. That leaves only two words for the two loop instructions. Even if a MOVEQ is used for initialization, the DBRA alone will require two words. Therefore, we are better off with the four NBCD instructions. While no one would expect a programmer to check each and every instruction combination to see which is faster or takes up less space, it is wise to be aware that such tradeoffs do exist. Sometimes it is obvious when such a decision should be made.

Exercises

1. What is meant by arithmetic precision?
2. You have a requirement to store monetary values from 0 to 1 billion dollars down to the nearest penny. What scaling is required, and what precision is required to store these values?
3. How are multiple precision values stored in memory?
4. Set up the value $5643278436667 as a double longword in memory.
5. Write the instructions necessary to add the above constant to the double longword variable ALPHA.
6. What are the multiplication and division instructions used with signed and unsigned numbers?

7. What is the precision of the result of a multiplication?
8. What is the sign of the remainder in signed division?
9. Where is it located?
10. Write the instructions necessary to multiply unsigned byte variables NUM1 and NUM2, placing the result in NUM2. Ignore overflow.
11. Write the instructions necessary to divide unsigned word variable COUNT by 25.
12. Write the instructions necessary to sign-extend a byte in register D0 to a full longword.
13. How many decimal digits can be stored in a byte using BCD representation?
14. What is a nibble?
15. What is the binary value for 75_{10} in BCD representation?
16. What is the decimal equivalent for the BCD value 10010110_2?
17. What addressing modes are allowed with the ABCD and SBCD instructions?
18. Write the instructions necessary to add the constant 10 to a 10-digit BCD number at location LIMIT.

Answers

1. The number of bits that are used to represent a numeric value.
2. One billion is 1,000,000,000. If we scale by two decimal digits to include pennies, we must be able to accommodate numbers as large as 100,000,000,000. This requires 5 bytes. Two longwords or three words would be a reasonable choice for implementation.
3. In consecutive memory locations, with the high-order bytes first.
4.

```
CON:    DC.L    $00056432
        DC.L    $78436667
```

5.

```
MOVE.L  ALPHA+4,D0
ADD.L   CON+4,D0
MOVE.L  D0,ALPHA+4
MOVE.L  ALPHA,D0
MOVE.L  CON,D1
ADDX.L  D1,D0
MOVE.L  D0,ALPHA
```

6. MULU and DIVU for unsigned numbers and MULS and DIVS for signed numbers.
7. The sum of the precisions of the numbers being multiplied. Specifically for the 68000, the result is a longword.
8. The sign of the remainder is always that of the dividend.

9. The remainder is located in the high-order word of the destination register.

10.
```
        MOVE.B  NUM1,D0
        EXT.W   D0
        MULU    NUM2,D0
        MOVE.B  D0,NUM2
```

11.
```
        MOVE.W  COUNT,D0
        EXT.L   D0
        DIVU    #25,D0
        MOVE.W  D0,COUNT
```

12.
```
        EXT.W   D0
        EXT.L   D0
```

13. Two.
14. The upper or lower four bits of a byte.
15. 01110101_2.
16. 96_{10}.
17. Both source and destination as registers or address register indirect with predecrement addressing.

18.
```
        LEA     CON+5,A0
        LEA     LIMIT+5,A1
        MOVE.W  #4,D0
        MOVE.W  #4,CCR
NEXT:   ABCD    -(A0),-(A1)
        DBRA    D0,NEXT
        .
        .
CON:    DC.B    0,0,0,0,$10
        .
        .
LIMIT:  DS.B    5
```

CHAPTER 12

EXCEPTION PROCESSING, SYSTEM CONTROL OPERATIONS, AND I/O

In this chapter we will cover a number of topics and instructions that don't fit into the category of general programming instructions. I mentioned in Chapter 2 that the 68000 doesn't have any input/output instructions. This is not quite true. A number of instructions are used to process interrupts, a certain type of exception which is a vital part of I/O activity. In addition, a special version of the MOVE instruction is provided to make certain kinds of I/O easier and faster. I also mentioned in Chapter 2 that the 68000 has a user and supervisor mode of operation. The system control operations are used to coordinate these two modes.

The Status Register and System Control

When we are in the supervisor mode, the condition code register, CCR, is part of a 16-bit register known as the status register, SR. Let's take a closer look at the high-order bits of the register found on the following page. If the trace bit is set to a 1, the CPU is placed into *trace mode*. This special mode is used for debugging purposes. When in trace mode, an exception is generated for each instruction executed. We will discuss trace mode when we talk about exceptions.

If the supervisor state bit is set, we are in supervisor mode. However, this bit cannot be arbitarily set at any time. If we are in user mode (the supervisor bit clear), we can't modify the high-order bits of the status register. How then do we get into supervisor mode? There are two ways. The first is when we initially turn on our system, or push the reset button (if so equipped). This causes a system reset to supervisor mode. The second method is related to the handling of exceptions. When

Status Register

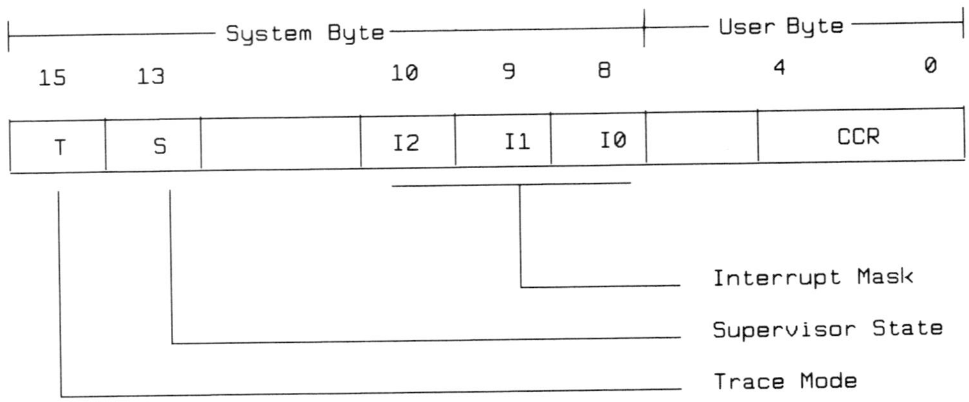

an exception condition occurs, we will wind up in supervisor mode. Exceptions are discussed in the next section.

The interrupt mask is a three-bit value that specifies the processor interrupt priority: if an interrupt from an I/O device has a priority greater than the interrupt mask, it will be allowed to generate an interrupt exception. The interrupt priority from the device is restricted to the range from 1 to 7. If the interrupt mask is set to 0, any interrupt will be allowed. If it is set to a 1, then only interrupts from devices with priorities from 2 through 7 will be allowed. An exception exists for processor interrupt priority level 7. This only inhibits device priorities below 7. Device priority 7 *will* cause an interrupt.

A number of instructions have been provided to manipulate the status register directly. The following are the only instructions that can be used with the SR:

```
MOVE    <ea>,SR (PRIVILEGED)
MOVE    SR,<ea>
ANDI    #xxx,SR (PRIVILEGED)
EORI    #xxx,SR (PRIVILEGED)
ORI     #xxx,SR (PRIVILEGED)
```

You will notice that all of these instructions are privileged if they can modify the SR. A program running in user mode can only look at, not change, the contents of the SR. These are all word instructions and all of the bits of the SR are affected.

A program running in user mode can always examine or modify the condition code register by using the following instructions:

```
MOVE    SR,<ea>
MOVE    <ea>,CCR
```

```
ANDI    #xxx,CCR
EORI    #xxx,CCR
ORI     #xxx,CCR
```

Notice that the MOVE from SR instruction is used to examine the CCR. With this exception, the instructions are all byte instructions.

Two other instructions involving the CCR not mentioned previously should be examined. Return and restore condition codes, RTR, is similar in operation to the RTS instruction except that the CCR is restored from the stack prior to the return. In other words, the RTR instruction is equivalent to

```
MOVE    (SP)+,CCR
RTS
```

If the CCR is pushed onto the stack at the beginning of a subroutine and the subroutine uses an RTR instead of an RTS, the subroutine will not result in any changes to the CCR. This is a simple way to make a subroutine transparent as far as the CCR is concerned.

The other instruction is actually a group of instructions. The Scc instructions are similar to the group of conditional branches, Bcc. The difference is that rather than conditionally branch, this instruction will set its effective address to TRUE or FALSE depending on the particular condition tested. TRUE and FALSE are defined as all ones for TRUE and all zeros for FALSE. The effective address must always be a byte. The following conditions can be tested:

```
CC carry clear              LS low or same
CS carry set                LT less than
EQ equal                    MI minus
 F false                    NE notequal
GE greater or equal         PL plus
GT greater than              T true
HI high                     VC overflow clear
LE less or equal            VS overflow set
```

This instruction is especially useful for remembering the outcome of a test without taking immediate action. For example, we might want to remember if a calculation overflowed. We can set a flag byte OVFL using the SVS instruction:

```
         <perform calculation>
         SVS     OVFL     SET FLAG BYTE
         <do something else>
         TST.B   OVFL
         BNE     OVERFLOW
         .
         .
OVFL:    DS.B    1        OVERFLOW FLAG BYTE
```

There is one more instruction that should be mentioned before going on to exceptions. Recall from Chapter 2 that there are really two register A7's. One A7 is for the user in user mode, and the other A7 is for the system in supervisor mode. These are designated USP (user stack pointer) and SSP (system stack pointer). If a user wants to change her stack pointer she merely references it as A7 or SP. If the system in supervisor mode wants to change its stack pointer, the SSP, it can do so also by referencing A7 or SP. It is not permissible for a user to modify, or even to examine, the SSP. However, it is normally the responsibility of the system to set up a valid initial stack pointer for the user. A special instruction is required for this purpose. The MOVE to USP instruction:

```
MOVE    USP,An
MOVE    An,USP
```

This is always a longword instruction and it is privileged.

Exception Processing

An *exception* is an event that causes the normal flow of a program to be suspended and a special piece of program code to be given control. This special piece of code, or *exception handler*, is designed to respond to the condition causing the exception by taking whatever steps are necessary and then returning control to the program for the program to continue, if possible. The condition causing an exception can be generated by an I/O device external to the CPU, by an error condition within the program like a divide by zero, or by the program itself using special instructions known as *traps*.

When the CPU detects an exception condition, it must locate the special piece of code to handle that specific exception. It does this by looking into a special table of *exception vectors*. These exception vectors are located at the very bottom of memory. They take a total of 1024_{10} bytes. Each exception vector requires 4 bytes. This conceptually allows a total of 256_{10} different vectors. However, vector numbers 0 and 1 serve a special purpose, that of system reset, giving a total of 255 unique vectors. Not all of these are assigned. Each entry contains the 32-bit address of the exception handler. The format is:

	Even Bytes | Odd Bytes
Word 0	New Program Counter (High)
Word 1	New Program Counter (Low)

Vector Number(s)	Dec	Address Hex	Space	Assignment
0	0	000	SP	Reset: Initial SSP[2]
1	4	004	SP	Reset: Initial PC[2]
2	8	008	SD	Bus Error
3	12	00C	SD	Address Error
4	16	010	SD	Illegal Instruction
5	20	014	SD	Zero Divide
6	24	018	SD	CHK Instruction
7	28	01C	SD	TRAPV Instruction
8	32	020	SD	Privilege Violation
9	36	024	SD	Trace
10	40	028	SD	Line 1010 Emulator
11	44	02C	SD	Line 1111 Emulator
12[1]	48	030	SD	(Unassigned, Reserved)
13[1]	52	034	SD	(Unassigned, Reserved)
14	56	038	SD	Format Error[5]
15	60	03C	SD	Uninitialized Interrupt Vector
16-23[1]	64	040	SD	(Unassigned, Reserved)
	95	05F		–
24	96	060	SD	Spurious Interrupt[3]
25	100	064	SD	Level 1 Interrupt Autovector
26	104	068	SD	Level 2 Interrupt Autovector
27	108	06C	SD	Level 3 Interrupt Autovector
28	112	070	SD	Level 4 Interrupt Autovector
29	116	074	SD	Level 5 Interrupt Autovector
30	120	078	SD	Level 6 Interrupt Autovector
31	124	07C	SD	Level 7 Interrupt Autovector
32-47	128	080	SD	TRAP Instruction Vectors[4]
	191	0BF		
48-63[1]	192	0C0	SD	(Unassigned, Reserved)
	255	0FF		–
64-255	256	100	SD	User Interrupt Vectors
	1023	3FF		–

NOTES:

1. Vector numbers 12, 13, 16 through 23, and 48 through 63 are reserved for future enhancements by Motorola. No user peripheral devices should be assigned these numbers.
2. Reset vector (0) requires four words, unlike the other vectors which only require two words, and is located in the supervisor program space.
3. The spurious interrupt vector is taken when there is a bus error indication during interrupt processing. Refer to Paragraph 4.4.2.
4. TRAP #n uses vector number 32 + n.
5. MC68010 only. See Return from Exception Section. This vector is unassigned, reserved on the MC68000, and MC68008.

Figure 13 Exception vector assignments. (Courtesy of Motorola, Inc.)

The exception vector assignments are shown in Figure 13. Each vector is assigned a number. The address of the particular vector number is four times the vector number.

Before we discuss the various types of exceptions, let's see just what happens when an exception occurs. The following events take place:

1. An internal copy is made of the status register. This is used in step number 3. The CPU is forced into the supervisor mode by setting the

S bit in the status register. The tracing bit, T, is negated to prevent tracing. If the exception is an interrupt, the interrupt priority mask is updated.
2. The vector number of the exception is determined. This either comes from an external fetch, in the case of an interrupt, or is determined internally by the CPU.
3. The current program counter and the saved status register are pushed onto the supervisor stack using the supervisor stack pointer, SSP. Some additional information is stacked for certain types of exceptions and for the 68010, 68020, and 68030 processors.
4. The address of the exception handler is fetched from the vector location and placed into the program counter. Execution continues within the exception handler.

The exception handler can perform any operations it deems necessary. It will be executing in supervisor mode so that it has access to all the system and CPU resources. Once its work has been done, it can optionally return to the program that was originally interrupted. This is done by executing the instruction RTE (return from exception). This instruction has no operands. It reverses the steps listed above:

1. The saved status register is popped from the supervisor stack and placed in the status register.
2. The saved program counter is popped from the stack and placed into the program counter.
3. Execution continues with the next instruction in the interrupted program.

The whole process of handling an exception looks very much like a subroutine call except that the calling program doesn't issue a JSR or BSR instruction. If the exception is an external interrupt, then no instruction is executed that can be associated with the exception.

To cover all the details concerning exceptions would require many pages of explanation and would probably confuse many novice readers. Since most programmers will only require a casual knowledge of exceptions, I am only going to cover the really important exceptions for general programmers. For more specific details on the remainder of the exceptions, refer to the appropriate Motorola documentation.

Reset is not a standard exception in that it requires two vector entries. When you initially power up your computer, or press a reset button, the reset exception is generated. This exception is normally used to cause a boot of your operating system. The program counter and supervisor stack pointer are loaded from the vector addresses, and control proceeds at the

PC location. Normally this is to an area of read only memory (ROM) that contains a small bootstrap program to load the complete operating system from disk. In some cases, the bulk of the operating system is contained in ROM, and little or no information is obtained from disk. In either case, the program flow ends up in your operating system, usually at command level.

Interrupts that are generated by external devices cause exceptions in either of two ways. The first method is one in which the particular device provides the vector number ranging from 64 to 255. The particular vectors used for particular devices is system-dependent. The second method is to use the autovector feature. The autovectors are 25 through 31. The particular vector selected is determined from the device's interrupt priority.

Bus error, address error, illegal instruction, zero divide, and *privilege violation* are exceptions caused by errors in a program. A bus error is generated when you try to reference a non-existent area of memory. An address error results when you try to access a word, longword, or instruction from an *odd* memory address. The illegal instruction exception is generated if the CPU tries to execute a word bit pattern that doesn't correspond to any valid instruction. One very specific instruction, ILLEGAL, *always* generates this exception. In a sense it is the only legal instruction that generates an illegal instruction exception. A zero divide exception results from a DIVU or DIVS instruction when you divide by zero. Certain instructions are executable only in the supervisor mode. If one of these instructions is executed in the user mode, the privilege violation exception occurs.

Traps

Exception vectors numbered 32 through 47 are associated with the TRAP instruction. Its format is:

```
TRAP    #<vector>
```

where <vector> is a number from 0_{10} through 15_{10}. The operand value of the TRAP instruction is added to 32_{10} to determine the actual exception vector. Execution of this instruction causes an immediate exception to be generated, with control passed to the appropriate exception handler. If the handler subsequently executes an RTE instruction, the program will continue with the instruction following the TRAP.

TRAPS are sometimes called *software interrupts* and are the method that many operating systems use to provide user services. There are a couple of advantages to this method:

1. Execution of the TRAP instruction will result in the CPU being placed into supervisor mode.
2. By use of a vector number, rather than the specific address of the operating system service, the actual address within the operating system can change without the user reassembling his programs. The operating system merely ensures that the proper address is placed into the exception vector at the time the system starts up.

A special trap instruction, TRAPV, can be used to test the result of a computation for an overflow condition. If the overflow condition is set, the TRAPV instruction will cause an exception to vector number 7. If we have an appropriate exception handler, this instruction is quite useful. For example, if we perform an addition and then wish to trap on an overflow, all we have to do is write the following instructions:

```
ADD.L   D0,D1
TRAPV
```

Along the same line as the TRAPV instruction is the CHK (check register against bounds) instruction:

```
CHK     <ea>,Dn
```

The word in register Dn is first checked to see if it is below zero. If it is, an exception is generated. If the word in Dn is zero or greater, it is compared with the source operand. If it is greater than the source operand, an exception is generated. The exception vector is number 6.

If the T bit in the status register is set to 1, we enter the trace mode. In trace mode, every instruction generates an exception *after* it completes, but before the next instruction begins. This is very useful for debugging a program. In effect, we can single-step a program. Remember that the T bit is reset before the exception handler gets control so that the handler itself will not generate further exceptions. When the RTE is executed, the T bit will assume its value before the exception, and execution will continue with the next instruction in the program. The trace exception is vector number 9.

Setting up an exception handler is quite simple. All that is needed is to place its address in the appropriate exception vector location. However, this requires access to the vector area of memory. Some systems restrict access to this area in the user mode. In this case, we must somehow get into supervisor mode. That means an exception of some sort. Usually an operating system has a specific service that allows entry into supervisor mode for a short time. If the operating system is very secure, or is multi-user, it might not allow a user to do anything in supervisor mode. This is not a disadvantage, but one of the intended features of the 68000 family. Unlike many microprocessors, including the 8086, the 68000 does allow the writing and implementation of a secure multi-user operating system. Here is how to set up an exception handler for the TRAP #0 instruction:

```
TRAPOV: EQU     32*4               TRAP 0 VECTOR ADDRESS
*GET INTO SUPERVISOR MODE IF NOT ALREADY IN IT
        LEA     TOHAND,A0          GET ADDRESS OF HANDLER
        MOVE.L  A0,TRAPOV          STICK IN VECTOR
        .
        .
        .
*TRAP 0 HANDLER
TOHAND: MOVEM.L ....,-(SP)         SAVE REGISTERS WE USE
        .
        .
        .
        MOVEM   (SP)+,....         RESTORE REGISTERS WE USED
        RTE                        END WITH AN RTE
```

Notice that the exception handler saves and restores any registers it uses. This is important because they are not automatically saved and restored by the exception mechanism—only the program counter and the status register/condition codes are. Forgetting to save and restore registers has major consequences.

Serial I/O

In Chapter 2 the concept of *memory mapped I/O* was introduced. All input/output on the 68000 is via I/O devices with control and data registers that are present as addresses in the 68000's address space. This has the advantage that rather than being restricted to a small number of input/output instructions, the 68000 programmer can use any memory reference instruction with input/output devices as well as actual physical memory locations.

To cover the wide variety of I/O devices that can be connected to the 68000 would take up a book in itself. Additionally, so many system-dependent aspects of these devices would make the topic almost limitless in scope. Instead, in order to give you an idea of how to program an I/O device, we will take a look at one very popular I/O chip, the MC6850 Asynchronous Communications Interface Adapter (ACIA).

Many microcomputers are equipped with serial communications interfaces. Your CRT terminal or printer can be connected via a serial interface. Another popular interface is the parallel interface. The terms *serial* and *parallel* refer to the methods used to transfer data from the input/output device to the interface. A parallel interface transfers a complete byte or word at a time. A serial interface transfers a byte or word a single bit at a time. The advantage of a serial interface is that fewer wires are needed to make the connection. A parallel interface requires at least one wire for each bit. A disadvantage of a serial interface is that data cannot be transferred as rapidly as with the parallel interface.

At the heart of the serial interface is a chip commonly known as a universal asynchronous receiver transmitter (UART). Each byte of data is sent or received as a stream of bits. Two additional bits are included for each byte of data. A start bit is included to tell the UART that a byte is to follow. A stop bit is used to verify to the UART that we are finished with the current byte. Without start and stop bits, the UART would not be able to ensure *framing*. When a framing error occurs, some of the bits from one byte are mixed up with some of the bits from a previous byte. Figure 14 shows this typical asynchronous serial format. The most popular format is for eight data bits, one start bit, and one stop bit, giving a total of 10 bits for each byte of data sent or received.

If each byte is to represent an ASCII character code, an extra bit is available. This bit can be permanently set to a 1 or 0, or it may be used as a *parity bit*. A parity bit is used to help verify that the data has been received without error. The way a parity bit is used is very simple. We

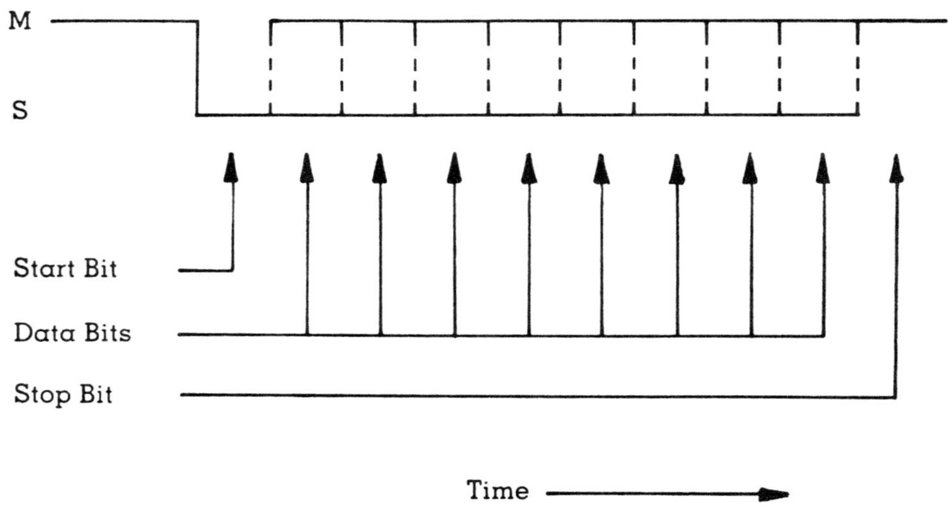

M—Marking or a logical one.
S—Spacing or a logical zero.

Figure 14 Asynchronous serial I/O format.

count up the number of data bits that are ones. We include the parity bit, but not the start and stop bits. If we have an even number we have *even* parity. If we have and odd number we have *odd* parity. Most serial interfaces allow a programmer to specify if even, odd, or no parity is required. The interface normally generates and/or checks the parity if desired.

Now let's take a look at the MC6850 in particular. This chip is a member of the older 8-bit family of interface devices used with the MC6800 CPU. However, it is still a very popular device for use with the MC68000. It is inexpensive, simple to program, and interfaces directly to the 68000 using the CPU's 8-bit compatibility feature. You will find this chip used on many 68000-based systems. The 6850 ACIA consists of four internal 8-bit registers. These are:

1. Transit Data Register
2. Receive Data Register
3. Control Register
4. Status Register

The transmit and receive data registers are located at the same address. The appropriate register is selected, depending on whether the register is being read or written. The transmit data register is *write only* and the receive data register is *read only*. A similar situation exists for the control and status registers. These normally occupy the address two bytes greater than the data registers. The control register is write only and the status register is read only.

The interpretation of the bits in these registers is as follows:

Transmit and Receive Data Registers

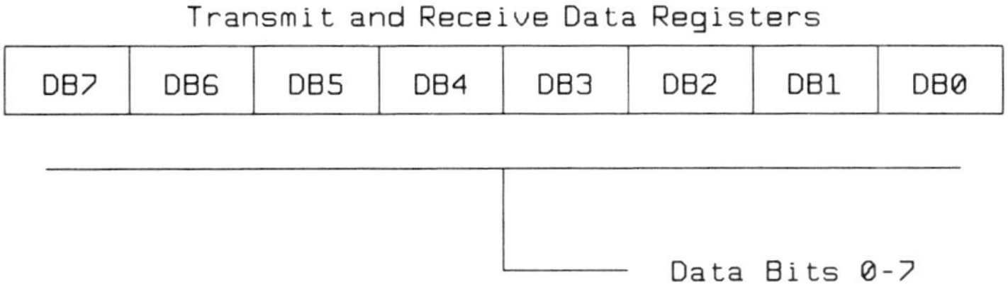

Control Register

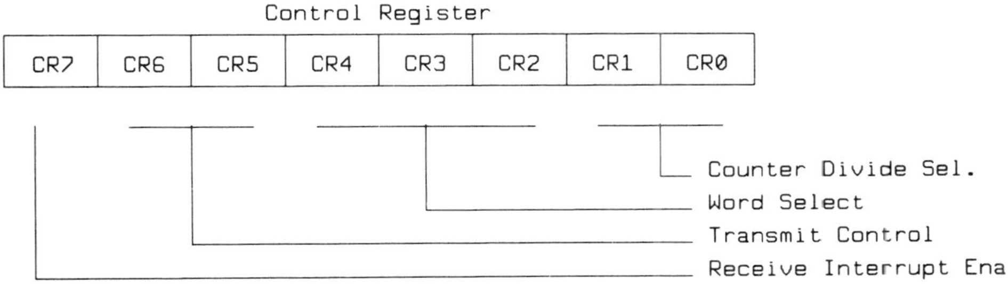

Status Register

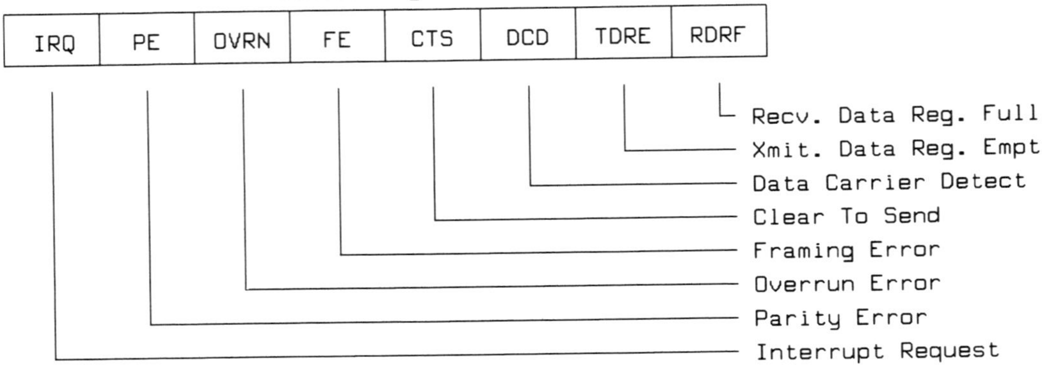

<u>Counter Divide Sel.</u>

CR1	CR0	Function
0	0	Divide by 1
0	1	Divide by 16
1	0	Divide by 64
1	1	Master Reset

<u>Word Select</u>

CR4	CR3	CR2	Function
0	0	0	7 bits, even parity, 2 stop bits
0	0	1	7 bits, odd parity, 2 stop bits
0	1	0	7 bits. even parity, 1 stop bit
0	1	1	7 bits, odd parity, 1 stop bit
1	0	0	8 bits, 2 stop bits
1	0	1	8 bits, 1 stop bit
1	1	0	8 bits, even parity, 1 stop bit
1	1	1	8 bits, odd parity, 1 stop bit

<u>Transmit Control</u>

CR6	CR7	Function
0	0	RTS low, transmit disable low
0	1	RTS low, transmit interrupt enabled
1	0	RTS high, transmit interrupt disabled
1	1	RTS low, transmit a break, transmit interrupt disabled

There are two methods of operating the ACIA; programmed I/O and interrupt-driven I/O. The 6850 is capable of both methods. We will discuss programmed mode, as it is much less complicated. This way we don't have to get involved with interrupts and an exception handler. The keys to using the 6850 are the RDRF (receive data register full) and TDRE (transmit data register empty) bits in the status word. The other control and status bits are used to set up the operating modes and to detect errors. If RDRF is set to a one, we have an input character already to be picked up. This would most likely be coming from a terminal's keyboard connected to the serial port. This character is available in the receive data register. If RDRF is not set to a 1, we have to wait. If TDRE is set to a 1, we are free to output a character to the transmit data register. If TDRE is not set to a 1, we have to wait.

To demonstrate the programming involved with the 6850, we will write three subroutines: one to initialize the port, one to output a character, and finally one to read a character. Let's assume that we want to operate our port with a standard clock divide rate of 16 (a system-dependent value), 8 data bits with no parity, 1 stop bit, and RTS low with transmit and receive interrupts disabled. Here are the three subroutines:

```
ACIATD: EQU      <addr. of port> THE TRANSMIT DATA REGISTER
ACIARD: EQU      ACIATD          THE RECEIVE DATA REGISTER
ACIAC:  EQU      ACIATD+2        THE CONTROL REGISTER
ACIAS:  EQU      ACIAC           THE STATUS REGISTER
CONTROL:EQU      #$15            THE PORT PARAMETERS
*
*INITIALIZE THE ACIA
*
INIT:   MOVE.B   #$3,ACIAC       DO A MASTER RESET
        MOVE.B   #CONTROL,ACIAC  INITIALIZE PARAMETERS
        RTS
*
*OUTPUT CHARACTER IN D0 TO THE ACIA
*
OUT:    BTST.B   #1,ACIAS        TRANSMIT DATA REGISTER EMPTY?
        BEQ      OUT             NO, TRY AGAIN
        MOVE.B   D0,ACIATD       YES, OUTPUT THE CHARACTER
        RTS
*
*INPUT A CHARACTER TO D0 FROM THE ACIA
*
IN:     BTST.B   #0,ACIAS        RECEIVE DATA REGISTER FULL?
        BEQ      IN              NO, TRY AGAIN
        MOVE.B   ACIARD,D0       YES, GET THE CHARACTER
        RTS
```

These subroutines are very straightforward. The BTST instructions are used to test the appropriate bits in the status register. If a particular bit is not set, we merely enter a loop and keep trying. This does have the disadvantage that we can't do any other useful processing while waiting for a character to be sent or received. If we were to use the interrupt capability of the 68000 and the 6850 ACIA, we could overcome this problem, and the CPU would be free for use. When a character arrived, an interrupt would be generated and we could then process the new character. In a similar manner, when the current character is output, an interrupt would be generated so that we could output the next character. Naturally, using an interrupt mode of operation requires character buffering and cooperation between the interrupt handler and the main program. Many textbooks on systems programming or operating system techniques describe these techniques.

There is one special instruction that has been provided just for interfacing with 8-bit peripheral devices. This is the MOVEP (move peripheral data) instruction. Its general forms are:

```
MOVEP[.<size>]  Dx,d(Ay)
MOVEP[.<size>]  d(Ay),Dx

<size> = W, L
```

Note that the only forms of the addressing modes it allows are register and register indirect with displacement. This instruction moves bytes of data to or from alternate bytes of a memory address. A longword transfer to/from an even address looks like this:

Register Contents

13 — 24	23 — 16	15 — 8	7 — 0
hi-order	mid-upper	mid-lower	low-order

Contents of Memory

15 — 8	7 — 0
hi-order	
mid-upper	
mid-lower	
low-order	

A word transfer to/from an even address looks like the illustration at the top of the following page.

Miscellaneous Instructions

In this section we will discuss a few miscellaneous instructions not covered in previous chapters.

The NOP instruction is an instruction that does absolutely nothing. It stands for No OPeration. It takes a minimum amount of time to execute, since there are no operands. It occupies one word of memory. It can be used as a place holder. For example, if you are using a debugger and

Register Contents

31 ... 24	23 ... 16	15 ... 8	7 ... 0
		hi-order	low-order

Contents of Memory

15 ... 8	7 ... 0
	hi-order
	low-order

find that an instruction is to be substituted by one that requires one less word in memory, a NOP can be used to fill the excess word.

The RESET instruction can only be used in supervisor mode. When it is executed it asserts the hardware reset line. This normally causes all external devices to be reset. The exact results of using this instruction will depend on what sort of devices are connected to the hardware reset line. Normally this instruction is executed by the operating system to ensure an initialized state for all external devices. Unless you are writing an operating system, you should never have need for this instruction. If you execute it by mistake in the user mode, a trap will be generated.

The STOP instruction has the general form:

```
STOP     #xxx
```

The STOP instruction must be executed when in the supervisor mode or else a trap will be generated. The immediate operand of the STOP instruction is moved into the entire status register, the program counter is advanced to the next instruction, and the CPU stops executing. However, if an interrupt occurs with a priority higher than the current interrupt priority level in the SR, then an interrupt exception will be generated; otherwise nothing happens. If the exception handler executes an RTE, the next instruction following the STOP will be executed. If an external reset is generated, the processor will execute the standard reset sequence.

The test and set instruction, TAS, is primarily used in a multi-processor environment. The general form of the instruction is:

```
TAS      <ea>
```

The operand size used with the TAS instruction must be byte. It first tests the byte at the effective address and sets the N and Z bits of the CCR accordingly. It then sets bit 7 of the operand to a 1. This instruction is special in that a read-modify-write bus cycle is used so that the test and set operation can be performed in an indivisible manner. In other words, only one CPU at a time can perform a TAS in a multiple CPU system. No two TAS's can overlap.

This instruction is normally used for locking operations. If a processor wants to place a lock on some item, it can execute the following code:

```
L:        TAS     LOCK
          BNE     L
```

It might look as if this loop would go on forever. This is not the case if the lock was zero to begin with. Remember, the test operation is performed *before* the set takes place. After a processor is finished with the locked item, it must reset the lock and therefore allow other CPU's to access the data, one at a time. This unlock operation is performed by:

```
          CLR.B   LOCK
```

The byte variable LOCK must be initially cleared or no CPU will ever be able to access the item.

The particular items protected by locks can vary all over the place. A lock could be placed on a record of a file, an area of memory, and so on. Since the use of a TAS involves a *busy wait*, an operating system normally uses this instruction to implement *higher level* methods of ensuring mutually exclusive access. Consult a good operating systems text for these details.

Exercises

1. How large is the status register?
2. In addition to the CCR bits, what extra bits are in the SR?
3. Can the status register be accessed when in user mode?
4. What is the range of values for the interrupt mask?
5. Write an instruction to clear the carry bit in the CCR. All other bits should remain the same.
6. What is the purpose of the RTR instruction?
7. Write an instruction to set the byte at location MINUS if the result of a calculation is negative.
8. Assume your program is in supervisor mode. Write the instructions necessary to initialize the USP to location USTACK.
9. What is an exception?
10. Where are the exception vectors located?
11. What is the difference between an RTE instruction and an RTS instruction?
12. What happens when you try to access a word or longword at an odd memory address?

13. What exception vectors are associated with the TRAP instruction?
14. Is an exception generated for an overflow condition?
15. What happens if the trace bit is set in the status register?
16. Does the 68000 restrict the user to specific instructions for I/O?
17. What is the difference between a serial and a parallel interface?
18. What is the purpose of a parity bit?
19. What two methods can be used to program the 6850 ACIA?
20. What is the purpose of the MOVEP instruction?
21. What instruction is normally used as a place holder?
22. After the STOP instruction has been executed, is it possible for the CPU to start up again?
23. What instruction is used in a multi-processor system for locking operations?

Answers

1. Two bytes.
2. The 3-bit interrupt mask, the supervisor state bit, and the trace mode bit.
3. It can be read but not written using the MOVE from SR instruction.
4. The interrupt mask can range from 0 through 7.
5.
```
ANDI #$FE,SR
```
6. The RTR instruction is used to restore the saved CCR bits from the stack and return. It allows the writing of a transparent subroutine.
7.
```
SMI MINUS
```
8.
```
LEA     USTACK,A0
MOVE    A0,USP
```
9. An event that causes the normal flow of a program to be suspended, and control given to a special handler.
10. In memory, starting at location zero, for a total of 1024 bytes.
11. The RTE is used to return from an exception. The SR as well as the return address are popped from the stack. The RTS is used to return from a subroutine and only the return address is popped from the stack.
12. The address error exception is generated.
13. Vector numbers 32 through 47.
14. No, but the TRAPV instruction can be used to generate one.
15. An exception is generated after every instruction execution. Vector number 9 is used.

16. No, any memory reference instruction can be used, since the 68000 employs memory-mapped I/O.
17. A serial interface transfers a bit at a time, while a parallel interface transfers a byte or word at a time.
18. A parity bit can be used to detect errors in data transmission.
19. The 6850 can be operated using programmed I/O or interrupt-driven I/O.
20. The MOVEP instruction is used to transfer data to alternate byte addresses. This is helpful for certain I/O devices.
21. The NOP instruction.
22. Yes, if an interrupt is generated from an external device.
23. The TAS (test and set) instruction.

CHAPTER 13

THE 68010

The MC68010 is the next step up the ladder in the 68000 family. This microprocessor is not radically different from the 68000. Most programmers will never have to be aware that their program is running on a 68010 and not on a 68000. The 68010 is primarily designed to make it easy for designers to build systems that use *virtual* concepts. The most popular virtual concept is that of *virtual memory*. A secondary but also very important use of 68010-type processors is in implementing *virtual machines*. By "virtual" we mean giving the illusion that something is there when it really isn't. For example, we can give the illusion of a large physical memory when, in fact, we have only a small physical memory. A virtual machine can be used for a number of purposes. One of these is to allow the concurrent execution of two or more different operating systems. This might be desirable when we want to test a new operating system while running an old one. Also, different users might want different operating systems. The 68010 allows all of these things to be accomplished by some relatively minor changes to the basic architecture.

Virtual Memory and the Bus Error Exception

You may recall from Chapter 12 that a *bus error* is a particular exception that occurs when a program tries to access an address in memory that doesn't exist. A bus error may occur when the CPU tries to access the instruction itself or when accessing one of the instruction's operands. It all depends on what is in the real physical memory and what is addressed at non-existent memory locations. If a bus error occurs on the 68000, an exception is generated and control will be passed to an appropriate exception handler. There is not much the handler can do about the situation. Normally the program is aborted and an appropriate notice is given to the user. Even if it can somehow be arranged for memory to be subsequently made available at the address that caused the bus error (this is the basis of virtual memory management), we have no way of restarting the instruction without the potential for error. A simple example will serve to illustrate. Suppose the following instruction generates a bus error on the destination operand, MEMLOC.

```
MOVE.L   (A0)+,MEMLOC
```

If we try to re-execute this instruction, the address in A0 will be in error. We have already postincremented the value. What we would really like to be able to do is to restart the instruction just where it left off—in this case, just after having fetched the source operand. Unfortunately, the 68000 does not have this feature. And so, now enters the 68010, which of course *does* give us this capability.

The secret to being able to recover midstream from a bus error on the 68010 comes from the way in which information is placed on the stack during a bus error exception. The 68010 places 22 words of additional information on the stack concerning the intermediate state of an instruction execution. Therefore, when the RTE instruction is executed, everything can be put back just as it was *before* the bus error. The instruction can continue execution without ever knowing that it was interrupted. You don't have to be concerned with the specific details of this additional information, since the RTE instruction takes care of if all when it is executed.

One issue needs to be briefly explained: just how does memory get managed such that we can make physical memory available at a particular address that was formerly not available? There are many techniques to do this. In all cases some form of memory management hardware must be added "between" the CPU and the physical memory. The Motorola MC68851 Paged Memory Management Unit is a single chip available for this purpose. The 68851 is actually a coprocessor, and although specifically designed for the MC68020 CPU, it can be used with other CPU's, including the 68010. Other hardware can also be used. Regardless of the specific hardware, the basic concept of virtual memory is that we map an address in the *virtual address space* into an address in the *physical address space*. The virtual address is the address your instruction uses. This address is in turn converted or mapped to a physical address that may or may not be the same. All forms of virtual memory management map blocks of memory rather than specific addresses. Otherwise the mapping would be very complex and inefficient.

The most popular form of memory management is called *paging*. With paging we divide the virtual memory up into equal sized blocks called *pages*. Physical memory is likewise divided up into *page frames* that are the same size as those of the virtual memory. The memory management hardware is responsible for mapping a virtual page to a physical page frame. The offset or displacement within a virtual page is always the same as the offset in the page frame that it is mapped to;

the tenth word in the virtual page corresponds to the tenth word in the physical page. Since the virtual address space is normally much larger than the physical memory, it is necessary to temporarily store the pages that won't fit into physical memory. For example, we might have just 1 megabyte of physical memory, while the 68010 can address up to 16 megabytes. Normally a disk memory is used to store the pages that are not in physical memory. This is sometimes called a *backing store*. The backing store does not have to be as large as the addressing capability of the CPU if the size of the virtual address space is reduced.

Now we can tie up the loose ends. If an instruction references an address that is mapped to physical memory, the memory management hardware makes that address immediately available and no bus error is generated. If a reference is made to an address that is not currently mapped, a bus error exception will occur. This is normally called a *page fault* when paging is used. The operating system now gets control. It is responsible for finding the proper page on the backing store and bringing it into memory. Once it is in memory, the operating system can execute the RTE instruction with the stack pointer pointing at the same place it was when the bus error was initially processed. This will return control to the instruction that generated the bus error, and it will now be able to access the address.

This may sound simple, but an operating system has a lot of bookeeping to do in order to get all the pages mapped correctly. Many operating systems textbooks will provide more information on the techniques used to implement paging. Figure 15 shows a possible mapping of virtual pages to physical page frames. Notice that some of the pages are not mapped. Any reference to an address in one of these pages will generate a bus error and hence a page fault.

Virtual Machines

Like virtual memory, a virtual machine provides the illusion of a bare-bones machine. In other words, it appears to the user that *all* the functionality of the machine is available. The user must not be aware that a virtual machine operating system is running underneath her own operating system.

In order to implement a true virtual machine, not only does the CPU have to appear as a bare CPU, but any input/output devices must also be made available to each user. Virtual memory can provide the illusion of a specific physical memory (all users must have access to the same addressing range). Since input/output devices are memory-mapped, they can be replicated or shared for each user and appear at the same physical

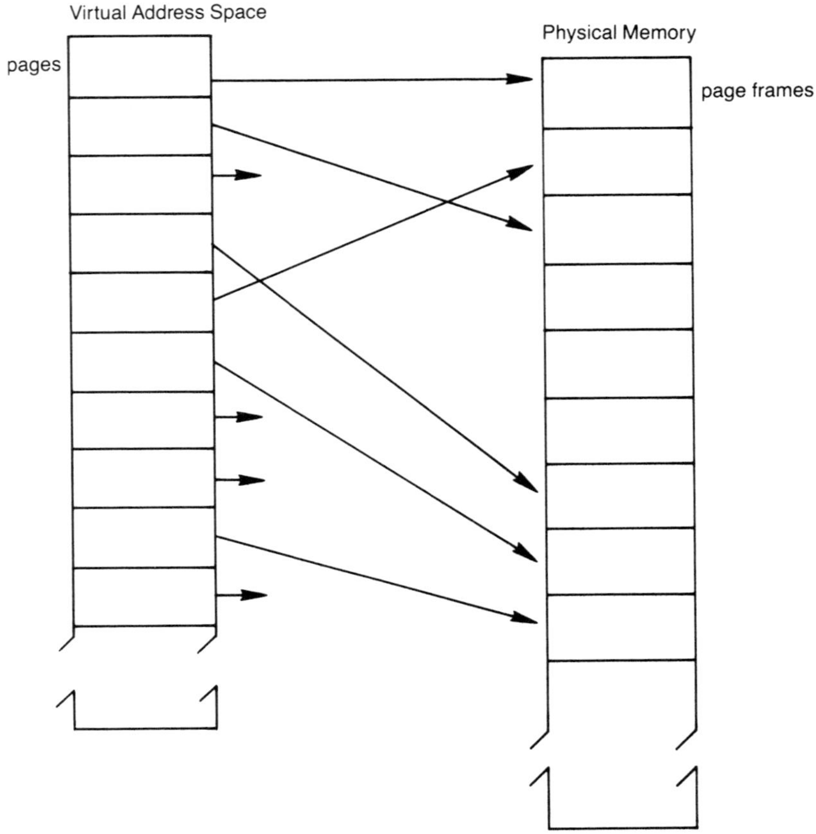

Figure 15 Virtual memory mapping.

addresses. The CPU is another matter. Each user must think she has access to all of the CPU's capabilities, including user and supervisor states. However, in order for the virtual machine operating system to maintain control, the user must always run in user mode. We must be able to fool a program into thinking that it is running in supervisor mode when it actually isn't.

Let's say that a program is running in the user mode and executes a privileged instruction. An exception will be generated and the virtual operating system can take control. It can then verify and simulate the execution of the privileged instruction. The user program will never know that the instruction was not executed directly. The one problem that can not be handled in this manner is the manipulation of the status register, SR. A user on the 68000 can execute

```
MOVE    SR,<ea>
```

to examine the processor state. This instruction is not privileged on the 68000. The user could then tell that she was really in the user state.

To correct this deficiency, the 68010 makes the MOVE from SR instruction privileged. The virtual operating system can then "fool" the program into believing that it is in the supervisor state when it is actually in the user state. It can simulate the execution of the instruction and return the status register contents with the supervisor bit set. One minor change was also made: a new instruction was added, the MOVE from CCR. Its general form is

```
MOVE    CCR,<ea>
```

The contents of the condition code register is moved to the destination operand. This instruction is not available on the 68000 and it is not privileged on the 68010. It allows a user-mode program on the 68010 to access the CCR without generating a privilege exception. You will find a summary of the new and changed instructions at the end of this chapter.

Reference Classifications

Three additional output lines are provided with both the 68000 and the 68010 CPU. These lines are used to classify the type of memory reference. They are interpreted as follows:

FC2	FC1	FC0	Reference Class
0	0	0	N/A
0	0	1	User Data
0	1	0	User Program
0	1	1	N/A
1	0	0	N/A
1	0	1	Supervisor Data
1	1	0	Supervisor Program
1	1	1	Interrupt Acknowledge

N/A = not generated by a normal instruction

A computer system based on the 68000 family can use these lines to control access to certain areas of memory. Separate areas can be reserved for user and supervisor states. A further distinction can be made between data and program references. Bus errors can be generated if incorrect references are made. All this must be accomplished with external hardware.

With the 68000 there is no way to override the use of the three function class bits. However, the 68010 provides two new registers and two new instructions to be used in conjunction with the function class output lines. A source function code register, SFC, and a destination function code register, DFC, are available in the supervisor state. These registers are 3 bits each, each bit corresponding to a bit of the function class lines. A new privileged instruction, the move to/from control register, is provided on the 68010. Its general form is:

```
MOVEC    Rc,Rn
MOVEC    Rn,Rc

Rc = SFC, DFC, VBR, USP
Rn = D0-D7, A0-A7
```

It is always a 32-bit transfer, with unused bits read as zero. This instruction can also be used to access the user stack pointer, USP, or the vector base register, VBR (discussed below), or to set up the SFC or DFC with any relevant value.

A second privileged instruction, move to/from address space, can now be used to access the memory location in the address space specified by the source or destination function registers. The general form of this instruction is:

```
MOVES[.<size>]  Rn,<ea>
MOVES[.<size>]  <ea>,Rn

<size> = B, W, L
Rn = D0-D7, A0-A7
```

The SFC or DFC is used, as appropriate, depending on whether <ea> is the source or destination of the instruction.

The Vector Base Register

You will recall from Chapter 12 that for the 68000 the exception vectors start at memory location 0_{16} and continue through $3FF_{16}$. This is normally the case for the 68010 as well. However, the 68010 provides a method of relocating the exception vectors to any place desired. A special register, the vector base register, VBR, is provided for this purpose. This 32-bit register is initially set to zero upon a system reset. A program running in the supervisor mode can change the contents of this register by use of the MOVEC instruction described above. The contents of the VBR is always added to the address that would normally be used to process the exception. You may recall that this address is four times the exception number. For example, the TRAP #0 instruction will generate exception number 32_{10}. The actual vector location will be at 128_{10} or 80_{16}. If the VBR contains 4000_{16}, the TRAP #0 exception vector is located at 4080_{16}. The following instructions can be used to set the VBR to 4000_{16}:

```
MOVE.L  #$4000,D0
MOVEC   D0,VBR
```

The VBR can be used for many purposes. The implementation of a virtual machine is made much easier by the use of the VBR. Each different user of the virtual machine must think that he/she has his/her own set of exception vectors. These should appear to be located at address zero. However, when the program runs, these vectors really can't be used since the virtual machine operating system requires complete control. The virtual machine operating can use the VBR to set up an alternate address for the actual vectors. If an exception occurs that the virtual machine operating systems wants to pass to the user it can re-vector through the address found in the vectors based at zero. The VBR can also be used to make a debugger appear more transparent to the program it is debugging.

RTD and Loop Mode

Two other minor features that exist for the 68010 are the RTD instruction and loop mode. The RTD instruction works exactly like the RTS instruction except that a constant is added to the stack pointer after the return address is fetched. This constant value is normally used to clear the stack of any parameters passed to the subroutine. As discussed in Chapter 8, this is normally the responsibility of the caller. To see how this instruction works, let's say that subroutine MYSUB is called with three longword arguments. The following call would be used:

```
MOVE.L  ARG3,-(SP)
MOVE.L  ARG2,-(SP)
MOVE.L  ARG1,-(SP)
JSR     MYSUB
.
.
.
```

Normally the caller would use an ADDA.L #12,SP following the JSR to clean up the stack. With the 68010, the following instructions can be used such that the subroutine can clean up the stack upon its return:

```
MYSUB:  .
        .
        .
        RTD     12
```

Loop mode is an enhancement to the operating speed of the 68010 that the user doesn't even have to be aware of. To understand the advantage of loop mode, we will have to take a closer look at the factors that govern the speed of execution of an instruction. As I mentioned in Chapter 2, a CPU requires a clock to generate timing for the overall execution of instructions. The speed of this clock depends on the particular chip being used and also on the design of the computer it is used with. Each instruction requires a particular number of clock cycles to execute. This number varies with the particular operand addressing modes used with the instruction. The reference documentation for the particular member of the 68000 family you are using will have tables giving the exact number of cycles for each instruction and addressing mode. All you need to know is the speed of your clock and you can figure out the execution time for any instruction. There is one minor problem that can throw off your calculations: The 68000 is designed to accommodate memory of any speed. If your memory is slower than the required speed for maximum CPU speed, the CPU adds *wait states,* extra clock cycles to slow down the CPU until the memory catches up. You will have to get the technical details about your particular machine.

Since loops in a program may be executed hundreds or thousands of times, it may be important to design the instructions inside the loop so that they execute in the fastest time. This may mean sitting down with paper and pencil to consult the manual to add up the total cycles for all the instructions, and then trying various combinations until the best set of instructions is obtained. Now back to the 68010 loop mode. If you understand how this special mode works, you can plan some loops to make them execute faster. The increased speed is obtained by entering loop mode for only certain loops. The loop must contain only a single word long instruction. The addressing modes of this instruction must be such that no extension words are required. This would eliminate such instructions as MOVE.L COUNT,D1. The reason the 68010 can execute these small loops with greater speed is that it has a two-word prefetch queue, plus the instruction decode register. This means that all three words of the entire loop can be held in the CPU. No additional memory references are required for the instruction fetches once the loop is set up. The memory references are then only those required by the loop instruction. A prefetch queue is a special set of internal CPU registers that are used to "look ahead" into memory and obtain the next few words before they are actually needed. The MC68020 explained more fully in the next chapter, makes extensive use of this technique.

Generally, any memory reference instructions can be used for loop mode. These include the arithmetic and logical/shift rotates. The operands must use one or more of the following addressing modes:

```
Dx
(An)
(An)+
-(An)
```

You may recall that the DBcc instruction on the 68000 first checks the terminating condition. If it is true, execution continues with the next sequential instruction; if the test condition is false, the loop counter is decremented and the result is checked against −1. If it is not equal to −1, the loop branch is taken and we stay in the loop; otherwise, we continue with the next sequential instruction. Under the 68010 loop mode, the sequence is slightly different. The 68010 first decrements the contents of the count register. It does this internally without actually changing the value in the register. If the result is −1, this value is stored in the count register and execution continues with the next sequential instruction. If the result is not −1, the terminating condition is checked. If it is true, the temporary count is discarded and execution continues with the next sequential instruction. Otherwise, if the terminating condition is false, the branch is taken.

A very fast memory move can be implemented using loop mode with the following:

```
        LEA     SOURCE,A0
        LEA     DEST,A1
        MOVE.W   COUNT,D0
NEXT:   MOVE.L  (AO)+,(A1)+
        DBRA    D0,NEXT
```

Summary

Here is a summary of the new or changed instructions and registers for the 68010:

Instruction	Comments
MOVE from CCR	68010 only
MOVE from SR	Privileged on 68010
MOVEC	68010 only
MOVES	68010 only
RTD	68010 only
RTE	68010 restores intermediate instruction state

New Registers	
SFC	Source function code register
DFC	Destination function code register
VBR	Vector base register

Exercises

1. What is a virtual memory?
2. What is a bus error?

3. In what way does the 68010 handle bus errors differently than the 68000?
4. What is the purpose of memory management hardware?
5. What is the most popular form of memory management for implementing virtual memory?
6. What is a page fault?
7. What is the purpose of a virtual machine?
8. Is a MOVE from SR instruction privileged on the 68010?
9. Write a 68010 instruction to copy the contents of the CCR to register D0. This instruction should not generate an exception in user mode.
10. What output lines are provided for reference classifications?
11. What new registers are provided on the 68010 to allow overrides to the reference classification?
12. Write the instructions necessary to reference absolute location $1000 in the supervisor data space. Read the longword at this location into register D0.
13. What is the function of the vector base register?
14. What does the RTD instruction do?
15. What addressing modes are allowed with the single instruction used inside the loop in loop mode?

Answers

1. A virtual memory is the illusion of a large physical memory when in actuality a much smaller memory is available.
2. A bus error is an exception that is generated when a reference is made to non-existent memory.
3. The 68010 allows an instruction to be restarted where it left off after a bus error is processed. This is accomplished by stacking additional state information during the exception processing.
4. Memory management hardware provides the necessary mapping between the logical address and the physical address.
5. Paging.
6. A page fault is generated if a memory reference is made to a page that is currently not in physical memory.
7. A virtual machine can be used to allow execution of several different operating systems on the same CPU or to provide a simulation capability for features that don't actually exist.
8. Yes, but not on the 68000.
9. `MOVE CCR,D0`
10. `FC0, FC1, and FC2.`

11. The SFC (source function code) register and the DFC (destination function code) register.

12.
```
        MOVE.L   #5,D0
        MOVEC    D0,SFC
        MOVES.L  $1000,D0
```

13. The vector base register allows moving the exception vectors to any location in memory.
14. RTD performs like an RTS except that a constant is also added to the stack pointer after the return address is popped. This can be used to clear the stack of any arguments passed to the subroutine.
15. Dx, (An), (An)+, and −(An).

CHAPTER 14

THE 68020

The MC68020 is a dramatically improved member of the 68000 family with a plethora of new features. Not only is the basic core performance of the processor much improved, but the new features expand the functionality of this chip so much that it brings it into serious competition with mini- and super minicomputers. The major enhancements can be summarized as:

1. A full 32-bit address bus
2. An instruction cache for faster execution
3. Built-in coprocessor support
4. New addressing modes
5. New and enhanced instructions
6. 8-, 16-, and 32-bit data bus interface

The 68020 is a true 32-bit architecture. With the 32-bit data bus capability and internal 32-bit operations, the 68020 can operate at its maximum potential with 32-bit operands. Even though the 68000 performs 32-bit operations, the data bus path is restricted to 16 bits at a time. For this reason the 68000 is sometimes classed as a 16-bit micro. The 68020 is clearly a 32-bit architecture in *every* way. In order to allow the 68020 to be used in systems that are restricted to an 8- or 16-bit data bus, the 68020 provides the option of using 8-, 16-, or 32-bit data bus widths. Unfortunately, you can't just plug in a 68020 where a 68000 was. The physical construction is very different. The 68020 uses a 114-pin grid array, whereas the 68000 uses the more conventional dual in-line package (DIP).

Along with the expanded addressing capability comes an added bonus: the restriction that word or longword data must be aligned on even-byte boundaries is relaxed. Words and longwords can start on any byte address. However, the restriction that instructions start on even bytes has not been removed.

Instruction Caching

Besides using full 32-bit operands both internally and via the data bus, the 68020 gains additional performance improvement by introducing an instruction *cache*. A cache is very similar to a small internal memory. Since it is internal, it can operate at register speeds. This means that an access to the cache takes less time than an access to the physical memory. The cache on the 68020 is used to store instructions. If an instruction is found in the cache there is no need to look for it in physical memory. There is an additional benefit however; while the instruction is being fetched from the cache, an operand can be accessed in memory. If this situation occurs, then the instruction fetch is actually for free. This is because the two accesses are overlapped.

The operation of the instruction cache is invisible to the programmer. The cache is automatically updated according to an internal algorithm in the CPU. The real advantage of the instruction cache comes into play when a small loop is executed. If all the instructions of the loop will fit into the instruction cache, once we have gone through the loop the first time, the instruction fetches for each additional pass through the loop will be from the instruction cache. The instruction cache on the 68020 is 256 bytes. This is enough to hold a significant number of instructions. Since the length of an instruction varies from 2 to 10 bytes, it is not possible to know the exact number of instructions that will fit in the cache, but a rough estimate is around 50. Since most loops don't involve more than 50 instructions, the instruction cache almost always speeds up loops. The loop mode on the 68010 is a very limited version of the 68020 instruction cache.

Figure 16 shows the operation of the 68020 instruction cache. The cache stores 32-bit longwords that are aligned on even-word addresses. Bits 2 through 7 of an address are used to index into the cache. This allows 64 longwords to be stored in the cache. Bits 8 through 31 and the high-order bit of the 3-bit function code are stored as a tag in the cache entry along with the 32-bit value at that address. You will recall from Chapter 13 that the function code specifies the address space. Only user and supervisor program spaces are stored in the instruction cache. The high-order bit of the function code determines which is which. If this bit is set, it indicates a supervisor program address. The two lower-order bits of the function code must be 10. Every address accessed by the CPU is compared with the contents of the cache. The entry is selected by bits 2 through 7. If the tag field matches, then the data in the cache, rather than a fetch to memory, is used. If the tag doesn't match and the reference is a program reference, then the actual memory location is accessed and the cache is updated.

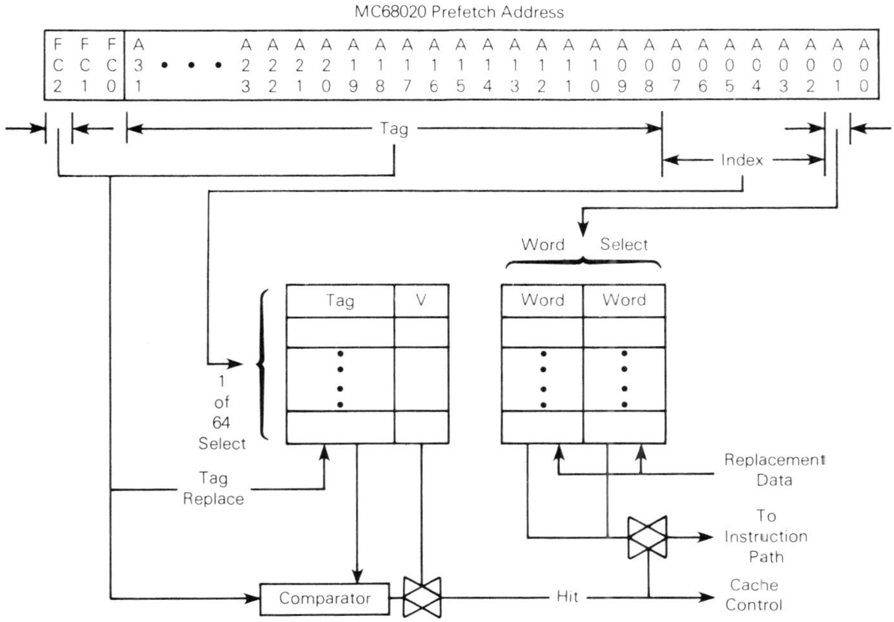

Figure 16 Instruction cache. (Courtesy of Motorola, Inc.)

In order to control the operation of the instruction cache, two new registers were added to the 68020; the cache control register, CACR, and the cache address register, CAAR. They are both 32 bits, but not all the bits are used. The CACR only uses the low-order 4 bits.

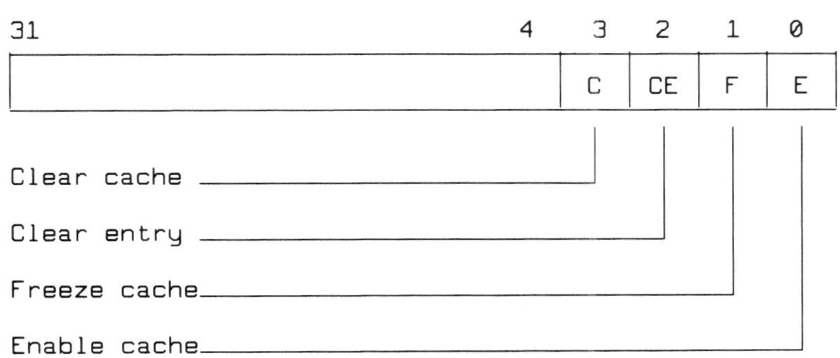

When the hardware is reset, the cache is initially disabled. In order to enable the cache, the E bit in the CACR must be set. The MOVEC instruction has been expanded on the 68020 to include the cache registers.

```
MOVE.L  #1,D0
MOVEC   D0,CACR
```

does the job nicely. The other bits can be manipulated in a similar manner. Remember, MOVEC is a privileged instruction, so this operation can't be accomplished when in user mode. The cache can be enabled or disabled at will.

The F bit will freeze the cache. The cache will still operate, but its contents will not change. This is useful for certain types of applications when a function is being emulated. The C and CE bits are used to clear the entire cache or just a particular entry. The cache should be cleared every time the the contents of program memory are changed. If program memory is changed without the cache being cleared, the contents of the cache will not reflect the actual contents of memory, and errors in execution may result. This operation would normally be performed by the operating system when it loads a new program. To clear a specific entry we place the cache index value in the CAAR. The cache index value is determined by using bits 2 through 7 of the corresponding memory address. This value is placed in bits 2 through 7 of the CAAR. It doesn't matter what the other bits are, they are ignored. The CAAR is structured like this:

31 … 8	7 … 2	1	0
	INDEX		

This last operation is provided only for the most sophisticated applications. If a specific memory address in program space is modified, only the specific cache entry that corresponds to it need be modified; the entire cache does not have to be cleared. Since self-modifying programs have fallen out of vogue, it is unlikely that clearing a specific entry has any value except for very sophisticated machine emulation applications.

Additional Addressing Modes

The 68020 provides six additional addressing modes besides the 12 that already exist for the 68000. These new addressing modes form two groups of three. The operation of the two groups is very similar. The first group extends the 68000's address register indirect with index mode. The second group extends the 68000's program counter with index. You will recall from Chapter 6 that these two modes are quite similar. The program counter with index mode functions exactly like the address register indirect with index, with the address register being replaced with the program counter.

For these two basic 68000 modes, the effective address is computed by taking the address register or program counter and adding the contents of either the full 32 bits of a general register or the sign-extended low-order word of a general register. To this intermediate result the sign-extended value of an 8-bit displacement is added. This final result is used as the address of the operand. In assembler, these modes were written as d_8(An,Rn.<size>) and d_8(PC,Rn.<size>), with <size> either W or L. Along with the new 68020 addressing modes, Motorola introduced a slightly different assembler syntax for these addressing modes as well as for the new ones. You will have to check your 68020 assembler manual to find out the syntax required of your own assembler. The new syntax for these 68000 addressing modes is (d_8,An,Rn.<size>*<scale>) and (d_8,PC,Rn.<size>*<scale>). As you can see, these are very minor changes. <scale> is an optional scale factor that is available with the 68020. It can be 1, 2, 4, or 8. If the scale factor is present, it is used to multiply the value in the index register Rn. This makes indexing into word and longword arrays much easier. For example, a scale factor of 4 would be used to access an array of longwords. Let's say we want to access the 25th entry of a longword array pointed to by A0. We can do it with the following instructions:

```
MOVE.W  #24,D0
MOVE.L  (0,A0,D0.W*4),D1
```

Remember, the first entry in the array will be at offset zero.

The first really new addressing mode on the 68020 is almost like the address register indirect with index. The difference is that an optional sign-extended 16- or 32-bit displacement, rather than an 8-bit displacement, is allowed. In fact, the address and index registers are also optional. Two versions of this mode are available, one for use with an address register and one for use with the program counter. These addressing modes have the following assembler formats:

```
(bd,An,Rn.<size>*<scale>)
(bd,PC,Rn.<size>*<scale>)
```

As before, the optional scale factor can be 1, 2, 4, or 8. These addressing modes are formally known as address register indirect with index (base displacement) and PC register indirect with index (base displacement).

The second and third new modes are forms of memory indirect. The ultimate effective address of these modes is found by referencing the contents of a memory location. The value found there is actually an address. This may seem complicated, but it is actually quite simple. Without these addressing modes, in order to take an address from memory and use it to access the contents of the location it points to, we would first have to place the pointer in an address register and then use a register indirect mode. The new 68020 modes make this operation a thing of the past. Figure 17 shows the calculation of the effective address for the versions using an address register. The versions of these modes for use with the program counter are identical if the PC is substituted for the address register. In this case the memory address pointed to by the PC is that of the first extension word. The two versions of the addressing mode are very similar. The major difference is whether post-indexing or pre-indexing is used.

The assembler syntax for these forms are:

```
([bd,An],Rn.<size>*<scale>,od)   post-indexed
([bd,An,Rn.<size>*<scale>],od)   pre-indexed
([bd,PC],Rn.<size>*<scale>,od)   post-indexed
([bd,PC,Rn.<size>*<scale>],od)   pre-indexed
```

With the post-indexed versions, the memory location calculated by adding An or PC to bd is used as the memory indirect location. This is the memory location containing the pointer. The index register, appropriately scaled, is added to this pointer as well as the outer displacement, od. This final value is the effective address. With the pre-indexed versions the sequence is slightly modified. The location of the memory indirect pointer is determined by adding the address register or PC to the base displacement, bd, and the scaled index register. The outer displacement is added to the pointer to compute the final effective address. All four of the specified values are optional. This actually provides 16 different combinations.

Only the most advanced assembly language programmers will need these advanced addressing modes. However, the pre-indexed versions are especially useful when you have an array of pointers. You might keep this in mind as you start programming with the 68020.

Instruction Extensions

The extensions to existing instructions generally fall into two categories: increase in the size of allowable displacements, and increased functionality.

The 68020 allows a full 32-bit displacement to be used with the branch instructions BRA, BSR, and Bcc. Formally, the addressing range was restricted to a 16-bit displacement. This extension allows us to reach anywhere in memory with these instructions.

The CHK instruction will now operate with both word and longword sources. Recall that the CHK instruction checks the contents of an address register against a bound that is stored in the source operand. You must specify the size of the bound using the usual method of appending .W or .L to the instruction mnemonic.

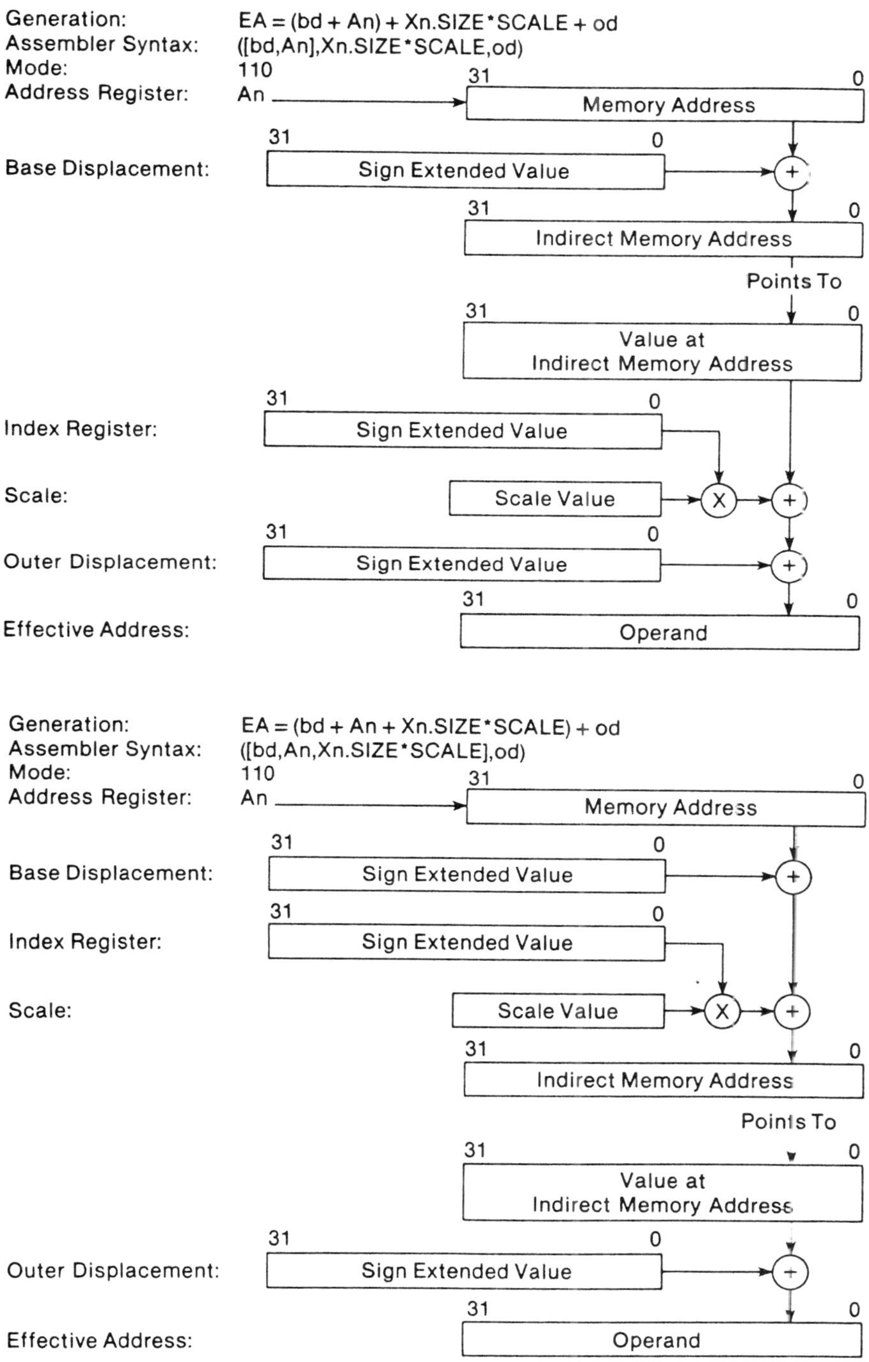

Figure 17 Effective address calculation. (Courtesy of Motorola, Inc.)

The CMPI and TST instructions now allow all of the PC relative addressing modes. However, this extension only applies when word or longword operands are used.

The divide and multiply instructions, DIV and MUL, have been greatly expanded. Recall that the four forms of these instructions were:

```
DIVU    <ea>,Dn
DIVS    <ea>,Dn
MULU    <ea>,Dn
MULS    <ea>,Dn
```

The divide instructions require a 16-bit source and 32-bit destination operand. The result is a 32-bit value consisting of a 16-bit quotient and a 16-bit remainder. The multiply instructions multiply two 16-bit operands, yielding a 32-bit result. The expanded divide instructions have the following forms:

```
DIVS.W  <ea>,Dn         DIVU.W  <ea>,Dn         32/16->16r:16q
DIVS.L  <ea>,Dq         DIVU.L  <ea>,Dq         32/32->32q
DIVS.L  <ea>,Dr:Dq      DIVU.L  <ea>,Dr:Dq      64/32->32r:32q
DIVSL.L <ea>,Dr:Dq      DIVUL.L <ea>,Dr:Dq      32/32->32r:32q
```

The operation of these instructions is relatively straightforward. The first form is the form found on the 68000. This is the default if no size is specified. The three extended forms vary in the sizes of the operands and/or the result. Notice that a register pair is required for operands/results that require more than 32 bits total. The notation Dr/Dq refers to the quotient and remainder registers. These can be any of the data registers.

The expanded multiply instructions have the following format:

```
MULS.W  <ea>,Dn         MULS.W  <ea>,Dn         16X16->32
MULS.L  <ea>,Dl         MULS.L  <ea>,Dl         32X32->32
MULS.L  <ea>,Dh:Dl      MULS.L  <ea>,Dh:Dl      32X32->64
```

The first form is the old 68000 form. In this case two 16-bit operands are multiplied to yield a 32-bit result. The expanded forms allow the multiplication of two 32-bit operands to yield either a 32-bit or a 64-bit result. In the case of a 64-bit result, Dh and Dl refer to the registers used to hold the high-and low-order 32 bits of the result.

The EXT instruction has been expanded. Recall that the EXT.W sign extends a byte to a word, and the EXT.L sign extends a word to a longword. In order to sign-extend a byte to a longword, both of these instructions had to be used. The 68020 allows a sign extension from byte to longword with a single instruction. A slightly different mnemonic has to be introduced. This is not really a different instruction, but an expanded form of EXT. The new instruction format is EXTB.L. This is the exact format that must be used. For example, to sign-extend the byte in D0, you would issue an EXTB.L D0 instruction.

The LINK instruction was formally restricted to use a sign-extended 16-bit displacement to offset the stack pointer. The 68020 allows a full 32-bit offset to be added to the stack pointer.

New Instructions

The 68020 has a relatively small number of totally new instructions. Since these instructions are fairly well spread out over the overall functionality of the 68020, I will cover them in alphabetical order.

Bit Field Instructions BFxxx The first new instruction is actually a group of instructions. They each manipulate a *bit field.* A bit field is a group of 1 to 32 contiguous bits in either a register or memory. The bit field is specified by a field width and offset. The assembler language format recommended by Motorola is {offset:width}. Offset can be an immediate value of 0 to 31 or a value in a data register. If a data register is used, it has a range of -2^{31} to $2^{31}-1$. The offset is the bit offset from the *high-order bit.* In other words, an offset of 0 specifies a bit field starting at bit number 31. Width can be an immediate value of 0 to 31 or a value in a data register. If a data register is used, the value is taken modulo 32. In either case, a value of 0 represents a field width of 32. The specific assembler syntax can vary, so be sure to check your assembler manual. This is especially important concerning whether an immediate field width of 32 is allowed and automatically converted to 0.

Here is a list of the bit field instructions and their functions:

```
BFCHG    <ea>{offset:width}      One's complement the bit field
BFCLR    <ea>{offset:width}      Clear the bit field
BFEXTS   <ea>{offset:width},Dn   Bit field->Dn, sign extended
BFEXTU   <ea>{offset:width},Dn   Bit field->Dn, zero extended
BFFFO    <ea>{offset:width},Dn   Search for first bit set, offset->Dn
BFINS    Dn,<ea>{offset:width}   Dn->bit field
BFSET    <ea>{offset:width}      Set all bits to one
BFTST    <ea>{offset:width}      Set N and Z conditions, treat the
                                 bit field as a signed number
```

Breakpoint Instruction BKPT The BKPT (breakpoint) instruction is provided for use by debuggers and hardware emulators. In order for this instruction to be used, external hardware is required. When the BKPT instruction is executed, a special bus cycle is executed. The BKPT instruction has a single immediate mode operand. This operand is placed on address line A2–A4. The immediate value must be in the range 0–7. If external hardware is present, it can respond with an instruction word on the data lines that is executed in place of the BKPT. If the external hardware is not present, this instruction generates an illegal instruction exception.

CALLM/RTM The CALLM (call module) and RTM (return from module) instructions are used to support the 68020 concept of a *module*. A module is very similar to a subroutine except that it can be granted access rights that may be more extensive than those of the program calling the module. Access rights pertain to what portions of memory can be accessed. Since input/output devices on the 68000 family are memory-mapped, access to those areas of memory are necessary to perform I/O. The 68020 doesn't have the necessary hardware on the chip to fully support access rights. External hardware is needed to work along with the module concept for this to work.

Access rights are intimately tied in with the concept of address spaces. In Chapter 13 I discussed the concepts of address spaces and the use of the three function code lines. The decoding of these lines for the 68020 is as follows:

FC2	FC1	FC0	Reference Class
0	0	0	(Undefined, Reserved)
0	0	1	User Data Space
0	1	0	User Program Space
0	1	1	(Undefined, Reserved)
1	0	0	(Undefined, Reserved)
1	0	1	Supervisor Data Space
1	1	0	Supervisor Program Space
1	1	1	CPU Space

This mechanism provides a minimal number of access levels, primarily those offered by the supervisor or user modes. The module support allows the external hardware to implement a much larger number of access levels. An 8-bit access level number is associated with each module. The external hardware can be designed to interpret this access value any way it wants. When a module is called, a request can be made to change the current access level. This mechanism is rather complicated, and since it requires external hardware that doesn't exist in a general form, I will present a brief description of its operation. To use the module support feature, you will need to find out the exact details of the external hardware your system is providing.

The CALLM instruction has the following general form:

```
CALLM    #<data>,<ea>
```

<ea> is the address of an external module descriptor. <data> is an

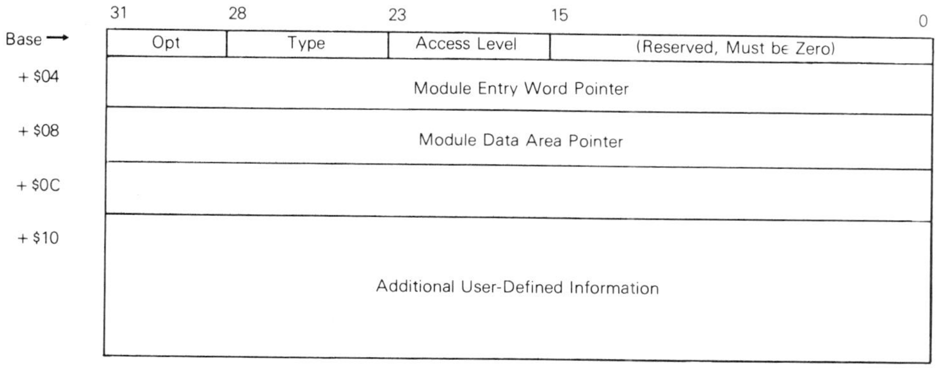

Figure 18 Module descriptor format. (Courtesy of Motorola, Inc.)

immediate operand specifying the number of arguments being passed to the module. These arguments are passed on the stack. Before the CALLM is executed, they must be pushed on the stack. Figure 18 shows the layout of a module descriptor. The OPT field is restricted to two values: 000 indicates that arguments are passed on the stack, 100 indicates that a pointer to the arguments will be provided on the stack. Only two values for the type field are used: 00 indicates that no change in access level is desired, 01 indicates that there may be a change in access rights. If type 01 is indicated, the called module is allowed to have a stack area that is independent of the caller's stack.

The access level field is passed to the external hardware to provide information for a possible change in access rights. The module data area pointer contains the address of the called module's data area. This is normally the value that will be loaded into the stack pointer. The module entry word pointer is the address of the module's entry word. This is a special word that precedes the first instruction of the module. Figure 19 show the layout of this word. It merely specifies an address or data register to be loaded with the module's data area pointer. Before the register is loaded, it is saved on the call stack. If this register is SP, the effect is that the module data pointer is ignored. This is because SP is overwritten with a new value following the execution of the CALLM. Figure 20 shows the module call stack frame.

The RTM instruction has the following form:

```
RTM     Rn
```

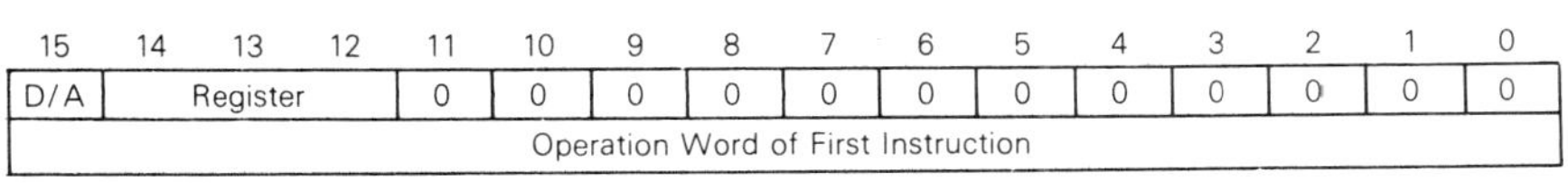

Figure 19 Module entry word. (Courtesy of Motorola, Inc.)

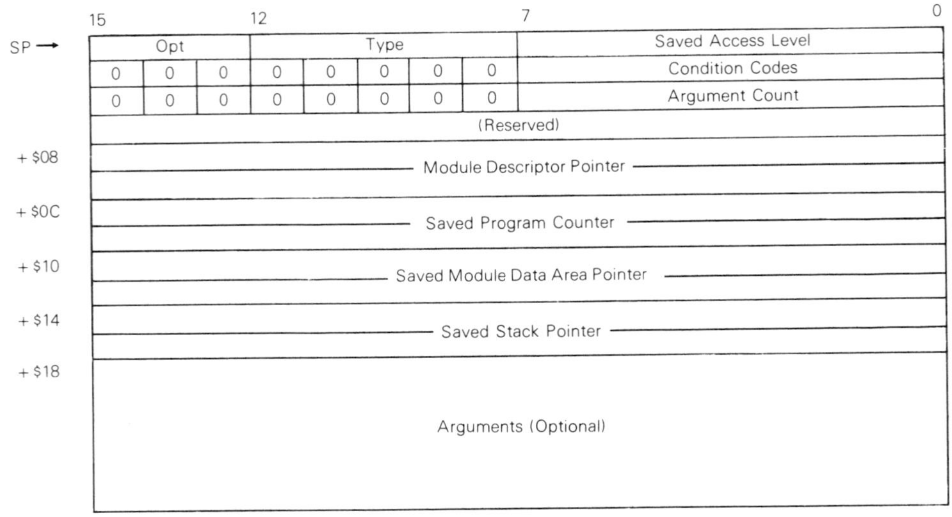

Figure 20 **Module call stack frame. (Courtesy of Motorola, Inc.)**

Rn specifies the register to beloaded with the saved module's data pointer obtained from the stack. If SP is specified, this restored value is overwritten by the updated value of SP. Rn would normally be chosen to match the register specified by the module entry word. A nice feature of the RTM is that it increments the stack pointer by the number of arguments that were specified in the CALLM.

CAS and CAS2 The 68020 provides two new instructions that are extensions to the mechanism provided by the test and set instruction, TAS. Before you continue, it would be a good idea to review the TAS instruction covered in Chapter 12. The TAS instruction only provides a binary-type operation on a lock—in other words, the lock is set or it isn't. The compare and swap with operand instructions, CAS and CAS2, have a much greater functionality. Their general forms are:

```
CAS     Dc,Du,<ea>
CAS2    DC1:Dc2,Du1:Du2,(Rn1):(Rn2)
```

Dc and Du represent the compare and update registers. The CAS instruction first compares Dc and <ea>. If they are equal, the contents of Du is placed in <ea>. If they are not equal, the contents of <ea> is copied to register Dc. If you think about it, this is actually a test and set type of operation. The entire operation is performed in an atomic fashion—no other processor or interrupt routine can execute bus cycles while this instruction is executing. A typical application of the CAS instruction would be the implementation of a counting semaphore. What we want to be able to do is to increment the value of a semaphore in such a manner that no other process or interrupt routine interferes. Here is how we would use the CAS instruction:

```
          MOVE.W   SEM,D0
LOOP:     MOVE.W   D0,D1
          ADDQ.W   #1,D1
          CAS.W    D0,D1,SEM
          BNE      LOOP
```

The CAS2 instruction operates in a similar manner to the CAS except that it has additional operands, and two compares are performed instead of just one. Both comparisons must show a match for the update registers to be stored in the destination addresses. The destination addresses must be specified using register indirect addressing with either a data register or an address register. If one or both of the compares fails, the destination operands are copied to the compare registers just as in the case of the CAS. The CAS instruction allows byte, word and longword operations. The CAS2 is restricted only to word or longword operations.

CHK2 The CHK2 instruction is an extended version of the CHK instruction. CHK2 will check a data value in either a data register or an address register against a pair of bounds. The general form of this instruction is:

```
CHK2[.<size>]    <ea>,Rn

<size> = B, W, L
```

The effective address must be to a pair of memory operands. The first is the lower bound. It is a byte, word, or longword. The second is the upper bound. This is located at the next byte, word, or longword in memory above the lower bound. If the register, Rn, is less than the lower bound or greater than the upper bound, an exception is generated. The exception vector is the same as for the CHK instruction. The CHK2 instruction can be used for both signed and unsigned operands.

CMP2 The CMP2 instruction is very similar to the CHK2 instruction. It has the same general form:

```
CMP2[.<size>]    <ea>,Rn

<size> = B, W, L
```

The operands are identical to the CHK2 instruction. The difference is that this instruction does not generate an exception if the register is out of bounds; instead, the condition codes are used to indicate the success or failure of the operation. The carry condition is set if the register value is out of bounds. The zero condition is set if the register value is equal to either the upper or lower bound. Here is how to test for whether the value in register D0 is greater than 100 or less than −100:

```
          CMP2.L   BOUNDS,D0
            .
            .
BOUNDS:   DC.L     -100,100
```

Coprocessor Support Instructions The 68020 provides direct coprocessor support. A coprocessor is a special purpose chip that operates in conjunction with the main CPU chip to provide additional features not available on the main CPU. Examples of coprocessors for the 68000 family are the MC68881 floating point arithmetic coprocessor and the MC68851 paged memory management unit. Each coprocessor has a set of instructions that are unique to it. If a particular coprocessor is present in your system, the 68020 allows you to write the coprocessor instructions directly.

Without presenting the details of specific coprocessors it is not possible to present specific coprocessor instructions. However, all coprocessor instructions for the 68020 fall into specific types. Here is a brief list of the 68020 coprocessor support instructions.

```
cpBcc      <label>       Branch on Coprocessor Condition
cpDBcc     Dn,<label>    Test Coprocessor Condition Decrement
                         and Branch
cpGEN      <params>      Coprocessor General Function
cpRESTORE  <ea>          Coprocessor Restore Functions
cpSAVE     <ea>          Coprocessor Save Function
cpScc      <ea>          Set on Coprocessor Condition
cpTRAPcc   [#<data>]     Trap on Coprocessor Condition
```

You will have to consult the appropriate coprocessor manual to obtain the specific information you will need to program the coprocessor.

PACK and UNPK In decimal arithmetic, discussed in Chapter 11, a decimal number is represented as two binary-coded decimal (BCD) digits per byte. In order to perform BCD arithmetic, we had to convert ASCII digits to BCD digits and pack two of them in each byte, and perform the reverse operation on output. The PACK and UNPK instructions will perform these operations for us. PACK has the following two general forms:

```
PACK    -(Ax),-(Ay),#<adjustment>
PACK    Dx,Dy,#<adjustment>
```

<adjustment> is a 16-bit value. Both forms of this instruction take two bytes, either from memory using predecrement addressing or from the low-order 16 bits of the register, and add the adjustment. The resulting 16-bit value is packed into a single byte. This is done by taking the low-order four bits from each of the two bytes and concatenating. The adjustment can be used to convert the data from ASCII, or some other character code, to BCD representation. If a negated value is used for the adjustment, it will effectively be subtracted from the two digits. For ASCII conversion we would form an adjustment such that the ASCII code for the character 0 is subtracted from each byte. Here is how we would write a PACK instruction to do this, assuming that the data is referenced by A0 and placed in a byte pointed to by A1.

```
PACK     -(A0),-(A1),#-$3030
```

UNPK has the following identical general forms:

```
UNPK     -(Ax),-(Ay),#<adjustment>
UNPK     Dx,Dy,#<adjustment>
```

UNPK simply reverses what a PACK does. A packed BCD byte is obtained from the source operand. It is then unpacked to two bytes. The adjustment is added in and the final result stored in the two bytes of the destination. The following instruction performs this conversion for ASCII output:

```
UNPK     -(A0),-(A1),#$3030
```

TRAPcc The TRAPcc instruction is very similar to the TRAP instruction except that it conditionally generates the exception. The characters cc in the instruction mnemonic can be any of the conditions used with the Bcc or Scc instructions. They are:

```
CC carry clear            LS low or same
CS carry set              LT less than
EQ equal                  MI minus
 F false                  NE notequal
GE greater or equal       PL plus
GT greater than            T true
HI high                   VC overflow clear
LE less or equal          VS overflow set
```

There are three general forms for the TRAPcc instruction:

```
TRAPcc
TRAPcc.W         #<data>
TRAPcc.L         #<data>
```

If either a word or longword operand is specified, this immediate operand is placed in one or two extension words immediately following the instruction word. The operand can be used to pass an argument to the trap handler. Exception vector 7 is used for this instruction. It is the same exception vector that is used by the TRAPV instruction discussed in Chapter 12.

Exercises

1. What is the width of the 68020's address bus?
2. What data bus sizes can be accommodated by the 68020?
3. Can a 68020 be plugged in in place of a 68000?

4. Can word or longword data begin on an odd address boundary when using the 68020?
5. What is the purpose of an instruction cache?
6. How large is the instruction cache on the 68020?
7. What is the size of the entries in the 68020 instruction cache?
8. What new registers are provided for control of the 68020 instruction cache?
9. Why is it necessary to clear the cache when the contents of program memory is changed?
10. What is purpose of the optional scale factor for the 68020's address register indirect with index addressing mode?
11. What are the allowed values for the scale factor?
12. What is the proper form for the 68020 address register indirect with index (base displacement) addressing mode?
13. For the above addressing mode, are any elements optional? If so, which?
14. What is memory indirect addressing?
15. What size displacement is allowed with the 68020 branch instructions?
16. What extensions are made to multiplication and division instructions with the 68020?
17. Write the 68020 instruction to sign-extend a byte in D0 to a full longword.
18. With the 68020 bit field instructions, how large can the bit field be?
19. Where can a bit field be located?
20. What is a 68020 *module?*
21. What new 68020 instructions support modules?
22. What new 68020 instructions expand the capabilities of the 68000's TAS instruction?
23. Write the 68020 instructions necessary to compare register D0 to determine if it is greater than 20 and less than 75. Branch to ERROR if it is not.
24. What is the normal purpose of the PACK and UNPK instructions?
25. Write an instruction to generate exception 7 if the negative condition is set.

Answers

1. A full 32 bits.
2. 8, 16, and 32.
3. No, it is physically impossible.
4. Yes, the 68000 even-byte restriction does not apply to the 68020.
5. An instruction cache is used to store a number of instructions inside the CPU in order to speed up the execution of loops.

6. 256 bytes.
7. 32 bits.
8. The cache control register, CACR, and the cache address register, CAAR.
9. The cache must be cleared so that it doesn't contain instructions that do not match the actual contents of memory.
10. It makes indexing into arrays much easier.
11. 1, 2, 4, or 8.
12. (bd,An,Rn.<size>*<scale>)
13. Any element is optional.
14. The 68020 addressing modes that use the contents of a memory location as the address of the actual data.
15. A full 32-bit displacement.
16. Various combinations of 16-, 32-, and 64-bit operands are allowed.

17.
```
        EXTB.L DO
```

18. A bit field must be 32 bits or less.
19. In a register or memory.
20. A section of code similar to a subroutine that can be granted access rights.
21. The CALLM (call module) and the RTM (return from module) instructions.
22. The compare and swap instructions CAS and CAS2.

23.
```
                CMP2.L   BOUNDS,D0
                BCC      ERROR
                  .
                  .
        BOUNDS:          DC.L     21,74
```

24. To convert to and from ASCII and BCD.

25.
```
        TRAPMI
```

CHAPTER 15

THE 68030

In the latter part of 1986 Motorola announced its latest member of the 68000 family, the MC68030. This new super chip should be in full production during 1987. This second-generation 32-bit microprocessor is actually a combination of an enhanced MC68020 and a subset of the MC68851 paged memory management unit. The combination really gives awesome capability to one single tiny chip.

Programming the 68030 will be no different from programming the 68020 unless you are involved with the PMMU (paged memory management unit) portion of the chip. In that case, you would need to know the details of the MC68851 coprocessor subset. I will not present all these details; rather, I will give an introduction to the concepts of memory management so that you can read the manufacturer's documentation on the 68030 or 68851 with less difficulty. At the time of this writing only preliminary documentation on the 68030 was available. The information presented here is as accurate as possible with this preliminary documentation.

The 68030 operates at 20 MHz, compared to a top speed of 16.7 MHz for the 68020. However, the 68030 actually has an effective speed which is twice that of the 68020. This is accomplished by a combination of data and instruction caches and a pipelined architecture. You will recall from Chapter 14 that the 68020 has an instruction cache. Its purpose is to reduce the access time to instructions in memory. It is most effective for program loops that are small enough to be entirely contained in the cache. The operation of the instruction cache in the 68030 is similar to that of the instruction cache in the 68020. However, the addition of a data cache allows a greater improvement in speed. Both the instruction cache and the data cache are 256 bytes. Figure 21 shows the block diagram of the 68030. You will notice that there are two internal address and data buses. This duplication allows simultaneous access to the instruction and data caches.

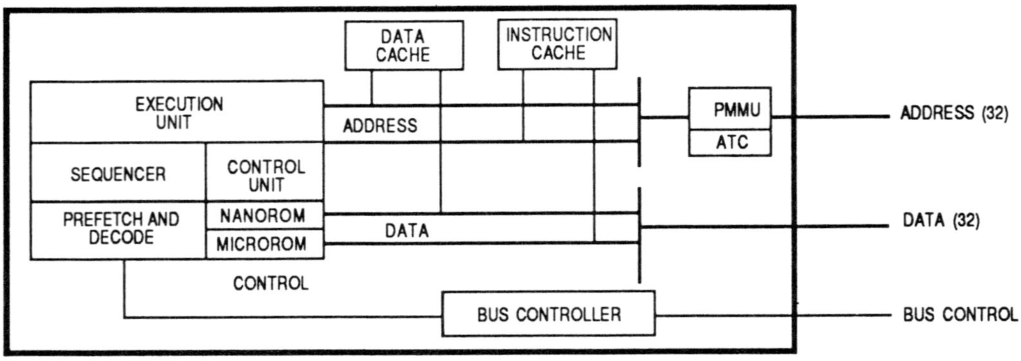

Figure 21 68030 Block diagram. (Courtesy of Motorola, Inc.)

Instruction and Data Caches

Figure 22 shows the organization of the 68030 data cache. The cache consists of 16 entries. Each entry contains four longwords. A valid bit is provided for each of these four longwords. If the valid bit is set, it indicates that the data in the cache entry is valid for access. A reference to this longword by a program would then obtain it from the cache rather than from the physical memory. The organization of the instruction cache is identical. These cache organizations differ slightly from the 68020. The 68020 instruction cache consists of 64 longword entries. This yields a cache of the same size, but with a different organization. Studies that Motorola performed have indicated that the organization used with the 68030 has a better performance.

A problem exists with a data cache that doesn't exist with an instruction cache. Since an assumption is made that the instructions of a program can never be modified by the program itself, the information contained in the instruction cache never has to be written back to memory. No such assumption can be made about data. In fact, a program that didn't modify any memory locations containing data would be highly unlikely. Since the stack can contain data, the memory occupied by the stack falls into this category. If we allow the data contained in the data cache to be modified, we must take steps to assure that the actual memory location is modified as well.

A number of techniques exist to make sure that cache contents and memory contents are updated correctly. One method is to modify only the contents of the cache when a write operation is issued. As long as the entry remains in the cache, subsequent reads will have the correct results. If an entry is replaced in the cache, the updated data can be written to physical memory at that time. An alternate approach is to update the contents of physical memory as soon as a write is issued. This means that

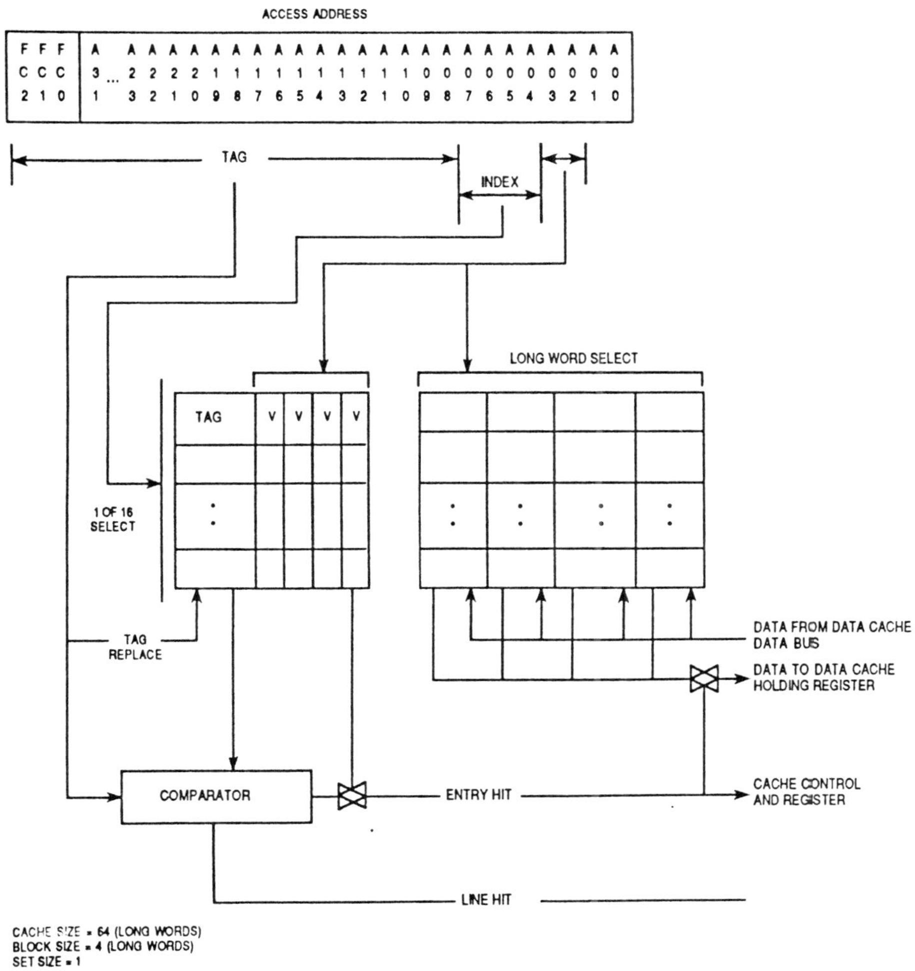

Figure 22 68030 Data Cache. (Courtesy of Motorola, Inc.)

we update both the cache and the physical memory for each write to an address contained in the cache. This latter technique is called a *write through*.

The first technique has the advantage that fewer writes to physical memory are needed if the data in the cache is updated more than once. Only one physical update is needed for many cache updates. The disadvantage is that considerably more complex hardware is required. The processor must keep track of which addresses in the cache have been modified. The write through cache is a simpler design. Since the normal programming method is to use registers for counters and addressing inside loops, the penalty for the write through cache is not as great as one might think.

Pipelined Architecture

Pipelining is a technique used on high performance CPU's such as mainframes. With pipelining, the CPU can execute operations for several instructions in parallel. Instructions are fed into a prefetch queue or pipe. The 68030 contains an instruction pipe capable of holding three 16-bit values. These three words can represent from one to three complete instructions. The 68030 has three independent arithmetic logic units (ALU's). These are used to calculate instruction addresses and operand addresses, and to perform data operations. In combination with the instruction pipe, these three ALU's allow concurrent operations to be performed. Arithmetic operations are not always performed concurrently, but when possible they are. The CPU does this automatically, with the end result of a faster overall operating speed. The more concurrency the better. The fact that the instruction and data caches allow additional concurrency adds to this effective speed even more.

Paged Memory Management

As Figure 21 showed, the PMMU is added in between the internal address buses and the external address bus. If the PMMU is not activated on the 68030, the physical addressing is identical to the 68020. The address bus is a 32-bit bus. This allows direct access to 4 gigabytes of physical memory. This is truly an enormous amount of memory by today's megabyte standards. However, consider that a 68030 processor might support many users simultaneously, that we might actually have substantially less than the maximum permitted memory, and that this memory would have to be divided up among these users. The more users, the less actual physical memory is available to each user. The only way to allow a user to seemingly occupy more memory than is actually available is to implement a *virtual memory*, briefly discussed in Chapter 13. It is possible to implement a virtual memory with either the 68010 or the 68020. However, they would both require external hardware. The PMMU of the 68030 gives us a built-in capability for a virtual memory.

The 68030 PMMU implements a rather sophisticated version of paging. Before we discuss the specifics of the 68030, let's take a look at how a basic paging mechanism works. Paging divides the virtual or logical address space into equal size blocks called pages (Chapter 13). We do the same for the physical memory. Each page in the logical address space is mapped to a corresponding page frame in the physical address space. Each byte in the page corresponds to the same byte in the physical page frame. This requires that pages and page frames be the same size. It is customary for the page size to be a power of 2. This makes it easy to take a binary logical address and partition it into a page number and an offset within the page.

Logical Address (example)

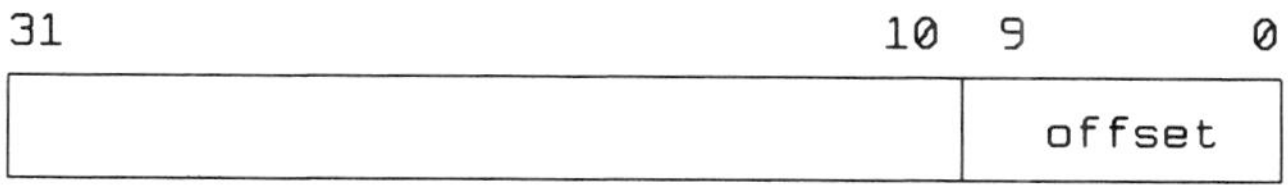

Since addresses on the 68030 are all 32 bits, we can divide the logical address into two pieces as long as the sizes add up to 32. For example, if we desire pages to be 1K (1024 bytes), the offset requires 10 bits, leaving 22 bits for the page number. Therefore, there would be 2^{22} pages, each 1024 bytes long.

How do we then map the pages into the corresponding physical page frames? Also, what if all the pages are not currently in memory? When we implement a virtual memory, we store the pages that are not currently in memory on a secondary storage device such as a disk. The hardware must be aware of what pages are actually in physical memory at a given time. Both of these problems are solved by the use of a *page table*. A page table is simply a translation table. The physical frame number corresponding to a particular page can be found by looking it up in the page table. A simple organization of a page table is that of an array of frame numbers. The page number is used as an index into the array.

The problem of determining if a page is currently mapped to physical memory is solved by providing an extra bit with each page table entry. This bit can be set if the frame number is valid and reset if the page is not in memory. In the latter case, the frame number can be used to provide information to the operating system about where the page is located on secondary storage. The hardware doesn't handle this case. The hardware only handles the mapping of pages to physical memory. What the hardware does when it encounters a non-resident page is to generate a *page fault*. This page fault is detected by the operating system, the missing page is brought into memory, and the instruction that caused the page fault is allowed to continue. This time it will find the missing page. On the following page is an example of the first few entries of a page table. It is easy to see that page 0 is mapped to frame 23, page 1 is mapped to frame 12, and page 3 is not in memory.

While this scheme seems simple, the implementation is rather complex. For each memory reference, the CPU must determine what page is being referenced, find the proper entry in the page table, compute the actual physical address by adding the offset to the frame's location, and finally perform the memory access. Two subtle problems emerge when

	V	Frame no.
0	1	23
1	1	12
2	1	0
3	0	-
4	1	123
5		

some thought is given to this process. First, if the page table is located in memory, an extra memory reference must be made for each and every desired memory reference, thereby reducing effective memory speed by a factor of two. The second problem concerns the necessity of having a page table with as many entries as there are pages in the logical addressing space. If the number of possible pages is large, this table might not fit in memory, or at the very least it may be quite large. The 68030 solves both of these problems.

The problem of speed is normally solved by the use of a special set of registers variously known as associative registers, content addressable memory, transaction lookaside buffers, or an address translation cache. The 68030 implements an address translation cache (ATC). This ATC can hold 64 translations of page to frame. The operation of this cache is similar to the instruction and data caches except that current page table entries are stored in the cache. The time taken to access the information in the ATC is very much faster than a memory lookup. If it turns out that the majority of pages can be mapped by the cache, the effective speed of memory is not significantly compromised. This is generally the case due to what is known as *locality of reference*—in simple terms, a property of a program that results in references to only a small portion of its total addressing space over particular intervals of time. As the program advances, new addresses are referenced and old addresses are abandoned. The current set of pages a program is referencing is known as its *working set.* A large amount of theoretical work has been done in investigating locality of reference. Suffice it to say that it works, and an ATC can be tremendously effective.

The 68030 handles the problem of large page tables by allowing the use of a tree-structured page table. Only a portion of the tree structure need be in memory at a particular time. The operating system can handle moving the portions of the tree structure between main memory and the disk. (In the following discussion of the details of these tree-structured tables, Motorola's terms for the entries of a page table, *translation descriptors*, and for an individual table in the tree, *descriptor table*, are used.)

In order to implement the tree structure, the page number in the logical address can be divided up into from one to four sub-fields. In addition, the size of the total page number field can be specified. In essence, this feature allows reducing the size of the logical address space to less than 32 bits. If there is only one field present, the value of this field specifies the actual page number. It is used as an index into the descriptor table to obtain the translation descriptor. In this case there is only one descriptor table. If two fields are present, the value in the first field is used to determine the location of the descriptor table to be used for the second field. This is done by indexing into the first descriptor table by the field value. The descriptor at this index does not correspond to a page translation but rather to the location of the second-level descriptor table. The value in the second field is used to index into the second-level descriptor table. This operation can be repeated for up to four levels if all four fields are present.

This is the general form of the logical address:

31					0
I	A	B	C	D	OFFSET

The I field is the *initial shift* field and is essentially the portion of the logical address to be ignored. This field can range from 0 to 15 bits. The A field must always be present. It can range from 1 to 15 bits, and specifies the first level of address translation. If fields B, C, and D are absent, the A field specifies particular pages. Fields B, C, and D can each range from 0 to 15. They must be present in increasing alphabetical order—in other words, if field D is present, then fields A, B, and C must also be present. The widths of all the fields present must add up to 32: I+A+B+C+D+OFFSET=32. The size of the OFFSET field determines the page size. All of these field sizes are set by values contained in the translation control register, TC.

Let's look at a simple example. Assume that the first field of the page number, A, is 2 bits. This means that it can specify four items. Furthermore, assume that a second field, B, is present and that it is 3 bits long. If there are only two fields present, the first field specifies four descriptor tables and the second field specifies eight pages. This means there are 32 pages in the virtual addressing space. Figure 23 shows how this particular tree would look. Not all of the descriptor tables or pages have to be in memory at the same time. If a reference is made to a

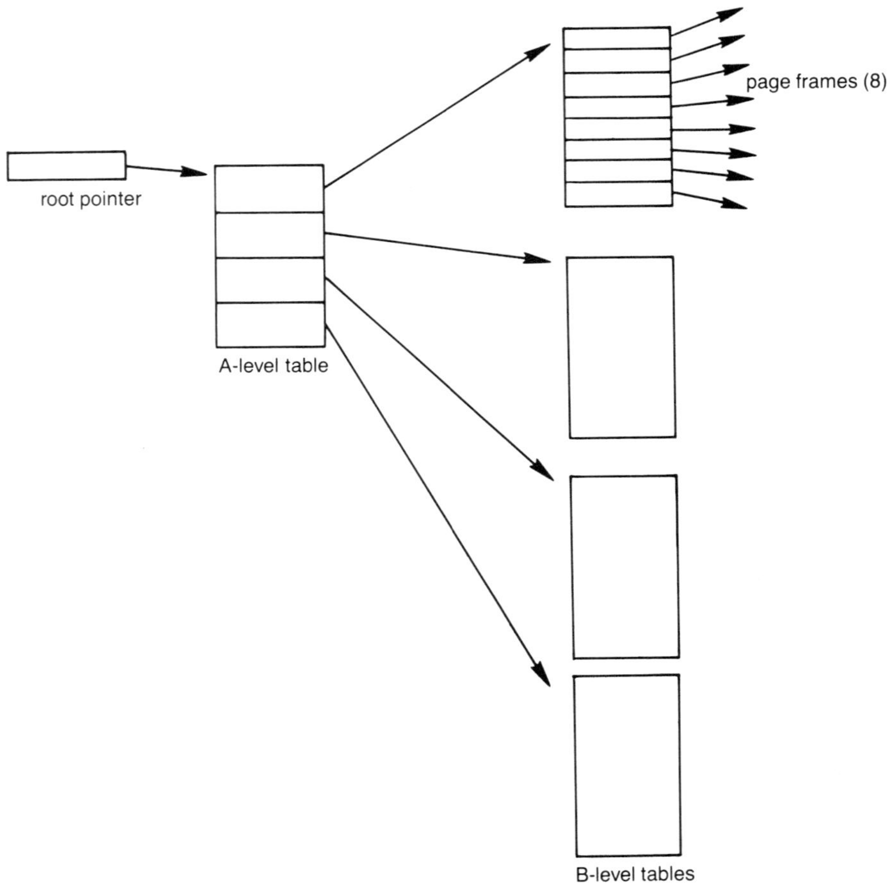

Figure 23 Example address translation tree.

non-existent table or page, the operating system will get control by an exception and can handle the situation.

In order to perform an address translation from the logical address to the physical address, we must know the location of the address translation tree in physical memory. In other words, we must have a starting point to apply the translation specified by a particular logical address. The 68030 allows us to have two distinct translation trees active at one time. Two CPU registers specify the location of these two trees. Refer to Figure 24. The CPU root pointer, CRP, is the pointer normally used for all references. The supervisor root pointer, SRP, can be set up to cause all supervisor mode references to use a different translation tree. The use of the SRP can be turned on and off by a special bit, SRE, in the translation control register, TC.

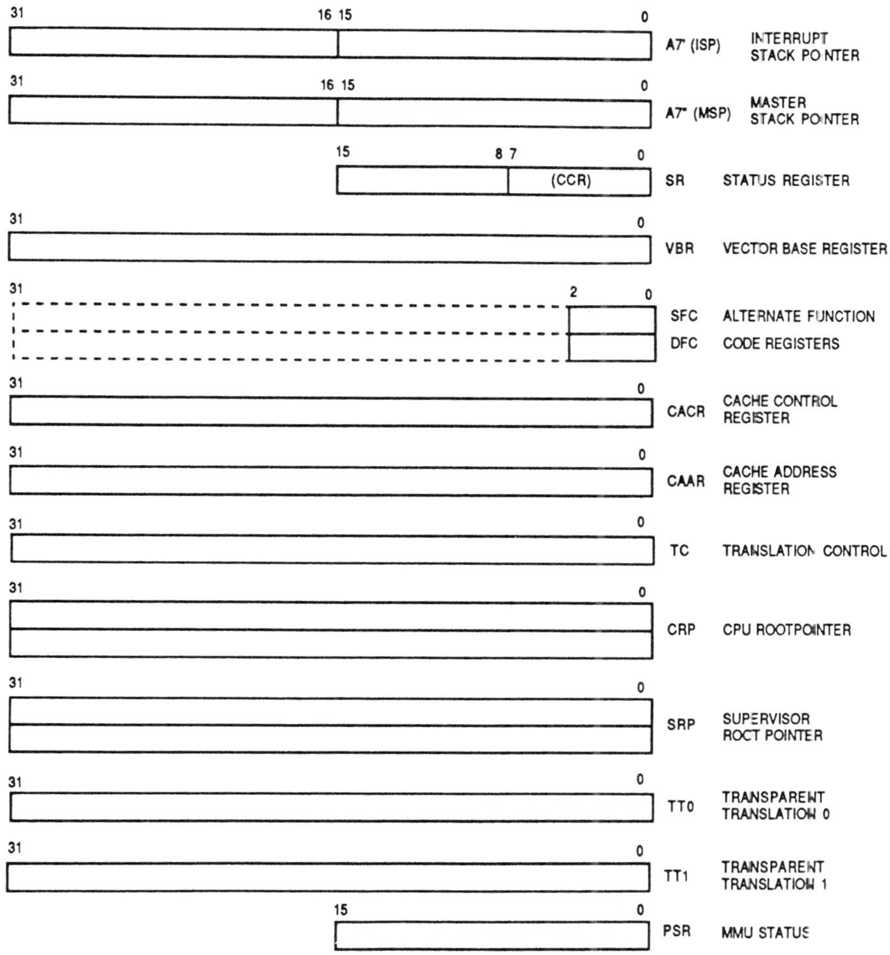

Figure 24 Supervisor Programming Model Supplement. (Courtesy of Motorola, Inc.)

68030 Instructions

The 68030 executes all of the instructions of the 68020 plus a handful of additional instructions needed to manage the PMMU. These instructions are a subset of the coprocessor instructions of the 68851. These are briefly summarized below:

PTEST Takes a virtual address and searches the ATC or the translation tree for the corresponding entry. The PMMU status register, PSR, is set according to the results of the search.

PLOAD	Takes a virtual address and searches the translation tree for the corresponding page descriptor entry. The ATC is then loaded with this entry.
PFLUSH	Flushes the ATC by function code, or function code and logical address. This instruction is used when a translation tree or table is changed in order to ensure that false information is not retained in the ATC.
PFLUSHA	Similar to PFLUSH except that *all* ATC entries are flushed.

Even after this brief introduction to the powerful 68030, I am sure you can see that this microprocessor is destined to become a dominant influence on future system designs. One can't help but wonder what a 68040 or 68050 might look like.

Exercises

1. Other than an enhanced 68020 core, what major feature does the 68030 have?
2. How much faster is the 68030 than the 68020?
3. How large are the instruction and data caches in the 68030?
4. What method is used by the 68030 to keep the contents of memory consistent with the data cache?
5. How many arithmetic logic Units (ALU'S) does the 68030 have?
6. What is pipelining?
7. How large is the 68030's instruction pipe?
8. What type of virtual memory does the 68030 PMMU implement?
9. What does a logical address consist of?
10. What is a frame?
11. What actions take place upon the occurrence of a page fault?
12. How are logical-to-physical addresses mapped?
13. What is the function of an address translation cache, ATC?
14. How many translations can the 68030 ATC hold?
15. What is locality of reference?
16. What is a working set?
17. What does Motorola call the entries of a page table?
18. What is the overall structure of the 68030's page table?
19. How many levels can there be to the descriptor tables?
20. How is the address translation tree located by the CPU?

Answers

1. A built-in capability for paged memory management.
2. About twice as fast.

3. Each cache is 256 bytes.
4. A write-through is used. Whenever a data location is modified in the cache, it is also modified in the corresponding memory location.
5. Three.
6. Pipelining is a technique that allows more than one instruction to be executing at a time.
7. The 68030 instruction pipe is three words long.
8. The 68030 PMMU implements a sophisticated version of paging.
9. A logical address consists of a page number and an offset into the page.
10. A frame is a unit of the physical memory that corresponds in size to a page in the logical address space. A frame can be used to hold any page.
11. An exception is generated so that the operating system can find the missing page on secondary storage, bring it into memory, and then allow the program to continue.
12. The page number is used as an index into a page table where the actual physical location (frame) of the page is found.
13. The ATC is used to speed up the process of page mapping by keeping current mappings in fast internal associative memory.
14. The ATC can hold 64 mappings.
15. Locality of reference is the property of a program that results in references to only a small portion of its total addressing space over particular intervals of time.
16. A working set is the set of pages a program is currently referencing. This is normally a subset of the total number of pages. The working set slowly changes as the program advances.
17. Translation descriptors.
18. A rooted tree.
19. Four.
20. By use of the CPU root pointer, CRP, or the supervisor root pointer, SRP. These are registers available in supervisor mode only.

APPENDIX A

ASCII CHARACTER CODES

Decimal	Octal	Hex	ASCII	Decimal	Octal	Hex	ASCII
0	000	00	NUL	32	040	20	SP
1	001	01	SOH	33	041	21	!
2	002	02	STX	34	042	22	"
3	003	03	ETX	35	043	23	#
4	004	04	EOT	36	044	24	$
5	005	05	ENQ	37	045	25	%
6	006	06	ACK	38	046	26	&
7	007	07	BEL	39	047	27	'
8	010	08	BS	40	050	28	(
9	011	09	HT	41	051	29	)
10	012	0A	LF	42	052	2A	*
11	013	0B	VT	43	053	2B	+
12	014	0C	FF	44	054	2C	,
13	015	0D	CR	45	055	2D	-
14	016	0E	SO	46	056	2E	.
15	017	0F	SI	47	057	2F	/
16	020	10	DLE	48	060	30	0
17	021	11	DC1	49	061	31	1
18	022	12	DC2	50	062	32	2
19	023	13	DC3	51	063	33	3
20	024	14	DC4	52	064	34	4
21	025	15	NAK	53	065	35	5
22	026	16	SYN	54	066	36	6
23	027	17	ETB	55	067	37	7
24	030	18	CAN	56	070	38	8
25	031	19	EM	57	071	39	9
26	032	1A	SUB	58	072	3A	:
27	033	1B	ESC	59	073	3B	;
28	034	1C	FS	60	074	3C	<
29	035	1D	GS	61	075	3D	=
30	036	1E	RS	62	076	3E	>
31	037	1F	US	63	077	3F	?

Decimal	Octal	Hex	ASCII	Decimal	Octal	Hex	ASCII
64	100	40	@	96	140	60	`
65	101	41	A	97	141	61	a
66	102	42	B	98	142	62	b
67	103	43	C	99	143	63	c
68	104	44	D	100	144	64	d
69	105	45	E	101	145	65	e
70	106	46	F	102	146	66	f
71	107	47	G	103	147	67	g
72	110	48	H	104	150	68	h
73	111	49	I	105	151	69	i
74	112	4A	J	106	152	6A	j
75	113	4B	K	107	153	6B	k
76	114	4C	L	108	154	6C	l
77	115	4D	M	109	155	6D	m
78	116	4E	N	110	156	6E	n
79	117	4F	O	111	157	6F	o
80	120	50	P	112	160	70	p
81	121	51	Q	113	161	71	q
82	122	52	R	114	162	72	r
83	123	53	S	115	163	73	s
84	124	54	T	116	164	74	t
85	125	55	U	117	165	75	u
86	126	56	V	118	166	76	v
87	127	57	W	119	167	77	w
88	130	58	X	120	170	78	x
89	131	59	Y	121	171	79	y
90	132	5A	Z	122	172	7A	z
91	133	5B	[	123	173	7B	{
92	134	5C		124	174	7C	|
93	135	5D	]	125	175	7D	}
94	136	5E	^	126	176	7E	~
95	137	5F	—	127	177	7F	DEL

APPENDIX B

PROGRAM SHELLS AND I/O SUBROUTINES

```
*************************************************************
* Shell for the Atari ST computers.
*
*************************************************************
*
        text
*
* Your program goes here
*
*
*       <PROGRAM>
*
*
*
* Return to system.
*
fini:   move.w  #0,-(sp)
        trap    #1
*
* Subroutines
*
putc:   movem.l d0-d7/a0-a6,-(sp)       save regs.
        andi.l  #$ff,d0                 make sure we have only a byte
        move.w  d0,-(sp)                push arg. on stack
        move.w  #2,-(sp)                dos function 2
        trap    #1                      trap to dos
        addq.l  #4,sp                   clean up stack
        movem.l (sp)+,d0-d7/a0-a6       restore regs.
        rts                             return
*
getc:   movem.l d1-d7/a0-a6,-(sp)       save regs.
        move.w  #1,-(sp)                dos function 1
        trap    #1                      trap to dos
        andi.l  #$7f,d0                 mask to 7 bits
        addq.l  #2,sp                   clean up stack
        movem.l (sp)+,d1-d7/a0-a6       restore regs.
        rts                             return
*
* The following subroutine to input a decimal number accumulates
* the number by multiplying the partially accumulated number by ten
* and adding in the current digit.  A double precision multiply is
* performed to allow a full 32 bit number to be entered.
*
indec:  movem.l d1-d2,-(sp)             save registers
        clr.l   d1                      initialize number to zero
indec0: jsr     getc                    get a character
        subi.b  #'0',d0                 make ascii into digit
        blt     indec1                  terminate if not a digit
        cmp.b   #9,d0                   not a digit i > 9
        bgt     indec1                  also terminate if so
        move.w  d1,d2                   save low order word of number
        clr.w   d1                      clear low order word
        swap    d1                      move high word to low word
        mulu    #10,d1                  multiply by ten
        swap    d1                      put result back in high word
        mulu    #10,d2                  multiply low order word of number by ten
        add.l   d2,d1                   add low order word to high order word
        add.l   d0,d1                   add in the current digit
        bra     indec0                  get another digit
indec1: move.l  d1,d0                   move number into d0
```

```
        movem.l (sp)+,d1-d2              restore registers
        rts                              return
*
* The following subroutine to output a decimal number performs this
* operation by successively dividing the number by ten to pick off the
* digits.  These digits are pushed onto the stack.  When the number
* has been converted, the digits are popped from the stack and output.
* A double precision divide is needed to accommodate a 32 bit number.
*
outdec: movem.l d0-d3,-(sp)              save reg. values
        move.w  #-1,-(sp)                push -1 onto stack
        tst.l   d0                       zero value?
        beq     outdecz                  yes, make sure we output a 0
* divide by ten to pick up digit value as remainder
* keep doing this until number is zero
outdec0:tst.l   d0                       finished?
        beq     outdec1                  yes, output the number
        move.w  d0,d2                    save low order word in d2
        clr.w   d0                       clear low order word
        swap    d0                       get high order word in low order word
        divu    #10,d0                   divide by ten
        move.w  d0,d3                    save remainder in d3
        move.w  d2,d0                    get low order word back
        divu    #10,d0                   divide by ten
        swap    d0                       swap quotient and remainder words
        move.w  d0,-(sp)                 save remainder as digit value
        move.w  d3,d0                    get old remainder in low order word
        swap    d0                       fix up so result is full 32 bit quotient
        bra     outdec0                  divide by ten again
*we now output the number
outdec1:move.w  (sp)+,d0                 get a digit from the stack
        bmi     outdec2                  terminate on -1
        and.l   #%1111,d0                mask
outdecz:add.b   #'0',d0                  make digit into ascii char
        jsr     putc                     output
        bra     outdec1                  continue to next digit
outdec2:movem.l (sp)+,d0-d3              restore registers
        rts                              return
*
cr:     equ     $0d                      ascii car ret
lf:     equ     $0a                      ascii line feed
newline:move.l  d0,-(sp)                 save reg. d0
        move.b  #cr,d0                   output a car ret
        jsr     putc
        move.b  #lf,d0                   output a line feed
        jsr     putc
        move.l  (sp)+,d0                 restore d0
        rts                              return
*
        end
```

```
***********************************************
* Amiga shell - This must run under the CLI
*               Link with amiga.lib
************************************************
*
* You may have to modify the following include if your
* include files are not in the same directory.
*
        include ":include/libraries/dos_lib.i"
*
        code
*
* External references
*
        xref    _AbsExecBase
        xref    _LVOOpenLibrary
        xref    _LVOCloseLibrary
*
* Initialization code to open the DOS library and the console device
*
        lea     DOSName,Al              get name of dos library
        clr.l   d0                      and latest version
        movea.l _AbsExecBase,a6         get base of exec
        jsr     _LVOOpenLibrary(a6)     open dos library
        move.l  d0,_DOSBase             save base address
        move.l  #1006,d2                new file
        move.l  #con,dl                 get console name
        movea.l _DOSBase,a6             dos lib base to a6
        jsr     _LVOOpen(a6)            open console
        move.l  d0,console              save file pointer
*
* Your program goes here
*
*
*       <PROGRAM>
*
*
*
* Code to clean up and exit to the CLI
*
fini:   move.l  console,dl              get file pointer
        movea.l _DOSBase,a6             dos lib base to a6
        jsr     _LVOClose(a6)           close console
        movea.l _DOSBase,al             dos lib base to al
        movea.l _AbsExecBase,a6         exec base to a6
        jsr     _LVOCloseLibrary(a6)    close dos library
        clr.l   d0                      indicate no error
        rts                             return to cli
*
* Standard I/O subroutines
*
getc:   movem.l dl-d7/a0-a6,-(sp)       save regs.
        move.l  console,dl              file pointer to dl
        move.l  #buff,d2                buffer pointer to d2
        moveq.l #1,d3                   count to d3
        movea.l _DOSBase,a6             dos lib base to a6
        jsr     _LVORead(a6)            read data
        clr.l   d0                      make sure high order bits clear
        move.b  buff,d0                 get the char.
        movem.l (sp)+,dl-d7/a0-a6       restore regs.
```

```
        rts
*
putc:   movem.l d0-d7/a0-a6,-(sp)       save regs.
        move.b  d0,buff                 put char. in buff
        move.l  console,d1              file pointer to d1
        move.l  #buff,d2                buffer pointer to d2
        moveq.l #1,d3                   count to d3
        movea.l _DOSBase,a6             dos lib base to a6
        jsr     _LVOWrite(a6)           write data
        movem.l (sp)+,d0-d7/a0-a6       restore regs.
        rts                             return
*
* The following subroutine to input a decimal number accumulates
* the number by multiplying the partially accumulated number by ten
* and adding in the current digit.  A double precision multiply is
* performed to allow a full 32 bit number to be entered.
*
indec:  movem.l d1-d2,-(sp)             save registers
        clr.l   d1                      initialize number to zero
indec0: jsr     getc                    get a character
        subi.b  #'0',d0                 make ascii into digit
        blt     indec1                  terminate if not a digit
        cmp.b   #9,d0                   not a digit i > 9
        bgt     indec1                  also terminate if so
        move.w  d1,d2                   save low order word of number
        clr.w   d1                      clear low order word
        swap    d1                      move high word to low word
        mulu    #10,d1                  multiply by ten
        swap    d1                      put result back in high word
        mulu    #10,d2                  multiply low order word of number by ten
        add.l   d2,d1                   add low order word to high order word
        add.l   d0,d1                   add in the current digit
        bra     indec0                  get another digit
indec1: move.l  d1,d0                   move number into d0
        movem.l (sp)+,d1-d2             restore registers
        rts                             return
*
* The following subroutine to output a decimal number performs this
* operation by successively dividing the number by ten to pick off the
* digits.  These digits are pushed onto the stack.  When the number
* has been converted, the digits are popped from the stack and output.
* A double precision divide is needed to accommodate a 32 bit number.
*
outdec: movem.l d0-d3,-(sp)             save reg. values
        move.w  #-1,-(sp)               push -1 onto stack
        tst.l   d0                      zero value?
        beq     outdecz                 yes, make sure we output a 0
* divide by ten to pick up digit value as remainder
* keep doing this until number is zero
outdec0:tst.l   d0                      finished?
        beq     outdec1                 yes, output the number
        move.w  d0,d2                   save low order word in d2
        clr.w   d0                      clear low order word
        swap    d0                      get high order word in low order word
        divu    #10,d0                  divide by ten
        move.w  d0,d3                   save remainder in d3
        move.w  d2,d0                   get low order word back
        divu    #10,d0                  divide by ten
        swap    d0                      swap quotient and remainder words
        move.w  d0,-(sp)                save remainder as digit value
```

```
        move.w  d3,d0                           get old remainder in low order word
        swap    d0                              fix up so result is full 32 bit quotient
        bra     outdec0                         divide by ten again
*we now output the number
outdec1:move.w  (sp)+,d0                        get a digit from the stack
        bmi     outdec2                         terminate on -1
        and.l   #%1111,d0                       mask
outdecz:add.b   #'0',d0                         make digit into ascii char
        jsr     putc                            output
        bra     outdec1                         continue to next digit
outdec2:movem.l (sp)+,d0-d3                     restore registers
        rts                                     return
*
cr:     equ     $0d                             ascii car ret
lf:     equ     $0a                             ascii line feed
newline:move.l  d0,-(sp)                        save reg. d0
        move.b  #cr,d0                          output a car ret
        jsr     putc
        move.b  #lf,d0                          output a line feed
        jsr     putc
        move.l  (sp)+,d0                        restore d0
        rts                                     return
*
        data
DOSName:        dc.b    'dos.library',0
con:    dc.b    '*',0           console name
*
        bss
buff:   ds.b    1               character buffer
_DOSBase:       ds.l    1       temp for dos lib pointer
console:        ds.l    1       temp for file pointer
        end
```

```
;**********************************************************;
; Macintosh shell.
;
;**********************************************************
;
; The following include files are needed:
;
        Include MacTraps.D
        Include SysEqu.D
;
        xdef    Start           ;starting address
;
; Equates
;
WIND_TOP        equ     40      ;window coordinates (GLOBAL)
WIND_LEFT       equ     4       ;
WIND_BOT        equ     338     ;
WIND_RIGHT      equ     508     ;
;
WINDHEIGHT      equ     WIND_BOT-WIND_TOP       ;window dimensions
WINDWIDTH       equ     WIND_RIGHT-WIND_LEFT
;
LMARG           equ     6               ;left margin
RMARG           equ     WINDWIDTH-10    ;right
TMARG           equ     15              ;top
BMARG           equ     WINDHEIGHT-15   ;bottom
;
BS              equ     8               ;ASCII backspace
CR              equ     13              ;ASCII car ret
LF              equ     10              ;ASCII lf
DASH            equ     45              ;ASCII minus sign
ZERO            equ     48              ;ASCII character for digit zero
NINE            equ     57              ;ASCII character for digit nine
;
TRUE            equ     1               ;boolean true
FALSE           equ     0               ;boolean false
;
FONTNUM         equ     4               ;default font code
FONTSTYLE       equ     0               ;plain style
FONTSIZE        equ     9               ;default font size
;
ASCENT          equ     0               ;offsets of fields in Fontinfo
DESCENT         equ     2               ;
WIDMAX          equ     4               ;
LEADING         equ     6               ;
; The window coordinates in local coordinates
WBoundsRect:    dc.w    WIND_TOP,WIND_LEFT,WIND_BOT,WIND_RIGHT
WScrollRect:    dc.w    0,0,WINDHEIGHT,WINDWIDTH
;
ScrollRgnH:     dc.l    0       ;handle for scroll region
FontInfo:       dcb.w   4,0     ;buffer for record ret. by _GetFontInfo
LineHt:         dc.w    0       ;buffer for height of line
WindowPointer:  dc.l    0       ;pointer to the window
;
EventRec:       ds.l    4       ;event record
;
Title:          dc.b    16,'Macintosh shell.'
;
; Initialization code.  Set up everything.
;
```

```
Start:  movem.l d0-d7/a0-a6,-(sp)       ;save regs.
        pea     -4(a5)                  ;space for Quickdraw
        _InitGraf                       ;init Quickdraw
        _InitFonts                      ;init font manager
        _InitWindows                    ;init window manager
        _InitMenus                      ;init menu manager
        clr.l   -(sp)                   ;no restart procedure
        _InitDialogs                    ;init dialog manager
        _TEInit                         ;init textedit
        _InitCursor                     ;set cursor to arrow
        lea     Title,a0                ;get title bar
        bsr     makewindow              ;make a window
;
; Your program goes here
;
;
;       <PROGRAM>
;
;
; Clean up and return
;
        movem.l (sp)+,d0-d7/a0-a6       ;restore registers
        _ExitToShell                    ;return to finder
;
; Subroutines
;
Makewindow:
        movem.l d0-d2/a0-a1,-(sp)       ;save regs.
        clr.l   -(sp)                   ;reserve space for window ptr.
        clr.l   -(sp)                   ;allocate
        pea     WBoundsRect             ;window size and location
        move.l  a0,-(sp)                ;window's title
        st      -(sp)                   ;vis flag = true
        clr.w   -(sp)                   ;document window
        move.l  #-1,-(sp)               ;window on top
        sf      -(sp)                   ;goaway = flase
        clr.l   -(sp)                   ;refcon = not used
        _NEWWINDOW
        lea     WindowPointer,a0        ;get address of window
        move.l  (sp),(a0)               ;save window ptr and pass
                                        ; to setport
        _SETPORT
        clr.l   -(sp)
        _NEWRGN
        lea     ScrollRgnH,a0           ;create a new region
        move.l  (sp),(a0)               ;save and pass along
        pea     WScrollRect             ;use same limits as WBoundsRect
        _RECTRGN                        ;required if scrolling
        move.w  #FONTNUM,-(sp)          ;default font number
        _TextFont                       ;set font selection
        move.w  #FONTSTYLE,-(sp)        ;default font style
        _TextFace                       ;set font style
        move.w  #FONTSIZE,-(sp)         ;default font size
        _TextSize                       ;set font size
        pea     FontInfo                ;get info. about font
        _GETFontInfo                    ;font dimension parameters
        move.w  FontInfo+ASCENT,d0
        add.w   FontInfo+DESCENT,d0
        add.w   FontInfo+LEADING,d0     ;compute font vert. size
        lea     LineHt,a0               ;get address
```

```
        move.w  d0,(a0)                 ;save vert info.
        move    #LMARG,-(sp)            ;horiz. pen pos.
        move    #TMARG,-(sp)            ;vert. pen pos.
        _MOVETO                         ;pen in upper left corner
        movem.l (sp)+,d0-d2,a0-al       ;restore regs.
        rts                             ;and return
;
FLASHTIME       equ     30              ;#ticks caret is on or off
EVENTKEY        equ     4               ;offset of key code in event record
EVENTMODIFIERS  equ     14              ;offset of modifier flags
;
getc:   movem.l dl-d4/a0-al,-(sp)
; local initializations
        move.l  #$0000ffff,d0           ;mask for all events
        _FlushEvents                    ;flush event queue
        move.l  Ticks,d3                ;d3 = time caret was on/off
        moveq   #0,d4                   ;caret off
; start of event loop, but must check if time to switch caret state
getcl:  move.l  Ticks,d0                ;get system time in ticks
        sub.l   d3,d0                   ;subtract time of last switch
        cmpi.l  #FLASHTIME,d0           ;if equal must switch
        blt.s   getc3                   ;if not eq then getc3
; switch caret state
        move.b  $'_',d0                 ;assume it was off
        tst.b   d4                      ;test if it was off
        beq.s   getc2                   ;if off write it
        move.b  #BS,d0                  ; if on erase by BS
getc2:  bsr     putc                    ;switch the caret
        move.l  Ticks,d3                ;update time switched
        not.b   d4                      ;flip state
; check the event queue for a key closure or auto-key event
getc3:  clr.w   -(sp)                   ;allocate space for result
        move.w  #$0028,-(sp)            ;mask
        pea     EventRec                ;pass address of event rec.
        _GetNextEvent
        tst.b   (sp)+                   ;system event or nothing?
        beq     getcl                   ;if nothing try again
; otherwise a key was held down and the caret must be erased, if visable
        tst.b   d4                      ;caret on?
        beq.s   getc4                   ;if not, getc4
        move.b  #BS,d0                  ;if on erase by BS
        bsr     putc                    ;switch the caret
; return the character code and echo
getc4:  move.w  EventRec+EVENTMODIFIERS,d0 ;get modifiers
        swap    d0                      ;into high word of d0
        move.w  EventRec+EVENTKEY,d0    ;get key and ASCII code
        bsr     putc                    ;echo
        andi.l  #$7f,d0                 ;mask to 7 bit ASCII
        movem.l (sp)+,dl-d4/a0-al       ;restore regs.
        rts                             ;return;
;
PenLoc: dc.l    0                       ;pen pos.
;
putc:   movem.l dl-d2/d5-d7/a0-al,-(sp) ;save regs.
        move.l  d0,d5                   ;char to d5
        pea     PenLoc                  ;get pen loc
        _GETPEN
        move.w  PenLoc+2,d7             ;x val to d7
        move.w  PenLoc,d6               ;y val to d6
        cmpi.b  #BS,d5                  ;backspace?
```

```
        bne     putcl                   ;if no jump past erasure
        cmpi.w  #LMARG,d7               ;else check left margin
        beq     putc4                   ;at margin, return
        lea     FontInfo,a0             ;get address of font data
        move.w  WIDMAX(a0),d0           ;get char width data
        neg.w   d0                      ;negate
        move.w  d0,-(sp)                ;push new x val difference
        move.w  #0,-(sp)                ;push new x val difference
        _MOVE                           ;move pen
        move.w  d7,-(sp)                ;bottom right corner
        move.w  d6,d0                   ;y val of pen pos.
        add.w   FontInfo+DESCENT,D0     ;add descender amount to y
        move.w  d0,-(sp)                ; val and push
        sub.w   FontInfo+ASCENT,d6      ;y val plus ascender
        sub.w   FontInfo+WIDMAX,d7      ;compute x val
        move.w  d7,-(sp)                ;push x val
        move.w  d6,-(sp)                ;push y val
        move.l  sp,a0                   ;push addr of erase rect.
        move.l  a0,-(sp)                ;
        _ERASERECT                      ;erase deleted character
        add     #8,sp                   ;pop rectangle values from stack
        bra     putc4                   ;exit
putcl:  cmp.b   #CR,d5                  ;CR?
        beq     putc2                   ;yes, go create new line
        cmp.w   #RMARG,d7               ;is pen past right hand margin?
        blt     putc3                   ;if no, jump past new line
; generate new line
putc2:  sub.w   #LMARG,d7               ;compute difference
        neg.w   d7                      ;negate difference x val.
        move.w  d7,-(sp)                ;push onto stack
        lea     LineHt,a0               ;get address of line height
        move.w  (a0),-(sp)              ;load new value
        _MOVE                           ;position cursor for new line
        cmp.w   #BMARG,d6               ;has pen moved past bot. margin?
        blt     putc3                   ;if no, bypass code to scroll
        pea     WScrollRect             ;push addr. of scroll rect
        move.w  #0,-(sp)                ;push zero
        lea     LineHt,a0               ;get address of line height
        move.w  (a0),-(sp)              ;load new value
        neg.w   (sp)                    ;negate top of stack value
        lea     ScrollRgnH,a0           ;get addr. of scroll region
        move.l  (a0),-(sp)              ;push on stack
        _SCROLLRECT                     ;scroll by one line's height
        move.w  #0,-(sp)                ;push zero
        lea     LineHt,a0               ;get address of line height
        move.w  (a0),-(sp)              ;load new value
        neg.w   (sp)                    ;negate top of stack
        _MOVE                           ;move pen too
;display character
putc3:  move.w  d5,-(sp)                ;push char code
        _DRAWCHAR                       ;display character
;exit
putc4:  move.l  d5,d0                   ;char to d0
        movem.l (sp)+,dl-d2/d5-d7/a0-al ;restore regs.
        rts                             ;return
;
;
; The following subroutine to input a decimal number accumulates
; the number by multiplying the partially accumulated number by ten
; and adding in the current digit.  A double precision multiply is
```

```
; performed to allow a full 32 bit number to be entered.
;
indec:  movem.l d1-d2,-(sp)             ;save registers
        clr.l   d1                      ;initialize number to zero
indec0: jsr     getc                    ;get a character
        subi.b  #'0',d0                 ;make ascii into digit
        blt     indec1                  ;terminate if not a digit
        cmp.b   #9,d0                   ;not a digit i > 9
        bgt     indec1                  ;also terminate if so
        move.w  d1,d2                   ;save low order word of number
        clr.w   d1                      ;clear low order word
        swap    d1                      ;move high word to low word
        mulu    #10,d1                  ;multiply by ten
        swap    d1                      ;put result back in high word
        mulu    #10,d2                  ;multiply low order word of number by ten
        add.l   d2,d1                   ;add low order word to high order word
        add.l   d0,d1                   ;add in the current digit
        bra     indec0                  ;get another digit
indec1: move.l  d1,d0                   ;move number into d0
        movem.l (sp)+,d1-d2             ;restore registers
        rts                             ;return
;
; The following subroutine to output a decimal number performs this
; operation by successively dividing the number by ten to pick off the
; digits.  These digits are pushed onto the stack.  When the number
; has been converted, the digits are popped from the stack and output.
; A double precision divide is needed to accommodate a 32 bit number.
;
outdec: movem.l d0-d3,-(sp)             ;save reg. values
        move.w  #-1,-(sp)               ;push -1 onto stack
        tst.l   d0                      ;zero value?
        beq     outdecz                 ;yes, make sure we output a 0
; divide by ten to pick up digit value as remainder
; keep doing this until number is zero
outdec0:tst.l   d0                      ;finished?
        beq     outdec1                 ;yes, output the number
        move.w  d0,d2                   ;save low order word in d2
        clr.w   d0                      ;clear low order word
        swap    d0                      ;get high order word in low order word
        divu    #10,d0                  ;divide by ten
        move.w  d0,d3                   ;save remainder in d3
        move.w  d2,d0                   ;get low order word back
        divu    #10,d0                  ;divide by ten
        swap    d0                      ;swap quotient and remainder words
        move.w  d0,-(sp)                ;save remainder as digit value
        move.w  d3,d0                   ;get old remainder in low order word
        swap    d0                      ;fix up so result is full 32 bit quotient
        bra     outdec0                 ;divide by ten again
;we now output the number
outdec1:move.w  (sp)+,d0                ;get a digit from the stack
        bmi     outdec2                 ;terminate on -1
        and.l   #%1111,d0               ;mask
outdecz:add.b   #'0',d0                 ;make digit into ascii char
        jsr     putc                    ;output
        bra     outdec1                 ;continue to next digit
outdec2:movem.l (sp)+,d0-d3             ;restore registers
        rts                             ;return
;
newline:move.l  d0,-(sp)                ;save reg. d0
        move.b  #CR,d0                  ;output a car ret
```

```
        jsr      putc
        move.l   (sp)+,d0                ;restore d0
        rts                              ;return

        end
```

68000-68020 INSTRUCTION SUMMARY

Mnemonic	Addr Modes: Src	Dest	Size	Attri-butes	Cond. Codes X	N	Z	V	C	Description
ABCD	Dn	Dn	B		S	ø	S	ø	S	Add Decimal
	-(An)	-(An)	B		S	ø	S	ø	S	Add Decimal
ADDA	<ea>	An	W,L		S	S	S	S	S	Add Address
ADDI	#data	<dea> Alterable	B,W,L		S	S	S	S	S	Add Immediate
ADD	<ea>	Dn	B,W,L	*1	S	S	S	S	S	Add Binary
	Dn	<mea> Alterable	B,W,L	*1	S	S	S	S	S	Add Binary
ADDQ	#d	<aea>	B,W,L	*1,*2	S	S	S	S	S	Add Quick
ADDX	Dn	Dn	B,W,L		S	S	S	S	S	Add Extended
	-(An)	-(An)	B,W,L		S	S	S	S	S	Add Extended
AND	<dea>	Dn	B,W,L		ø	S	S	0	0	And Logical
	Dn	<aea>	B,W,L		ø	S	S	0	0	And Logical
ANDI	#d	<dea> Alterable	B,W,L		ø	S	S	0	0	And Immediate
	#d	CCR	W,L		S	S	S	S	S	And Imm to CCR
	#d	SR	W,L	P	S	S	S	S	S	And Imm to SR
ASL	Dn	Dn	B,W,L	*3	S	S	S	S	S	Arith. Shift L
	#d	Dn	B,W,L	*4	S	S	S	S	S	Arith. Shift L
	<mea> Alterable		W		S	S	S	S	S	Arith. Shift L
ASR	Dn	Dn	B,W,L	*3	S	S	S	S	S	Arith. Shift R
	#d	Dn	B,W,L	*4	S	S	S	S	S	Arith. Shift R
	<mea> Alterable		L		S	S	S	S	S	Arith. Shift R
Bcc	<label>		16 bit displ.		ø	ø	ø	ø	ø	Branch Cond
Bcc.S	<label>		8 bit displ.		ø	ø	ø	ø	ø	Branch Cond Short
BCHG	Dn	<mea> Alterable	B,L		ø	ø	S	ø	ø	Test bit & Change
	#d	<mea> Alterable	B,L		ø	ø	S	ø	ø	Test bit & Change
BCLR	Dn	<mea> Alterable	B,L		ø	ø	S	ø	ø	Test bit & Clear
	#d	<mea> Alterable	B,L		ø	ø	S	ø	ø	Test bit & Clear
BFCHG	<ea>	-	-	*8	ø	S	S	0	0	Tst Bit Fld & Chg
BFCLR	<ea>{off,width}		-	*8	ø	S	S	0	0	Tst Bit Fld & Clr
BFEXTS	<ea>{off,width},Dn		-	*8	ø	S	S	0	0	Extrct Bit Fld Sin
BFEXTU	<ea>{off,width},Dn		-	*8	ø	S	S	0	0	Extrct Bit Fld Uns
BFFFO	<ea>{off,width},Dn		-	*8	ø	S	S	0	0	Fnd 1st 1 in bitfld
BFINS	<ea>{off,width}		-	*8	ø	S	S	0	0	Insert Bit Fld
BFSET	<ea>{off,width}		-	*8	ø	S	S	0	0	Set Bit Fld
BFTST	<ea>{off,width}		-	*8	ø	S	S	0	0	Test Bit Fld
BKPT	#d	-	-	*8	ø	ø	ø	ø	ø	Breakpoint
BRA	<label>		8 or 16 bit displ		ø	ø	ø	ø	ø	Branch Always
BSET	Dn	<mea> Alterable	B,L		ø	ø	S	ø	ø	Test bit & Set
	#d	<mea> Alterable	B,L		ø	ø	S	ø	ø	Test bit & Set
BSR	<label>		8 or16 bit disp		ø	ø	ø	ø	ø	Branch Subr.
BTST	Dn	<dea>	B,L		ø	ø	S	ø	ø	Test bit & Set
	#d	<dea>	B,L		ø	ø	S	ø	ø	Test bit & Set
CALLM	#d	<ea>	-	*8	ø	ø	S	ø	ø	Call Module
CAS	Dn,Dn,<ea>		B,W,L	*8	ø	S	S	S	S	Comp & Swap Op
CAS2	Dn:Dn,Dn:Dn,(Rn):(Rn)		W,L	*8	ø	S	S	S	S	Comp & Swap Op
CHK	<dea>	Dn	B,W,L	*8	ø	S	ø	ø	ø	Check Reg. Bounds
CHK2	<dea>	Rn	W		ø	ø	S	ø	S	Check Reg. Bounds

CLR	<dea> Alterable		B,W,L		ø 0 ø 0 0	Clear Operand
CMP	<ea>	Dn	B,W,L	*1	ø S S S S	Compare
CMPA	<ea>	An	W,L		ø S S S S	Compare Addr
CMPI	#d	<dea> Alterable	B,W,L		ø S S S S	Compare Imm.
CMPM	(An)+	(An)+	B,W,L		ø S S S S	Compare Mem.
CMP2	<ea>	Rn	B,W,L	*8 *1	ø ø S ø S	Compare Reg
cpBcc	<label>	-	W,L	*8	ø ø ø ø ø	Brnch Coproc Cnd
cpDBcc	<ea>	-	-	*8	ø ø ø ø ø	Tst,Decr,Br,CprC
cpGEN	Coprocessor specific operands		-	*8	S S S S S	Brnch Coproc Cnd
cpRESTORE	<label>	-	W,L	*8 P	ø ø ø ø ø	Coproc Restore
cpSAVE	<ea>	-	-	*8 P	ø ø ø ø ø	Coprocessor Save
cpScc	<ea>	-	B	*8	ø ø ø ø ø	Set on Coproc Cond
cpTRAPcc	-	-	W,L	*8	ø ø ø ø ø	Trap on CoprocCnd
	#d	-	W,L	*8	ø ø ø ø ø	Trap on CoprocCnd
DBcc	Dn	<label>	16 bit disp.		ø ø ø ø ø	Decr, Brnch Cond.
DIVS	<dea>	Dn	W		ø S S S 0	Divide Signed
DIVSL	<dea>	Dquotient	L		ø S S S 0	Divide Signed
	<dea>	Drem:Dquotient	L		ø S S S 0	Divide Signed
DIVU	<dea>	Dn	W		ø S S S 0	Divide UnSigned
DIVUL	<dea>	Dquotient	L		ø S S S 0	Divide UnSigned
	<dea>	Drem:Dquotient	L		ø S S S 0	Divide UnSigned
EOR	Dn	<dea> Alterable	B,W,L		ø S S 0 0	Exclusive OR
EORI	#d	<dea> Alterable	B,W,L		ø S S 0 0	Exclusive OR Imm
	#d	SR	W	P	S S S S S	Exclusive OR Imm
	#d	CCR	W		S S S S S	Exclusive OR Imm
EXG	Rn	Rn	L		ø ø ø ø ø	Exchange Regs
EXT	Dn	-	W,L		ø S S 0 0	Extend Sign
EXTB	Dn	-	L		ø S S 0 0	Extend B to L Sign
ILLEGAL	-	-	-		ø ø ø ø ø	Illegal
JMP	-	<cea>	-		ø ø ø ø ø	Jump Always
JSR	-	<cea>	-		ø ø ø ø ø	Jump Subr.
LEA	<cea>	An	L		ø ø ø ø ø	Load Eff Address
LINK	An	#d	W,L		ø ø ø ø ø	Link/Allocate
LSL	Dn	Dn	B,W,L	*3	S S S 0 S	Log. Shift Left
	#d	Dn	B,W,L	*4	S S S 0 S	Log. Shift Left
	<mea> Alterable		W		S S S 0 S	Log. Shift Left
LSR	Dn	Dn	B,W,L	*3	S S S 0 S	Log. Shift Right
	#d	Dn	B,W,L	*4	S S S 0 S	Log. Shift Right
	<mea> Alterable		W		S S S 0 S	Log. Shift Right
MOVE	<ea>	<dea> Alterable	B,W,L	*1	ø S S 0 0	Move Data
	<dea>	CCR	W	*5	S S S S S	Move to CCR
	CCR	<dea>	W	*5	ø ø ø ø ø	Move from CCR
	<dea>	SR	W	P	S S S S S	Move to SR
	SR	<dea> Alterable	W	P	ø ø ø ø ø	Move from SR
	USP	An	L	P	ø ø ø ø ø	Move from USP
	An	USP	L	P	ø ø ø ø ø	Move to USP
MOVEA	<ea>	An	W,L		ø ø ø ø ø	Move Address
MOVEC	Rc	Rn	L	*8 P	ø ø ø ø ø	Move Control Reg
	Rn	Rc	L	*8 P	ø ø ø ø ø	Move Control Reg
MOVEM	<reglist>	<cea> Alterable	W,L	*6	ø ø ø ø ø	Move Mult. Regs
	<cea>	<reglist>	W,L	*7	ø ø ø ø ø	Move Mult. Regs
MOVEP	Dn	d(An)	W,L		ø ø ø ø ø	Move Periph. Data
	d(An)	Dn	W,L		ø ø ø ø ø	Move Periph. Data

MOVEQ	#d	Dn	L		ø S S 0 0	Move Quick
MOVES	Rn	DFC<mea> Altrbl	B,W,L	*8 P	ø ø ø ø ø	Move Addr Space
	SFC<mea> Altrbl	Rn	B,W,L	*8 P	ø ø ø ø ø	Move Addr Space
MULS	<dea>	Dn	W		ø S S S 0	Multiply Signed
MULS.L	<dea>	Dh:Dl	L	*8	ø S S S 0	Multiply Signed
MULU	<dea>	Dn	W		ø S S S 0	Multiply UnSigned
MULU.L	<dea>	Dh:Dl	L	*8	ø S S S 0	Multiply UnSigned
NBCD	<dea> Alterable		B		S ø S ø S	Negate Decimal
NEG	<dea> Alterable		B,W,L		S S S S S	Negate
NEGX	<dea> Alterable		B,W,L		S S S S S	Negate Extended
NOP	-	-	-		ø ø ø ø ø	No Operation
NOT	<dea> Alterable		B,W,L		ø S S 0 0	Logical Complmnt
OR	<dea>	Dn	B,W,L		ø S S 0 0	Inclusive OR Log.
	Dn	<mea> Alterable	B,W,L		ø S S 0 0	Inclusive OR Log.
ORI	#d	<dea> Alterable	B,W,L		ø S S 0 0	Inclusive OR Imm.
	#d	SR	W	P	S S S S S	Inclusive OR Imm
	#d	CCR	W		S S S S S	Inclusive OR Imm
PACK	-(An),-(An),#<adjstmnt>		-	*8	ø ø ø ø ø	Pack
PEA	<cea>	-	L		ø ø ø ø ø	Push Eff. Addr
RESET	-	-	-	P	ø ø ø ø ø	Reset Ext. Device
ROL	Dn	Dn	B,W,L	*3	ø S S 0 S	Rotate Left
	#d	Dn	B,W,L	*4	ø S S 0 S	Rotate Left
	<mea> Alterable		W		ø S S 0 S	Rotate Left
ROR	Dn	Dn	B,W,L	*3	ø S S 0 S	Rotate Right
	#d	Dn	B,W,L	*4	ø S S 0 S	Rotate Right
	<mea> Alterable		W		ø S S 0 S	Rotate Right
ROXL	Dn	Dn	B,W,L	*3	S S S 0 S	Rotate L w/extnd
	#d	Dn	B,W,L	*4	S S S 0 S	Rotate L w/extnd
	<mea> Alterable		W		S S S 0 S	Rotate L w/extnd
ROXR	Dn	Dn	B,W,L	*4	S S S 0 S	Rotate R w/ext
	#d	Dn	B,W,L	*5	S S S 0 S	Rotate R w/ext
	<mea> Alterable		W		S S S 0 S	Rotate R w/ext
RTD	#d	-	-	*8	ø ø ø ø ø	Return/Deallocate
RTE	-	-	-	P	S S S S S	Ret from exceptn
RTM	Rn	-	-	*8	S S S S S	Ret from Module
RTR	-	-	-		S S S S S	Ret/Restore CCR
RTS	-	-	-		ø ø ø ø ø	Ret from Subr.
SBCD	Dn	Dn	B		S ø S ø S	Subtract Decimal
	-(An)	-(An)	B		S ø S ø S	Subtract Decimal
Scc	<dea> Alterable		B		ø ø ø ø ø	Set Conditionally
STOP	#d	-	-	P	S S S S S	Load SR, Stop
SUB	<ea>	Dn	B,W,L	*1	S S S S S	Subtract Binary
	Dn	<mea> Alterable	B,W,L		S S S S S	Subtract Binary
SUBA	<ea>	An	W,L		ø ø ø ø ø	Subtract Address
SUBI	#data	<dea> Alterable	B,W,L		S S S S S	Subtract Imm.
SUBQ	#d	<aea>	B,W,L	*1,*2	S S S S S	Subtract Quick
SUBX	Dn	Dn	B,W,L		S S S S S	Subtract Extended
	-(An)	-(An)	B,W,L		S S S S S	Subtract Extended
SWAP	Dn	-	W		ø S S 0 0	Swap Reg Halves
TAS	<dea> Alterable		B		ø S S 0 0	Test & Set Opernd
TRAP	#d	-	-		ø ø ø ø ø	Trap
TRAPcc	#d	-	W,L	*8	ø ø ø ø ø	Trap on Condition
TRAPV	-	-	-		ø ø ø ø ø	Trap on Overflow

TST	<dea> Alterable	B,W,L		ø S S 0 0	Test Operand
UNLK	An -	-		ø ø ø ø ø	Unlink
UNPACK	-(An),-(An),#<adjstmnt>	-	*8	ø ø ø ø ø	UnPack BCD
UNPK	Dn,Dn,#<adjstmnt>	-	*8	ø ø ø ø ø	UnPack BCD

Notes:

*1: If size is .B then Address Register Direct Addr. Mode is not allowed
*2: Immediate data occupies 3 bits representing values on 1 - 8.
*3: Source Data Reg. contains shift count. Value 0-63, 0 = shift 64 bits.
*4: The data is a shift count of 1-8.
*5: Only uses lower Byte of the Word.
*6: <cea> Alterable may be -(An).
*7: <cea> Alterable may be (An)+.
*8: 68020 only.
P: Privileged Instruction

Condition Code values:

S - Set or Cleared according to result of operation
1 - set
ø - not affected by this instruction
0 - always cleared

Addressing Mode Descriptions:

<ea> - effective address
<rea> - register effective address
<dea> - data effective address
<mea> - Memory effective address
<cea> - control effective address
<aea> - alterable effective address (data or memory)

MODE	ea	rea	dea	mea	cea	aea
Dn	X	X	X			X
An	X	X				X
(An)	X		X	X	X	X
(An)+	X		X	X		X
-(An)	X		X	X		X
d(An)	X		X	X	X	X
d(An,Xn)	X		X	X	X	X
A16	X		X	X	X	X
A32	X		X	X	X	X
d(PC)	X		X	X	X	
d(PC,Xn)	X		X	X	X	
#<data>	X		X	X		

68020 specific addressing modes

MODE	ea	rea	dea	mea	cea	aea
bd(An,Xn)	X		X	X	X	X
bd(PC,Xn)	X		X	X	X	
[bd,An],Xn,od	X		X	X	X	X
[bd,An,Xn],od	X		X	X	X	X
[bd,PC],Xn,od	X		X	X	X	
[bd,PC,Xn],od	X		X	X	X	

INDEX